Four Marys and a Jessie

Four Marys and a Jessie

The Story of the Lincoln Women

By C.J. King

signed: CJ King

Introduction by Harold Holzer

Friends of Hildene, Inc.

Manchester, Vermont

First Edition
© 2005 C.J. King
All rights reserved under International and Pan-American
Copyright Conventions. Published 2005.

Published in the United States by:
Friends of Hildene, Inc.
P.O. Box 377
Manchester, Vermont 05254

Printed by Daamen, Inc. Printing Company
West Rutland, Vermont

Cover image: Lee Krohn
Book design: Dave Lindberg

Library of Congress Control Number: 2005902565
ISBN 0-9754917-2-5 (SOFTCOVER)   ISBN 0-9754917-3-3 (HARDCOVER)

It always provokes me when people stare and say, "There's Lincoln's great-granddaughter." It's just my luck he was related to me.

— Mary Lincoln "Peggy" Beckwith

I wanted wild women, women who broke loose, women who lived life to the full, whatever that meant. What did it mean to live life to the full? How fully could a woman live? These were the questions I wanted biography and autobiography to answer... Merely to publish the life story of someone not famous challenged the accepted order, saying, with radical democracy, "This person counts, too."

— Phyllis Rose, *Norton Book of Women's Lives*

Contents

INTRODUCTION
By Harold Holzer

However sincere our democratic ideals, we Americans have always harbored a curious fascination, almost a yearning, for dynasties. Lacking royalty, we have lavished adoration on our reigning, and occasionally dysfunctional, "first" families—in the political, entertainment, and sports realms alike—all but canonizing generations of Roosevelts and Kennedys, and more recently the Fondas and Griffeys of the movie and baseball worlds, respectively.

This is hardly a new phenomenon, though the modern media has certainly intensified both public interest and public access. Generations earlier, at the close of the 18th century, artist Edward Savage had portrayed George Washington together with his wife and her children, in a painting that was quickly engraved and widely distributed, establishing the canonical image of our first First Family. It mattered little that the "Father of His Country" had in fact fathered no children of his own. Americans seemed to hope that the man who would not be king might somehow remain inspiringly in their midst, through his step-descendants, forever.

It is fair to say that few subsequent presidents came to office with less reverence for their own family histories than Abraham Lincoln. Of the "Fathers of the Republic" he spoke often in his political orations; it seemed in fact to many listeners that he often consciously aspired to join their ranks. About his own family, he said precious little.

When he finally touched on the subject of his ancestry for a brief 1859 sketch of his life, he wrote, almost dismissively: "My parents were both born...of undistinguished families—second families, perhaps I should say."[1]

Between his election and his inauguration, his handsome eldest son, Robert, became such a celebrity in his own right that the press began calling him "The Prince of Rails."[2] Civil War notwithstanding, Lincoln's frequently photographed wife and younger children became national figures, too, and Mary Lincoln a controversial one. When Lincoln's admirers were forced to grapple with his tragic death, they forged an emotional attachment approaching a first family cult, purchasing—by the thousands—composite photographs and newly minted prints of Lincoln, his wife, and children to decorate their own family homes. It was almost as if the country needed reassurance—however fanciful—that the beleaguered Lincoln had found solace in the bosom of his family during the grueling war years.

In truth, both Mary and Robert complained ruefully that the President had found little leisure to enjoy family life in the war-torn White House. Husband and wife scarcely had time for each other, not even when their middle son Willie died suddenly in 1862. And Robert later lamented with astonishing bluntness the sad fact that he and his father had not become "better acquainted."[3] Their admirers, however, preferred to remember the Lincoln family frozen in perpetual togetherness in engraved and lithographed parlor settings, grouped around a table or reading the Bible together. These scenes mocked reality but satisfied a deep emotional need in the public.

Most Lincoln admirers know the sad history of the Lincoln family thereafter. Robert refused to be lured into a race to return to the White House as president in his own right, content to amass wealth and perform public service from the safe fringes of the Cabinet and the Court of St. James's. His own greatest family hope —his aptly named son Abraham Lincoln II (actually the third to carry the name, since the President's grandfather was also "Abraham") died while still in his teens. The last male heir died in 1985—childless, and carrying the name of Beckwith, not Lincoln, to his grave.

So male-centric history has emphasized. No one could claim that the female side of the Lincoln family was more accomplished, or even more interesting, but there is no doubt that the Lincoln women have been woefully ignored by most historians, and deserve their day in the sun—even if all of them do not weather particularly well under the lens of the scholar's scrutiny. Now, at long last, C. J. King has filled in many blanks with a history of the Lincoln—and Todd—women across two centuries.

Readers will undoubtedly be struck by how much these four generations of women had in common—as well as how much they differed.

What, for example, can account for Robert's much-married daughter Jessie's incurable flirtatiousness? Perhaps it might be traced to Mary Todd Lincoln's earlier penchant for beaus and ballrooms in the days when libido had to be masked behind a fluttering fan. Why was the family's final Mary, "Peggy" Beckwith, so stubbornly informal—more apt to dress in overalls than in gowns? Questions about her sexual preference linger, but her mulish streak may well trace its roots to the first Mary, too. One can only conclude from reading these pages that Miss Beckwith's almost neurotic disdain for clothes could have been a direct reaction to her great-grandmother's neurotic need to own them. Surely she had heard the unpleasant stories of the truckloads of belongings that the family had been forced to unpack, identify, and distribute to public and private collections after the former First Lady died.

Most of the Lincolns in this book preferred to remain out of the public eye. The glare of publicity was not for them. But then, as now, disdain for the spotlight often intensifies its wattage. Think of Jacqueline Kennedy dodging photographers during her final 20 years, in the process growing into a national icon defined by her stoic silence. If the Lincolns did not quite attain that exalted status —they lacked, in the final generation, the element of glamour so crucial to modern celebrity—they did confront their past more often than we have been led to believe, as this book demonstrates. They simply chose not to take advantage of it.

There is no second chapter to immortality, and none of the subjects in this book would merit a line in history had they not been Lincolns. But this work does add a much-needed final chapter to Lincoln family history. Born into poverty, they grew into wealth. Raised in log cabins, they ended up in lavish mansions. Dedicated to education, they drifted into self-indulgence and lost their thirst for knowledge and curiosity for life. Why? Should we truly expect more from any family whose brightest stars are taken too soon?

Most children blame their parents for their shortcomings, and attribute their successes to their own hard work. The Lincolns turn out to be no different. The President's stepmother was "his best friend in this world," a relative once heard him say. But he did not feel friendly enough to invite her to his wedding, meet his wife or children, see the White House, or rescue her from isolated indigence.[4] He harbored so much antipathy for his father that he did not journey to his deathbed or pay for a headstone for his grave.

Robert could never really express anything but reverence for his martyred father, but there was likely more distance than intimacy between them. And once his mother lapsed into mental instability and nearly wrecked his own marriage, Robert seemed to break firmly with the past. It is said he even hated the thought that his father's log cabin had allegedly been discovered and placed on public view. He thought biographies should not mention his father's one-time sobriquet, "Honest Abe." It was undignified.

Ironies escaped the Lincoln family. The later Lincolns did not comprehend the fact that their effort to distance themselves from their ancestry made as little sense as Abraham Lincoln's struggle to distance himself from his own. They knew that Abraham Lincoln had launched a second American revolution with the Emancipation Proclamation, but later generations seem to have harbored indifference, at best, to aspirations for integration and equality.

In the irony of ironies in this book, Robert all but imprisons his daughter Jessie to prevent her from reuniting with the man with whom she has eloped. One Chicago newspaper immediately notes: "It was a pity when Abraham Lincoln freed the colored women of the south that he did not at the same time liberate the white ones of the north. The granddaughter of the great emancipator, sitting in her fortified chamber, in all probability wishes that her grandsire had declared the enthralldom of all women at an end, so that she might choose her life mate without consent of her father."

But "grandsire" Lincoln did not free white women.[5] So the Marys and Jessie in this book were destined to be, in a sense, forever shackled—by the high expectations of their illustrious past and the constrained prospects for their prescribed future. "I'm as far away from him as anyone else," Mary Lincoln "Peggy" Beckwith once admitted of the 16th President.[6] But thanks to this sympathetic but honest book, we can feel closer to the family than ever.

BIOGRAPHY

Harold Holzer, one of the country's leading authorities on Lincoln and the political culture of the Civil War era, is co-chairman of the U. S. Lincoln Bicentennial Commission and the award-winning author or editor of 23 books. His most recent book, *Lincoln at Cooper Union*, won the Lincoln Prize, the Barondess/Lincoln Award, and the Award of Achievement of the Lincoln Group of New York. A frequent guest on television, Holzer has appeared on the History Channel, PBS, and C-SPAN, including a February 11, 2005, live broadcast of a performance of "Lincoln Seen and Heard" with Sam Waterston, for President and Mrs. Bush at the White House. A prolific lecturer, Holzer gave two of the most prestigious lectures in the field in 2004: the NEH "Heroes of History" lecture at Ford's Theatre and the Fortenbaugh Lecture at Gettysburg College. In his day-to-day professional life, Holzer is Senior Vice President for External Affairs at The Metropolitan Museum of Art in New York City.

Preface

For most of you who read this book, it will be a story about the Lincoln family. For me, it's also a story about the Harlan family. My first introduction to the Harlan-Lincoln connection came through Mary Harlan Lincoln, President Lincoln's daughter-in-law, a distant cousin of mine. Mary Harlan Lincoln was a second cousin of my great-great grandfather. When my great-aunt Helen Harlan discovered this Harlan-Lincoln connection in the course of her genealogical research, in the late 1980s, I was a graduate student at the University of Massachusetts, Amherst, a couple of hours away from Hildene, the Lincolns' summer estate in Manchester, Vermont. My parents came to visit me, and we decided to visit Hildene.

Much of the Hildene tour focused on the President's son, Robert Todd Lincoln, who built Hildene at the height of his career. Although he always lived in his father's shadow, Robert Lincoln was quite accomplished, a well-respected lawyer who served as Secretary of War, minister to Great Britain, and president and chairman of the Pullman Palace Car Company. It was fitting for Hildene to be preserved in his honor, because that is what his granddaughter, Peggy Beckwith, wanted. The last owner and resident of Hildene before it was opened to the public in 1978, her will stated that she wanted the property to be a memorial to her family. But after the tour, I wanted to know more about Peggy, who was a farmer, a pilot, an artist, and more. My mother suggested I do some research, and the result of that research is this book.

A souvenir booklet for Hildene describes Peggy as "a lively, creative woman of wide-ranging interests...Original, outspoken, full of ideas and opinions...[she was] nevertheless a shy person who shunned public appearances." She was a gentlewoman farmer who liked tractors and fast cars. She loved all kinds of animals and had raccoons as pets. She played polo, developed her own pictures, made maple syrup, sculpted and painted. Born in 1898, her life spanned a time of great change for women, and she pushed against the social expectations placed on her as a Lincoln and as a woman. I liked her for her independent spirit, but also for her genuine, warm-hearted generosity to those around her. As I researched her, I thought a lot about the importance of family in shaping a personality, and the changes in women's lives over the past century and a half, and that led me to research the other Lincoln women as well.

And so, my story begins with Mary Todd Lincoln. For the descendants, there was no escaping the honor and the burden of the Abraham and Mary Todd Lincoln legacies. These two individuals so overshadow the rest of the family as to make them, with the exception of Robert Lincoln, nearly invisible. Every time I tell someone that I'm writing about the Lincoln women descendants, my listener inevitably turns the conversation to one of these original two. Of course, they are the only two Lincolns who are generally known. Except for Robert, the descendants did not achieve any national or international prominence or accomplish great things with far-reaching impacts on society. But they did live interesting lives, and they had positive ripple effects on those around them. Many people benefited from their generosity. This family story is an attempt to rescue these women from complete obscurity—not to glorify them, but to give them their own individual places in the family story.

Because this project has evolved over more than a decade, I worry about omitting someone as I acknowledge those who have helped me. I apologize for that, but I must attempt to express my gratitude for many acts of invaluable assistance. First, I want to remember my great-aunt, Helen Harlan, and my mother, Melba Harlan King, who started me on this family history quest. But the idea never would have developed without Oscar Johnson. He spent an afternoon with me in August 1991, taking me on my second tour of Hildene while telling me stories about the family. We went to the back gardens, where he showed me the outlines of the reflecting pool where Peggy used to sail her toy boats. Oscar dug in the weeds there and pulled out some rusted pieces of cast iron, remnants of a tiny wood stove that used to heat Peggy's playhouse there. I imagined her as a girl running through the tall grass and picking wildflowers. He took me to the edge of the cliff behind the house and showed me the field Peggy used as a runway to fly her planes in the 1930s. Through Oscar's many stories, Peggy and her family came alive for me, and I wanted to share their spirits with others.

On this trip, I also discovered 24 oral history tapes of interviews conducted by Alison Otis in 1979. I am so grateful to her, as this material became my starting point. Thanks to Hildene farm manager Ken Hill and the others who were interviewed by her, plus the many members of the Manchester community who shared stories with me directly.

In addition, I found primary sources in the form of letters, diaries, photographs, school records, house records, invitations from Queen Victoria and the Prince of Wales, dance cards, handwritten notes, cancelled checks, artwork, family memorabilia, and lots of old news clippings at four major historical collections: the Lincoln Museum Research Library in Fort Wayne, Indiana; the Chicago Historical Society; the Illinois State Historical Library (now the Abraham Lincoln Presidential Library) in Springfield, Illinois; and the Harlan-Lincoln House Collection and Iowa Wesleyan College Archives in Mount Pleasant, Iowa. These collections have been invaluable, and I am grateful to the staffs of these institutions, especially to Illinois State Historian Tom Schwartz; Iowa Wesleyan College's former president, the late Dr. Louis Haselmayer; and the Iowa Wesleyan College archivist, Lynn Ellsworth, for their help and encouragement. Thanks also to the many librarians in Iowa, Illinois, Indiana, Massachusetts, and Vermont who have helped me— librarians are the unsung heroes of every researcher.

There are many scholars with more breadth of knowledge about the Civil War era and women's history than me, but since none of them had studied these primary materials about the last three generations of Lincoln women, I dove in. For information about Mary Todd Lincoln's life and general information about U.S. history, though, I have generally relied on these scholars rather than primary sources. I am particularly grateful for the Mary Todd Lincoln biographies of Jean Baker and Ruth Painter Randall, for the collection of her letters by Justin and Linda Levitt Turner, and for the study of her insanity trial by Mark Neely, Jr. and R. Gerald McMurtry. Thanks to the late John Goff for sharing lunch and ideas, and for his research on Robert Todd Lincoln. Thanks to Harold Holzer, Frank Williams, and John Simon, the other Hildene Lincoln Women symposium speakers not already mentioned, and the speakers at other Hildene symposiums, for their ideas and encouragement. And thanks to Edwin Bigelow and Nancy Otis for their history of Manchester, Vermont, and to my tenacious cousin Alpheus Harlan, who spent more than two decades tracking down the first 200 years of history of the Harlan family in America.

I cannot finish without some more personal notes of thanks: to my U-Mass thesis advisor George Cuomo, who pushed me to do better; to Mary Hard Bort, who has supported me personally and answered many questions about Manchester history; to my dear friend Russell Burr Stanton, who taught me so much about history, research, writing, and life in general—how I wish you were here to see this; to Alan Fisher, who was always willing to read the many versions of this manuscript; to Beverly Fryer for her most generous hospitality; to Peg Gregory for patient listening and wise counsel; to Ellen Berkeley for mentoring; to my editor Kathleen James Ring, who has read this so many times and helped me with style and focus; to the past and present staff of Hildene for caring about this project as much as I do and for those who have backed it financially; to my mom and dad, for research assistance and so much more; and to my husband Ben Williams, who put up with me through this process and was perpetually encouraging. Many thanks to H.P.

C.J. King
Jamaica, Vermont
February 2005

The publishing of this book was supported
in part by Furthermore Grants in Publishing,
a program of the J.M. Kaplan Fund.

With special thanks to Kathleen James Ring,
whose donation of thoughtful and skillful editing
made this book far better.

THE HARLAN FAMILY

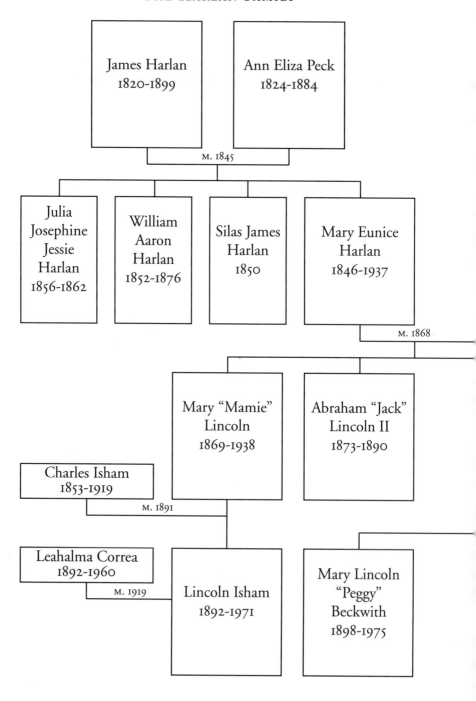

THE LINCOLN FAMILY

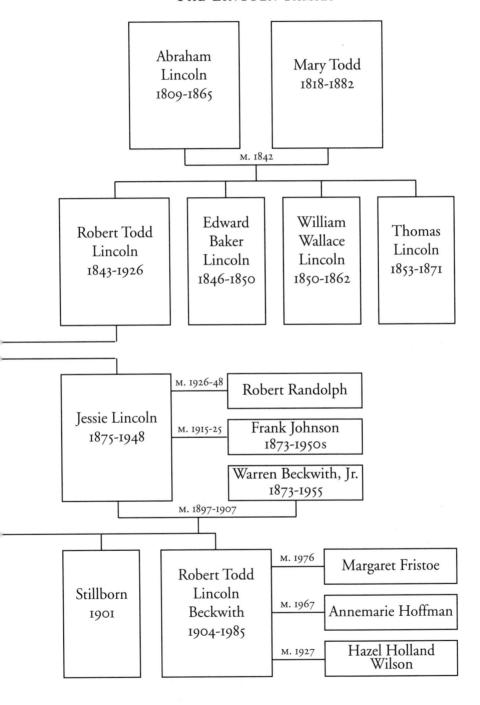

Four Marys and a Jessie

CHAPTER ONE:

"I Didn't Ask to Be Born a Lincoln"

Bennington County, Vermont, September 20, 1930

Vermont's fall foliage is so famous, people come from everywhere to see it. Vermonters are the lucky ones; they get to experience this parade of colors not as one majestic moment in early October, but as a steady series of magical transformations.

It always starts too soon—summers are too short in Vermont. After a cool night in August, some errand might take you up into the hill country, where you notice a stray red branch or an early tree blushing with color. You shiver a bit, thinking of the long winter to come. Then it turns warm again, and the hot summer sun lulls you into forgetfulness for a few weeks, during which time you try to pretend that summer isn't really nearly over.

By early September, it's undeniable—you can see the color creeping into the trees at higher altitudes. Then a week or so later, another cold spell comes, and suddenly you're aware that the color is all around you. You begin to watch the changes every day, as patches of green shrink and disappear, taking on every shade in an artist's palette from red and brown to orange and yellow.

It's beautiful everywhere, but the best views are those from way up high, looking down. From the mountaintops, it's spectacular, and those few who are truly lucky get to witness this miraculous view from the air.

On a sunny late-September afternoon in 1930, Mary Lincoln "Peggy" Beckwith was one of those lucky few. From the cockpit of her Fleet Model One biplane, she saw it firsthand. The descendants of Abraham Lincoln had been visiting Vermont since the height of the Civil War, and spending summers there for 25 years. For her predecessors, the advent of fall colors was a signal that it was almost time to go back south. Peggy would be the one to break this tradition and make Manchester, Vermont, her year-round home.

Flying over the long, narrow Valley of Vermont, with its rumpled carpet of color spread out beneath her, Peggy was witness to the drama of its geologic beauty. The fertile valley that is home to Manchester lies between two ancient ridges, the Green Mountains and the Taconics, which run side by side, north to south, for about 85 miles. Although they may appear to be parallel from the air, they aren't exactly. North of Manchester ten miles or so, near Emerald Lake, the valley is narrow, its walls steep and merely a few hundred yards apart, while at the southern end, near Bennington, the valley widens as the mountains soften, lose altitude, and spread out.

These mountains are so ancient it's incomprehensible, formed some 500 million years ago by the steady collision of the earth's tectonic plates. Dirt and rocks originally located southeast of Vermont were pushed up and over the emerging ridge that became the Green Mountains, forming a second ridge, the Taconics, to the west. Between them, glaciers helped carve a valley that once was connected to the Atlantic Ocean. The Taconics are rich in shale and slate, and both ranges have deep pockets of marble. These mineral deposits create a hospitable environment for an unusual mixture of plants and animals, nourished by the calcium-rich soil.[1]

On that sunny September day in 1930, Peggy Beckwith may have been pondering the eternity of geologic time, or the rich environment of flora and fauna, but more than likely she was just enjoying the view. She made another slow circle in the sky, waving from her window at another pilot, Henry Bradford, who was also circling over the parade route below.

Beneath them, a steady stream of cars crawled like ants along a brand-new stretch of concrete, running 37 miles from the Massachusetts border north to Manchester. Hundreds of people had gathered at the Vermont-Massachusetts border in Williamstown, Massachusetts, and all along the route, to participate in a celebration to open this new road. One section of the Ethan Allen Highway, it was intended eventually as a full route from the southern border of Vermont to its northern border with Canada.

The road represented a political victory for those who had spent the last ten years lobbying for it. It took a decade for enough people to be convinced a paved road was worth the tax dollars it would cost. The road would connect Vermonters to highways leading to Boston, New York, and other outside destinations. It would also bring outsiders in. Was that a good thing? The debate went on and on, but finally, a section at a time, the road won local support.

The parade included more than 60 floats and decorated cars, and more than 300 spectator cars, plus three bands and three drum corps. At the state border, they had lined up by towns, with those from the southernmost town, Pownal, going first, followed by those from Bennington, Shaftsbury, Arlington, Sunderland, and Manchester. A preview article from the *Bennington Evening Banner* had boasted that, "The motor parade promises to be one of the most impressive sights witnessed in this vicinity for a long time."[2]

Around 2 p.m., Legionnaires Curtis Crosier and James Hamilton had held a garland of chrysanthemums across the start of the road at the border, and William E. Bissell, one of the organizers, had cut the flower rope. A cannon was fired, and the road was officially open to traffic.[3]

The parade then headed north, stopping in each town along the way to re-enact some moment in history that had happened there, or to honor some important historical person who had once resided there. The road was named for Ethan Allen, leader of a band of Revolutionary War patriots who helped fight off the British throughout southwestern Vermont. In 1775, they single-handedly took Fort Ticonderoga from the British by surprising and surrounding them; the British gave up without a fight. In those days, the Ethan Allen Highway was a mere footpath in the wilderness. Several of the re-enactors quipped that the revolution would have been much easier with the broad, hard-surfaced road this path had become.[4]

Management of the parade traffic was quite a logistical challenge. In its preview article, the *Bennington Evening Banner* had warned that, "Traffic will be held up all along the route for the parade and no one will be permitted to pass in either direction once the line has started moving. Traffic going south will be forced to wait until the parade gets by while north bound traffic will have to follow the parade through to Manchester."[5] Three hundred passenger cars, 60 floats and decorated cars, three marching bands, three drum corps—imagine how long it took at parade speed for that crowd to cover 37 miles, especially with several stops along the way!

Airplanes, of course, can travel faster than cars. Even at their slowest throttle, it was difficult for the two pilots to keep pace with the parade, so they circled again and again. People along the route no doubt looked up whenever they heard the planes' engine noise. A mystique still surrounded flying in 1930. Charles Lindbergh's amazing cross-Atlantic solo flight was only three years past, and planes were still a novelty. The Bennington paper that carried the parade preview also had a story about the death of a female pilot who had just crashed while embarking on a transcontinental flight.[6] Many people were terrified at the thought of flying, but Peggy Beckwith wasn't afraid.

What did she like about flying? Was it the sense of adventure and risk, the mastery over atmosphere and gravity, or the absolute sense of privacy? We don't know for sure, but this daredevil sport of flying was unique and brand-new, something unexpected. And above all else, Peggy liked to defy expectations.

By 1930, the descendants of President Abraham Lincoln had moved far in station from his poor rural roots. Abraham Lincoln himself had left a sizeable estate, and his son, Robert Todd Lincoln, Peggy's grandfather, far surpassed his father in financial resources. The descendants were wealthy and could do what they wanted with their lives. And with the Lincoln name as part of their heritage, they all had access to elite circles of society. Doors opened for the descendants of President Lincoln, and people noticed when they arrived. But none of them, except Robert Todd Lincoln, chose public careers. With so many options open to them, why did they all choose such retiring lives?

Abraham Lincoln is the best-known and best-loved president in American history. His shadow and his reputation fell heavily over all of his descendants. Like the Kennedys, the Lincolns were always watched closely and treated as curiosities, and whatever they did, if it was good, the President somehow got the credit. Their successes were portrayed not as the result of their own hard work and determination, but as something expected of a Lincoln.

Abraham Lincoln didn't know how to fly an airplane. Horses and trains were the modes of transportation in his era. But in February 1930, the year the Ethan Allen Highway opened, a *National Tribune* reporter, writing the obligatory Lincoln's birthday story about his family and his legacy, discovered Peggy's "intense interest in aviation," which the reporter called "the first real 'news' in many a day regarding the Lincoln family."[7] A week earlier, another of these stories declared that, "The spirit of Abraham Lincoln lives, and in his great granddaughter, Miss Mary Lincoln Beckwith, many of his outstanding characteristics continue...she is now taking up aviation, owns her own plane, and is qualifying for her pilot's license."[8]

Peggy generally followed the family rule and avoided public appearances. She hated reporters who asked her questions just because she was a Lincoln. She knew they didn't really care about her as an individual, but were just looking for some reaction that seemed characteristic of Lincoln. "I didn't ask to be born a Lincoln," she once told a friend.[9] "I'm as far away from him as anyone else," she told a reporter.[10]

The shadow fell hardest on Peggy's grandfather. Robert Todd Lincoln biographer John Goff felt the need to argue in his book's subtitle that Robert Todd Lincoln was *A Man in His Own Right*. Everywhere Robert Lincoln went, he was always introduced as his father's son. By virtue of his roles as corporate lawyer, president and chairman of the Pullman Company, Secretary of War for President James Garfield and President Chester Arthur, and as minister to Great Britain under President Benjamin Harrison, he lived by choice in the public spotlight. But while he worked hard to be respected solely on his own merit, he never was. He would have been immensely pleased with his obituary in the *Chicago Tribune* that said, "Robert Todd Lincoln had no more distinguishing characteristic than his refusal to trade on the greatness of his parent..." and another from the Associated Press that said, "...Robert T. Lincoln, although living a retired life and avoiding any appearance of ever basking in the glow of his illustrious father's name, did render marked service to his country and built an enviable name for himself..." [11]

The other members of the Lincoln family lived privately; they did not pursue politics or business careers. They had homes in Chicago, Washington, New York, Virginia, Iowa, and Vermont, and wherever they went, they refused to flaunt their family name. They found refuge in small-town obscurity in Iowa and Vermont.

Even though she was asked to participate because of her illustrious family that September day in 1930, Peggy still had it the way she liked it. In her airplane, she was far above the crowds and reporters, way up in the sky and unreachable. This way, she could honor her great-grandfather while doing something she loved, without anyone paying her any particular attention.

Peggy did pose for one news photograph that day. She and Ethan Allen IV, great-grandson of Vermont's famous revolutionary hero, were photographed in front of her plane [PLATE 32]. Ethan Allen rode in a car for distinguished guests during the parade, and he attended all of the official proceedings, including a dinner afterward at Manchester's elegant Equinox House hotel. He was included in several news stories about the event. Peggy shared one paragraph with him in the *Bennington Evening Banner* and was mentioned in the *Manchester Journal*. Halfway through a long, detailed account, the *Banner* reported that:

> Of particular interest to the historically minded was the presence of three direct descendants of famous Americans: Ethan Allen, a New York broker, great grandson of Ethan Allen; Ray Stannard Baker of Amherst, Mass., great grandson of Remember Baker; and Miss 'Peggy' Beckwith of Manchester, [great]granddaughter of Abraham Lincoln... flew her plane over the course, accompanied by Henry Bradford in his bi-plane. [12]

The *Journal* gave her even less notice, stating only that, "Flying over the parade for its entire length were two airplanes, one belonging to Miss Mary L. Beckwith of Manchester, great-granddaughter of the martyred president, Abraham Lincoln, and the other belonging to Henry Bradford of Bennington."[13]

When the parade reached Manchester, several hours after it began, everyone marched to the fairgrounds, where the decorated cars and floats and bands went twice around the track. Prizes were awarded. Then Vermont Governor John Weeks congratulated the state highway board for making progress: The state had only 42 miles of paved roads in 1925, and now it had 348. State Chamber of Commerce Secretary James P. Taylor spoke, declaring (in the reporter's words) that roads form the "most intensive human interest factors in a commonwealth" and (direct quote) that he "who rides the roads of a state lives the life of its people."[14] The Massachusetts Highway Commissioner, the construction chief, and other members of the highway board also spoke, and Ethan Allen IV was introduced, but Peggy Beckwith did not appear on the program.

As hard as it was living in Abraham Lincoln's shadow, at least the shadow was from someone well loved. The female Lincoln legacy was more troubling.

Whenever people hear the name Mary Todd Lincoln, the first question most of them ask is whether she was insane. Maybe they recount the famous story of how her husband showed her the local mental hospital from a White House window after the death of their son, and said if she didn't get better soon they'd have to take her there. Or they repeat stories they've heard of her odd behavior later on—and there are plenty of these tales to tell. But many details of her story were still hidden from the public in 1930. Before he died in 1926, Robert Todd Lincoln, her oldest son, tied up a bundle of papers and labeled them "MTL Insanity Trial"—personal records he believed would vindicate his decision to have his mother committed. He stashed these papers in a secret compartment at Hildene, his summer home in Manchester, and they weren't discovered until after Peggy died in 1975 (she had inherited Hildene).[15] What most people knew about Mary Todd Lincoln before those papers were discovered was based half on rumor and half on fact.

What did the later Lincoln women know about their famous female ancestor? Four women in the family were named Mary Lincoln: Mary Todd Lincoln, Abraham Lincoln's wife; Mary Harlan Lincoln, the President's daughter-in-law; Mary Lincoln Isham ("Mamie"), the first-born Lincoln grandchild; and Mary Lincoln "Peggy" Beckwith, the only great-granddaughter and the last female Lincoln. Mamie's younger sister, Jessie, was Peggy's mother. Of all of these, only Mary Harlan Lincoln really knew Mary Todd Lincoln. At first, they were the best of friends, but in time their relationship soured. The only one of the next generations who had a chance to get to know the former First Lady was Mamie, the eldest grandchild, but she was only a girl when her grandmother died.

When Mamie was born, in October 1869, her grandmother was in Europe, and she didn't return for more than a year and a half. The family had a brief happy reunion in May 1871, when Mary Todd Lincoln and her youngest son Tad returned. They stayed briefly in Robert's home in Chicago and met the family's newest member. But then tensions arose between the mother-in-law and the daughter-in-law, some say over differing opinions on how to run the household.[16] Mary Harlan Lincoln left town to attend to her ailing mother near Washington, and Mary Todd Lincoln and Tad moved to a Chicago hotel. Tad, who had been suffering from what seemed like a cold ever since they arrived, quickly became very ill. He lingered for two months, his lungs filling up from pleurisy, and he died in July.

Mary Todd Lincoln had now outlived three of her four sons, as well as her beloved husband. This latest death put her over the edge, and she never fully recovered. She had always suffered physically from migraines and other persistent ailments, and she was by nature a highly emotional woman. Physical and mental problems plagued her almost constantly for the next decade. Things remained tense between Mary and her son and daughter-in-law, and there were long periods of separation as she spent the next few years traveling from health spa to health spa to soothe her physical ailments, and consulting spiritualists to soothe her unrelenting grief.

The spiritualists' claims that they could contact the dead were received with the same mix of skepticism, hope and belief in Mary Todd Lincoln's day as they are today, and some people were persecuted or even labeled insane for consulting with mediums. But there were other new and mysterious forces being introduced to American society in the mid-1800s, things like electricity, the telegraph, mesmerism, and belief in a sympathetic God. These strange new ideas influenced the society in which Mary Todd Lincoln came of age.

In 1842, when Samuel Morse asked Congress for $30,000 to build a telegraph line between Washington and Baltimore, one representative suggested the $30,000 be split, with half going toward the telegraph project, and the other half going to study mesmerism, a strange new medical practice that was invented in Vienna by Franz Anton Mesmer and brought to the United States by the mid 1840s. It used magnets and electrical currents to heal.[17]

The 1830s and '40s also saw the advent of a more sympathetic worldview, with progressive preachers espousing an end to strict Calvinistic beliefs like rigid predestination and infant damnation, allowing that one could convert to Christianity and thereby influence one's eternal destiny. Those who preached these gentler truths were sometimes censored by their church's hierarchy, as was Lyman Beecher, father of Henry Ward Beecher, Harriet Beecher Stowe, and Catherine Beecher. But despite pressures from within the church, these preachers believed they spoke from a higher authority, and those who heard them in revival tents across the nation passionately embraced their message, especially women, who had so little control over their lives, and welcomed the belief that they could control the fate of their souls, and the comforting idea that their infant children who died were not lost forever.[18]

Spiritualism was also gaining converts in the mid 1800s. In 1848, two young female mediums underwent a very closely controlled public experiment in Rochester, New York, that attempted to expose the "trick" of how they communicated with spirits by a series of audible raps received by "spiritual telegraph." The careful examiners could not find the source of these noises, and thus they could do nothing to discourage the growing practice of spiritualism. Other mediums did prove fraudulent, but still, many grieving persons turned to spiritualists.[19]

Was Mary Todd Lincoln insane for trying spiritualism, for dwelling on her many physical ailments, for her paranoiac worries about money, or for spending money as a means of emotional distraction? To her eldest son Robert, with his dignified and legalistic mind, it certainly seemed so. Some people have argued that he had her committed simply so he could control her money, but it can't be that simple, considering how carefully he accounted for her money while he was its conservator, how much he detested being in the public eye, and how impossible it would be to keep the insanity trial of President Lincoln's widow out of the papers.

Mary Todd Lincoln spent four months confined in a sanitarium,[20] during which time she turned all of her efforts toward getting out.[21] When she succeeded, she went to live with her sister in Springfield, Illinois, for a few months, then went back to Europe, maintaining her self-imposed exile until the fall of 1880, when general feebleness and two major injuries forced her return, once again to her sister's care.[22]

During her last year in Springfield, she mostly stayed in her room, keeping the shades drawn and complaining that light hurt her eyes. She spent hours digging through her 64 trunks full of possessions. She had few visitors, and those who did visit were quickly driven away by incessant recitations about her various medical conditions.[23] Finally, Mary Todd Lincoln collapsed on the anniversary of Tad Lincoln's death and died a day later, on July 16, 1882.[24]

Mrs. Lincoln did have one very important visit during that last year of her life. In May of 1881, Robert, who was serving as Secretary of War, traveled west to Fort Leavenworth on official business. He brought along his daughter Mamie,[25] who was by then 11 years old. Grandmother Lincoln was 63. At 11, Mamie had eyes and mind with enough maturity to see her grandmother's condition and to form a lasting impression. She had had no opportunity to get to know her grandmother in better times. She had visited with her grandmother several times before and during her confinement,[26] but that was at least four years past, when she was only seven. This visit would have more impact. What Mamie saw on this rare visit in 1881 was a frail but intimidating old woman, bent over from arthritis and back injuries, dressed in gloomy black clothes, sharp-witted but complaining. The darkened room in which they sat fit her grandmother's mood.[27] This was the last direct impression carried on to the next generations. This was what Mamie would remember when she thought about the woman who embodied her female Lincoln legacy.

CHAPTER TWO:

The Courtship of Mary Todd

What did the Lincoln descendants know about Mary Todd Lincoln's mental illness? How did they live with this legacy? Did they know about the secret papers stashed at Hildene? Was the last one alive supposed to "discover" the papers for posterity? Robert Todd Lincoln Beckwith, Peggy Beckwith's brother, was the last Lincoln alive after the summer of 1975, and he insisted that all of his grandfather's private papers had been destroyed. But Lincoln curator James T. Hickey, of the Illinois State Historical Library, was not discouraged. With Robert Todd Lincoln Beckwith's permission, he conducted a search of Hildene after Peggy's death in July of 1975, and he found the Robert Todd Lincoln "MTL Insanity File" stored in a double-locked closet.[1]

People generally are embarrassed to admit to insanity in their family, and perhaps this is especially true for a family as famous as the Lincolns. The descendants didn't talk publicly about the insanity trial, and they probably avoided discussing it among themselves as well.[2] We don't have any record of their opinions about Mary Todd Lincoln. Did Mary Harlan Lincoln ever reminisce to her children and grandchildren about the earlier, more pleasant times? In the beginning, she and her mother-in-law were dear friends, but later, after the trial, Mary Todd Lincoln accused her son and daughter-in-law of stealing things she had clearly given them as gifts, or of appropriating things she had stored away and forgotten. The relationship, once warm, then strained, was never fully healed.[3]

Mary Todd Lincoln certainly experienced a full share of life's tragedies. And because of her emotional makeup, she tended to respond emphatically to every insult and injury. Her early life may give us some clues as to why this was so.

Lexington, Kentucky, 1818–1835

Mary Todd was born on December 13, 1818, the third child of influential Lexington banker Robert Todd, and his wife, Eliza. Mary had two older sisters, Elizabeth and Frances.

In the 1820s, Lexington was admired as "the wealthiest, most sophisticated community west of the Alleghenies, excepting, of course, New Orleans," according to Mary Todd Lincoln biographer Jean Baker.[4] The Todds were among the original settlers of Lexington, and they helped to develop the city and to found Transylvania University there. They valued money, property, and education, and by example, they championed personal integrity and public service.[5]

Robert Todd, Mary's father, served in the military during the War of 1812 and as a state legislator. These ventures and regular business trips to New Orleans for his dry goods store kept him away from home for long periods of time. Sometimes he spent as much as one-third of the year away.[6]

Mary Todd's young mother, Eliza, admitted early on that she was ill prepared for the rigorous job of motherhood. She had spent her teenage years from age 12 to 18 doing what "proper" young ladies did—she rode in carriages, shopped, visited friends, attended parties, and gossiped about bachelors and marriage. Soon after her marriage to Robert, Eliza wrote a letter to her grandfather, stating that she had been "very busy for some time past preparing for house-keeping. I had no idea it was attended with so much trouble, it really is almost enough to deter girls from getting married."[7]

When Mary Todd was born, Eliza already had two children. As was common for women of the period, she continued to give birth approximately every two years. After Mary came Levi; then Ann; then Robert, who died at 14 months; then George Rogers Clark. Eliza died soon after this seventh birth, when Mary was six.

Typically, 10 to 20 percent of women died in childbirth,[8] but statistics do not matter to a six-year-old girl who has lost her mother.

At six, Mary probably felt no comfort from her family's Presbyterian belief that life in heaven would be better than life on earth.[9] She simply missed her mother.

Robert Todd had a newborn, plus five children to care for, and his business affairs to manage. He probably gave Mary no special attention during this difficult period, perhaps setting up a pattern for her to feel abandoned during times of grief. Her two older sisters were closer in age, perhaps making her feel excluded. Aunt Ann Todd, who ran the household after Eliza's death, doted on Mary's younger sister Ann, her namesake. Robert Todd and his brothers doted on the boys. "In age, circumstance, and temperament, she was most vulnerable," wrote biographer Baker.[10]

Mary felt utterly alone. Things did not improve when her father remarried. Plenty of other children had lost parents or siblings and endured being stepchildren, but Mary Todd later described her childhood as "desolate."[11] Baker's assessment of these first turbulent years of Mary's life was that:

> In her short, hectic life Mary had already encountered a series of family disruptions. At less than a year she had been abruptly weaned and had lost her place as the youngest to a first son. When she was four, a baby brother died. At five she lost part of her name [she was called 'Mary Ann' until the birth of her sister Ann, at which point her name was shortened to 'Mary'], at six her mother died, and now at seven a stranger absorbed her father's affections.[12]

Robert Todd was busy, and he needed a wife to manage his home. A year and a half after Eliza's death, when Mary was almost eight, Robert married Elizabeth "Betsey" Humphreys, of Frankfort, Kentucky. At 25, Mary's new stepmother was old enough to understand what was expected of her. She knew the circumstances of the Todd household, and she knew about the influence of the Widow Parker, Eliza's mother, just down the hill. During the early years of Eliza and Robert's marriage, Eliza's mother had helped to supervise their household, as well as her own, and frequently loaned them slaves. Grandma Parker was Mary's ally. She gave Mary special presents and extra money for clothes.[13]

Robert and Betsey added eight more children to the family (a ninth child didn't survive). Unlike Eliza, who had been timid and loving, Betsey was strict and stern and intimidating. All six of the original Todd children despised her.[14]

When Mr. Todd was gone, the new Mrs. Todd was in charge. This was quite an enterprise considering there were fourteen children and several slaves to manage, plus all the cooking and cleaning, and production of many of their daily necessities, such as soap, food and clothing. Betsey had to supervise all of this labor. In addition, several family members came for extended visits. Betsey's brother John spent summers with the Todds for many years, and her niece, Elizabeth "Lizzie" Humphreys, shared Mary's room for six years while the girls attended school together at Reverend Ward's Shelby Female Academy.

By the 1820s, progressive minds were beginning to agree that a certain amount of education was important for women. In these years, family life was beginning to change, with more and more men working outside the home. Urban areas were developing, as was the distinction between a man's realm and a woman's. Especially for more affluent families, home was becoming a place of nurturing retreat, not the site of cottage-industry production. While men concentrated on earning money from their efforts in the outside world, women increasingly were running the households, and education was seen as a way to create efficient and loving homes. Husbands tended to prefer intelligent, gentle companions who could read the Bible and help educate their children, women with enough schooling to support their husbands socially, to manage the household accounts, and to raise intelligent children.

Girls learned to be good wives and mothers by watching their elders' examples. This instruction was supplemented with ladies magazines and behavior manuals like the one written by Daniel Wise, *The Young Lady's Counsellor*, published in 1851. It explained the role of women like this:

...your sex is not necessarily inferior to the other, because it is called, by God and nature, to act in a different sphere. Your exclusion from the stage of public life does not imply your inferiority—only the diversity of your powers...What is the sphere of woman? Home. The social circle. What is her mission? To mold character—to fashion herself and others after the model character of Christ. What are her chief instruments for the accomplishment of her great work? The affections. Love is the wand by which she is to work moral transformation, within her fairy circle. Gentleness, sweetness, loveliness and purity are the elements of her power.[15]

An earlier version of this type of literature, Dr. John Gregory's *A Father's Legacy to His Daughter*, published in 1805, was still popular in Mary's day. Gregory credited women with "softness and sensibility of heart."[16] He stressed that wives were not to be "domestic drudges, or the slaves of our pleasures, but as our companions and equals; as designed to soften our hearts and polish our manners."[17]

New publications like *Ladies Magazine* and *Godey's Lady's Book* provided a steady stream of articles reminding women that they were the guardians of culture, the ones responsible for preserving manners and values. Women were very important to a democracy because they could create a virtuous society by producing ethical, hard-working children. Women were, of course, second in charge after their husbands. They must remember that they were junior partners in every marriage. Because they were not generally considered as wise as men, they should be submissive. "True feminine genius is ever timid, doubtful, and clingingly dependent," Grace Greenwood reminded her fellow women in a literary essay titled "The Intellectual Woman," written in 1846.[18]

In the first years of the new American republic and beyond, women were charged with raising the next generation of democratic citizens. For this reason, the arguments for women's education rang true. But others in Mary's day still feared that educating women was dangerous, countering that too much book-learning could make a woman unsuitable for marriage.[19]

Some declared that women's brains were inherently inferior, unable to process the same information as a man. "It is very certain, that they cannot, like the men, arrange, combine, abstract, pursue and diversify a long strain of ideas," John Bennett said about women in *Strictures on Female Education*, published just before the turn of the 18th century.[20] T.S. Arthur explained in *Advice to Young Ladies on Their Duties and Conduct in Life* that women's lack of reasoning power was due to an innate deficiency in their brains:

> A man's head is higher, and fuller in front, than a woman's; while a woman's head is broader and larger behind than a man's. From this it will be seen that man has a will and an understanding; and so has a woman;—that both are thinking and loving beings, but that in one the understanding or intellect preponderates, and in the other the will or affections...A man is not equal to a woman, nor a woman equal to a man...let any sensible woman reflect upon the nature of this difference, and she will at once see that the claim of equality which is set up is altogether an erroneous one, and that the attempt to make woman equal in the way some contend that she should be, would be to do the greatest possible wrong, both to herself and society.[21]

Eighteenth-century men sometimes spoke derisively about educated or literary women, calling them "blue stockings," but increasingly, 19th century writers urged men not to fear educated women as wives.[22] Benjamin Rush, in his essay "Thoughts on Female Education," explained that education would help make a woman "an agreeable companion for a sensible man" and help her fulfill her true calling in the new republic. "Let the ladies of a country be educated properly and they will form its manner and character," he wrote.[23]

From post-Revolutionary America to 1850 and beyond, educational opportunities increased rapidly for middle- and upper-class daughters. Literacy rose as well. In the late 1700s, probably half as many women as men could write their names; by the mid-1800s, literacy rates were nearly equal in the Northeast.[24]

Advocates of women's education continued to argue that it would enhance women's contribution to society. When Emma Willard petitioned the New York legislature for a women's academy in 1819, she argued that her school would help women be "the greatest possible use to themselves and to others." She stressed that her school would make women better homemakers and mothers, with sons ready to participate in a democratic society. New York did not grant her the money she requested, but the citizens of Troy, New York, did. The school opened in 1821.[25] Mary Lyon, founder of Mount Holyoke Female Seminary in South Hadley, Massachusetts, also declared that she could help rescue young ladies from "empty gentility" and could prepare them for a larger role in society. Her school first opened its doors in 1837.[26]

Girls from more financially able families went to this kind of academy, where they studied reading, writing, arithmetic, history, geography, and natural sciences along with "ornamentals" like French, embroidery, music, drawing, and painting. They were instructed in such social skills as dancing, etiquette, and letter writing. Many headmasters were also ministers, so lessons in religion, moral character, and personal ethics were emphasized. Academics were taught by recitation. Students were supposed to memorize a text, and then recite it back to the teacher through a question and answer format. Recitations included Bible verses and "homiletics" to remind them about a woman's place in society. The girls intoned phrases like, "Love is the essence of our being" and "Evil communications corrupt good manners; gentleness corrects," reciting these over and over. Independent thinking was discouraged.[27]

Mary's father supported women's education. His mother, his stepmother, his sisters, and both of his wives had all attended school, even though most girls still did not. Robert Todd had been exposed to Mary Wollstonecraft's *A Vindication of the Rights of Woman*, published in 1792, which argued that girls had both the mental faculty and a natural right to be educated. This book was in the family library when he was growing up. Of course, education would not be the center of his daughter's life. It was merely part of her preparation for a good marriage.[28]

From 1827 to 1832, Mary Todd and her step-cousin Lizzie attended Ward's, as Shelby Female Academy was generally called. Sessions ran from September to early January and from early March through July. Early every morning, the two girls climbed the hill between school and home, Mary often at a quick pace. Lizzie later recalled in a letter to the daughter of Mary's half-sister, who was preparing a family history, that Mary had a quick mind and was eager to learn. Recitations began early, before breakfast, and Mary was always in a hurry to get there. Once, a night watchman saw Mary running up the hill so early and so fast that he thought she must be eloping.[29]

Rev. Ward described his curriculum as a "complete system of female education." Accordingly, his classes did not include the traditionally male subjects of Greek, Latin, logic and oratory. After all, women were not allowed to enroll at Transylvania University, where these classics would be required for admission, and even the most brilliant wife and mother did not need to converse in these subjects.[30]

Rev. Ward shared teaching with his wife, Sarah, and his unmarried sister. Mrs. Ward was not particularly accomplished in the "ornamentals," but she was good at history, geography, and astronomy, offering Mary and the other girls a somewhat unusual example of female scholarship. She was an excellent cook, and she tried to pass this skill on to her students, taking the girls into the kitchen each afternoon to show them how to prepare various dishes.[31]

Mary was a good student who quickly mastered her lessons. Lizzie later described her as "happy, high-spirited, affectionate, and somewhat precocious."[32] She also described Mary as "far in advance over girls of her age in education; she had a retentive memory and a mind that enabled her to grasp and thoroughly understand that lesson she was required to learn."[33]

After her years at Ward's, she received two other significant forms of education. The Todds were politically well connected, and as Mary reached adolescence, she began to acquire her life-long interest in politics.[34] She had lots of opportunity to study the issues of the day and to form personal opinions, as her father was a friend of Henry Clay's, and he and other political guests often dined with the family.[35]

Shortly before her 14th birthday, Mary was enrolled at Madame Mentelle's School for Young Ladies, a Lexington academy run by two Parisian-born aristocrats who had escaped during the French Revolution. The school was only a mile and a half from home, but Mary boarded there during the week. Perhaps this helped relieve an overcrowded household, or gave space between stepmother and stepdaughter. The family coachman deposited her at Mentelle's on Monday mornings and retrieved her Friday afternoons. Charlotte Victoire Leclere Mentelle, the school's matron, described the school's program as follows:

> My price for tuition and boarding is $120 a year paid quarterly in advance. I give no other holydays than one week at Christmas, one day at Easter, and one at Whitsuntide [Pentecost]. We teach every branch of good education, French if wanted. The most particular care is taken of morals, temper, and health.[36]

Social activities at Mentelle's included dancing the polka, the schottische, the gallop, and the waltz in the parlor while Madame Charlotte played the violin. It also included acting and participating in local festivals and parades. One summer day, the girls dressed in white muslin, black sashes and veils, and took part in a memorial for the General Marquis de Lafayette, who had once visited this part of Kentucky; the county was named Fayette in his honor. Each girl represented one of the American states, plus France and America.[37]

In order to keep her charges in line, Madame Mentelle often told dramatic and terrifying stories about her childhood. She said her father, a wealthy Parisian merchant who had raised her like a son, regularly forced her to row across the Seine before breakfast. She said that once when she told him she was afraid of dying, he locked her up in a closet with the corpse of an acquaintance. She also described her frightening flight from France in 1792, with bloodthirsty revolutionaries at her heels. Whether these stories were completely true or exaggerated, they had their intended effect. The girls were entranced.[38]

Madame Mentelle's influence on the fertile ground of Mary Todd's teenage imagination was obvious. At Mentelle's, Mary acquired a lifelong fluency in French, a distaste for Lexington, a fascination with royalty, and a penchant for private theater. Lizzie remembered her as a "star actress" who was good at impersonation and mimicry. "Charlotte Mentelle, a grandmotherly sixty-two when Mary Todd enrolled, also conveyed indelible images of female independence, aristocratic snobbishness, and individual eccentricity," according to Jean Baker. Mary later remarked that she had found her "true" home at the Mentelle's.[39]

Springfield, Illinois, 1836–1842

Mary stopped attending Mentelle's in 1836, when she was 17. She was well-schooled in academics and the social graces, she had a quick and curious mind, and she didn't pretend otherwise. Her keen observations and strong opinions made her a lively conversationalist. Thus, she was ready to search for a marriage partner who could appreciate her own particular personality.

Springfield became the new Illinois state capital in 1837, so Springfield was the up-and-coming place to be. Mary's older sister Elizabeth had married and settled there, and Mary went to Springfield that year to visit her. This was the first of many visits. Elizabeth was the wife of Ninian Wirt Edwards, son of Illinois' first governor. Both Ninian Edwards and Mary's cousin John Todd Stuart, who also lived in Springfield, were considering bids for Congress. The Edwards home was often host to gatherings of young people who were interested in discussing local and national affairs.[40]

During her first visit, Mary's other older sister, Frances, was already visiting in the Edwards home and meeting available bachelors. Two years later, Frances would marry Springfield resident Dr. William Wallace, and a few years after that, Mary would marry wearing Fanny's wedding dress.[41]

Traveling from Lexington to Springfield was no easy task in 1837. Starting out one morning in early May, Mary took the train to Frankfort, then took a stagecoach to Louisville, then boarded a steamboat on the Ohio River traveling to St. Louis. From there, she rode the last hundred miles east in another bumpy stagecoach. The

trip took two weeks, according to Jean Baker, "if the proper connections were made, if the rain did not turn dirt roads into molasses,
if an axle did not fall off the wheel or the stage run off the road."[42]

Abraham Lincoln moved to Springfield the month before
Mary's first visit, in late April of 1837. Mary's cousin, John Todd
Stuart, had invited him to study and practice law in his firm. The
two men had met in service together during the Black Hawk War.[43]
Lincoln was also serving in the state assembly. Springfield, the
scruffy new state capital, had about 2,000 residents.[44] To Lincoln,
after living in the tiny village of New Salem 16 miles away,
Springfield was the big city. The capital was growing, attracting
politicians, lawyers, young ambitious Easterners, and a fair number
of Kentuckians.

Exciting as it may have seemed when he first arrived, Lincoln
was soon disillusioned. "This thing of living in Springfield is rather
a dull business after all, at least it is so to me. I am quite as lonesome here as I ever was anywhere in my life," Lincoln confided in
a letter to Mary Owens, whom he had courted in New Salem. He
felt awkward and out of place and was afraid to go to church
because, "I should not know how to behave myself."[45]

But Mary Todd was not lonely. Her sister's house was a lively
center of activity. She was busy visiting with friends, attending parties and dances, and discussing politics with the young people who
gathered in the Edwards' parlor. She attended speeches and public
events like the laying of the capital building's cornerstone.[46]
She had two close girlfriends, Mercy Levering, of Baltimore, who
was visiting a brother next door to Mary, and Julia Jayne, down the
hill, with whom Mary would later write and publish some controversial political satire in the local paper.[47] Mary kept busy with all
of this, and must also have helped Elizabeth with the Edwards'
newborn baby.[48]

After three months in Springfield, Mary returned to Lexington,
where she took advanced classes with her old teacher, Reverend
Ward. She served as a sort of apprentice and helped Mrs. Ward
teach the younger children.[49] Teaching was one of the few career

options for unmarried women, and perhaps Mary was preparing for possible spinsterhood. Teaching also offered some financial independence from her stepmother's authority. But she was back in Springfield by June of 1839, soon after Frances married and moved out of the Edwards' house.

Sometime during this first year back, Mary Todd became acquainted with Abraham Lincoln. No doubt, she had already heard of him. He was studying law with her cousin, and he was gaining a reputation around town as an excellent orator. She may have attended the speech he gave outside the Springfield courthouse in November, titled "On the Politics of the Time and the Condition of the Country." Stephen Douglas, another of her eventual suitors, also spoke that day.[50]

Lincoln eventually became a frequent guest in the Edwards' house. Like the others who gathered there, he liked to talk politics, and he couldn't help noticing Mary's passion for the subject. She read the papers, followed news of the candidates, and liked to make pronouncements about their chances and to discuss the issues. So did he, and gratefully, that gave him something to talk to her about, helping to relieve his shyness. Sometime during the 1840 presidential election campaign, pitting Whig William Henry Harrison (the eventual winner) against Democrat incumbent Martin Van Buren, Mary and Abraham found kinship in a common cause; they both supported Harrison. Much of the country was caught up in this election, and some 80 percent of the electorate voted.[51] Mary later confided to Mercy that during the election season, "I became quite a politician, rather an unladylike profession."[52]

The political discussions in the Edwards home provided a natural setting for Mary Todd to find a man who shared her interests. The social circle there allowed for an ease of conversation between men and women not altogether common in society. Sister Elizabeth later remarked that she often came into the parlor and found Abraham in rapt attention, listening to Mary talking. But there was no particular understanding between them early on about their future.[53]

Mary had other choices. She had a reputation for attracting men, and there were other suitors.[54] "Mary could make a bishop forget his prayers," her brother-in-law Ninian once said.[55] Abraham had his career to worry about, his developing law practice, his legislative duties, and the repayment of old debts for a bankrupt store in New Salem. These came first, before taking on the expense of a wife and family. Mary was attracting the attentions of at least three other eligible men, including Stephen Douglas, a Democrat who would one day be Lincoln's political rival.[56]

In the summer of 1840, Mary went to visit her uncle in Missouri and met a grandson of Patrick Henry, of Revolutionary War fame. While this man was a particularly attractive suitor, one with a "noble ancestor," Mary admitted in a letter to Mercy that, "I love him not, & my hand will never be given, where my heart is not."[57] She also kept company with a widower named Edwin Webb, a lawyer and state legislator she considered too old for her, but who served as insurance against spinsterhood.[58] In response to persistent rumors that they would marry, she told Mercy, "in your friendly & confiding ear allow me to whisper that my *heart can never be his,* I have deeply *regretted that his constant visits, attentions* && should have given room for remarks..."[59]

Lincoln was reluctant to ask for her hand because he was unsure that he could support a wife, especially Mary, who was used to luxuries. He couldn't afford to give the wrong impression, because in those days, a woman could sue over a broken marriage promise. Marriage was not just a practical contract—romantic passion and congeniality were expected to figure into the picture—but men were advised not to speak of marriage until they had the income to be dependable providers. "Love will not pay your rent bill, nor your board bill," John James warned in an article published in 1833.[60]

Lincoln was particularly sensitive to the importance of making a wife happy. He told Mary Owens that "whatever woman may cast her lot with mine, should any ever do so, it is my intention to do all in my power to make her happy and contented, and there is nothing I can imagine that would make me more unhappy than to fail in this effort."[61]

Mary's attraction to Lincoln also faced opposition from her family. Elizabeth warned Mary that she and Lincoln were too different to have a successful marriage. Elizabeth said that Abraham's manners were too rough and unrefined, that he was "defective in those little links that make up the chain of a woman's happiness."[62]

> I warned Mary that she and Mr. Lincoln were not suitable. Mr. Edwards and myself believed they were different in nature, and education and raising. They had no feelings alike. They were so different that they could not live happily as man and wife...Lincoln was unable to talk to women and was not sufficiently educated in the female line to do so.[63]

The time before marriage was a rare time of personal power for a woman, because for once she had some control over her destiny. Still, Elizabeth reminded her sister that a young woman's choice had practical as well as emotional consequences. But Mary saw something more in Abraham Lincoln. She saw the ethical, charismatic man described by a *Daily Union* reporter who interviewed Lincoln before the election in 1860:

> [Abraham Lincoln is a] tall, arrowy, angular gentleman, with a profusion of wiry hair...His presence is commanding...After you have been five minutes in his company you cease to think that he is either homely or awkward. You recognize in him a high-toned, unassuming, chivalrous-minded gentleman... sustained by the infallible monitor of commonsense.[64]

Mary saw this man when she argued with Elizabeth that she would marry "a good man, with a head for position, fame and power, a man of mind with a hope and bright prospects rather than all the houses and gold in the world."[65]

She would indeed, but not yet.

By December 1840, Mary and Abraham had reached an "understanding" and were talking openly of marriage. But, for some reason, the engagement was abruptly broken off on January 1, 1841. Lincoln would later call this date the "Fatal First."[66] No one knows for sure why they parted, but it seems Abraham was supposed to accompany Mary to a New Year's Eve party, but was late, and Mary went on without him. When he finally arrived at the party, she was flirting with someone, possibly Mr. Douglas or Mr. Webb. The next day, Abraham came to visit her, waiting for hours to talk to her, then argued with her, and they parted.[67]

Lincoln, who had never been absent from his duties at the state legislature, missed the next six days straight. He was clearly still depressed when he finally returned. Ninian said he was "crazy as a Loon," and others described him as "incoherent" and "distraught." Lincoln wrote that he was "the most miserable man living."[68]

Months went by, and the two still stayed apart. In June, Mary wrote Mercy that she was sad, but not angry. She spoke of "lingering regrets over the past which time can alone overshadow with its healing balm,"[69] and compared Lincoln to a Shakespearean king, who "deems me unworthy of notice, as I have not met him in the gay world for months...I would that the case were different, that he would once more resume his Station in Society, that 'Richard should be himself again,' much, much happiness would it afford me..."[70]

The following February, the wound still had not healed. Lincoln wrote his friend Joshua Speed that he was happy for his friend's recent marriage, but not happy for himself because of the "never-absent idea, that there is one still unhappy who I have contributed to make so. That still kills my soul."[71]

They stayed apart for a year and a half, much to the relief of Elizabeth and Ninian, but others could see that the separation continued to make them both miserable, so friends did what they could to get the couple back together. Lincoln's friend, Dr. Anson G. Henry, made a point of assuring him of Mary's lasting affection. Finally, Simeon Francis, editor of the local Whig paper, and his wife Eliza successfully reunited them with a surprise meeting at their house early in 1842. Both were invited separately, not knowing the other would attend. They were startled to see each other, so Mrs. Francis reportedly urged them to "be friends." Over the next few months, they continued to meet at the Francis home and at other friends' homes, including Dr. Henry's.[72] During that time, they began following election campaigns together. In fact, they wrote some political satire that led to Lincoln being challenged to a duel.

Mary and Abraham and her friend Julia Jayne wrote several pieces of satire that criticized a local politician. They sent the pieces to Simeon Francis' paper, the *Sangamon Journal*, which published them. In one piece, the politician was called a "fool as well as a liar."[73] Lincoln may have taken the blame for something Mary wrote, or he himself may have reproved the politician. The man promptly challenged Lincoln to a duel. The fight was scheduled, and Lincoln tried to prepare. In the end, Lincoln's legal mind prevailed—he set up conditions for the duel that were so impossible that a last-minute reconciliation was reached.[74] After that, Lincoln never wanted anyone to speak of the incident again. But the political activity gave Mary and Abraham a chance for frequent contact. They started seeing each other again, and they began secretly planning to marry.[75]

Six weeks after the almost-duel, on the morning of November 4, 1842, the day of their secretly arranged wedding, Mary and Abraham finally told Elizabeth and Ninian they planned to marry that evening in the home of the minister. Elizabeth relented, insisting the event should take place in the family parlor.[76]

Etiquette books generally recommended that a bride give her guests at least a week's notice, but Mary and Abraham gave less than that. Because the wedding had been kept secret, Mary had not made the customary bed linens and tablecloths for her new home. Elizabeth had little time to prepare a wedding supper and no time to order macaroons from Watson's, the Springfield confectioner famous for this traditional matrimonial feature.[77]

Mary wore her sister Frances' white satin skirt with a blouse and a simple pearl necklace. The accounts say nothing about Lincoln's attire. Dr. Charles Dresser performed the ceremony in front of 30 family members and friends. Lincoln gave his bride a gold ring with the words "Love Is Eternal" engraved inside. Family tradition says that when the couple cut their wedding cake, it was still warm.[78]

After the ceremony, the couple climbed into a carriage and rode across town, through a blinding rainstorm, to the Globe Tavern, the boarding house they would call home for most of the next year.[79]

"Why is it that married folks always become so serious?" Mary had asked her friend Mercy in a letter dated December 1840.[80] She was about to find out.

CHAPTER THREE:

"Ease, Grace and Fashionability"

Washington, D.C., Friday, March 8, 1861

On the evening of Mrs. Lincoln's initial White House reception as First Lady, her seamstress Elizabeth Keckley arrived late with her dress.[1] Impatient, Mary frantically paced the floor. How people would talk, late for her own party! She knew that the society people of Washington already gossiped mercilessly about her and her husband, labeling her ignorant and vulgar, calling her husband rough and undignified.[2] These Southern sympathizers couldn't imagine anyone from the Illinois frontier with good taste and fine manners! Always sensitive, Mary took the criticisms to heart. She knew she was from a cultured and highly respected family. She knew she was well educated. She needed that dress to prove her detractors wrong.

It had taken almost two decades of marriage to arrive at this pinnacle of success. Mary Todd Lincoln's faith in her husband's abilities had been vindicated by his election to the nation's highest office in November. Throughout the early years of their marriage, he had worked hard to build his reputation as a wise and eloquent lawyer, so well respected that other lawyers asked him to argue their cases before the Illinois Supreme Court.[3] Working his way up the political ladder, he had served in the Illinois state legislature, the U.S. Congress, and now in the White House. Mrs. Lincoln had supported all of his ambitions while raising their four sons.

She was not a newcomer to Washington, even though she was often treated like an outsider. She had lived there briefly during part of her husband's 1847–1849 term as U.S. Representative. Abraham Lincoln had long been involved in both state and national politics through his work with the Whig party, and she had always followed politics, too. Above all, she was now the wife of the President. Whatever they thought of her personally, she thought the ladies of Washington should have accepted her invitations and invited her for rides in their carriages, but these social duties were left undone.[4]

On a shopping trip to New York before the inauguration, she and her cousin, Elizabeth Todd Grimsley, had overheard several gentlemen at a nearby dining table discussing the President-elect, worrying that "his western gaucherie" would be a national embarrassment.[5] How she had wanted to speak up! When they first were married, she might have agreed. Mr. Lincoln was raised on a farm, with barely any formal schooling, without decent clothes. When she met him, he wore his pants legs too short, his socks didn't match, and he was very shy around ladies. This was quite a contrast to her genteel upbringing and her education at two of Lexington's exclusive female academies.[6]

In the early years of their marriage, she constantly had watched over Mr. Lincoln's manners, reminding him to wear matching socks, to put on his coat when answering the door, and not to wipe his hands on his trousers. She had to tell him these things many times before they became habit.[7] But since then, he'd become quite polished. The American people had no reason to be embarrassed by Abraham Lincoln's manners now. He looked absolutely distinguished in his black swallowtail coat, and he knew how to hold his top hat and gloves.

Mary Lincoln had been dreaming of the role of First Lady her whole life. She had always had a passion for politics; at the age of thirteen, she had burst into a dinner party being held by Henry Clay, her father's friend and a presidential candidate, to show him her new pony and to tell him she supported his bid for President. She told him that she too hoped to live in the White House someday. "I begged my father to be President but he only laughed and said he would rather see you there than to be President himself," she told her host, adding, "My father is a very, very peculiar man, Mr. Clay. I don't think he really wants to be President."[8]

Mary was a natural hostess who loved to meet all kinds of people. All along the 12-day trip to Washington, whenever the President-elect's train had stopped for long enough, she had organized little parties and receptions in local hotels.[9] Genuinely curious and easily sympathetic, she had enjoyed meeting the American people and talking to them about their lives. She would say a few words of welcome and then try to meet as many individuals as possible. Some thought she was immodest for playing such a public role in mixed groups of both men and women.

Some members of the media criticized her for making speeches. Others recognized that she had a gift for making people feel warm and welcome, and so the presidential train also left a series of positive reports in its wake.[10] One reporter noted Mrs. Lincoln's "ease, grace and fashionability."[11] The *New York Tribune* described her as "amiable and accomplished, gracious...a sparkling talker."[12] Historian George Bancroft wrote this after meeting her:

> Mrs. Lincoln was just dismissing a visitor or two so I was left to a tête-à-tête...She tells me she is a conservative, repudiates the idea that her secessionist brothers can have any influence on her...She told what orders she had given for renewing the White House and her elegant fitting up of Mr. Lincoln's room—her conservatory and love of flowers... and ended with giving me a gracious invitation to repeat my visit and saying she would send me a bouquet. I came home entranced.[13]

Ante-bellum America was a particularly difficult time to be a President's wife, with so many people arguing for the right to continue slavery and some threatening to secede from the Union. The abolitionists were just as adamant about their position. In this time of conflicting loyalties, it was hard to know who could be trusted. In Springfield, she had found that even though women gossiped, they could at least be counted on to keep their word. The same wasn't true in Washington. Servants betrayed her secrets. Messages sent were never received. The ladies of Washington ignored her invitations to tea. Later, she wrote that:

> Women who knew the wire-pulling at Washington, whose toilet arts and social *pretensions,* society-lobbying and opportunity-seeking, taught them to lie in wait and rise in the social scale by intimacy at the White House, these basely laughed at the credulous woman who took counsel from them, and struck aside the ladder of her friendship by which they alone had been able to climb.[14]

It was hard to remember that the animosity directed at them was often not so much personal, but a reflection of the times. The Lincolns represented the government. True, many people feared the consequences of Abraham Lincoln's election. Even before their arrival in Washington, rumors about assassination plots circulated. Mr. Lincoln had received many insulting letters, and even Mrs. Lincoln had received threats that her husband would be killed if he took office. Just before Christmas, they received a sketch in the mail, showing Mr. Lincoln tarred and feathered and hanging from a noose.[15]

Considering these threats, Lincoln and some of his officials thought it would be safer for the President-elect and his family to travel separately to Washington. Mr. Lincoln left Springfield with his eldest son, seventeen-year-old Robert, but without Mary and their other two sons, ten-year-old Willie and seven-year-old Tad. General Winfield Scott was persuaded to change his mind and allow Mrs. Lincoln and the boys to rejoin her husband a day later in Indianapolis, but the family separated again in Harrisburg, Pennsylvania. Chicago detective Allan Pinkerton had received reliable reports that Lincoln's train would be attacked going through Baltimore, so Lincoln heeded his warning and arranged to travel secretly on another train in the middle of the night. He got on board and tried to make his tall frame as inconspicuous as possible.

Upon arrival in the nation's capital, he cabled to tell Mary he was safe. Thank God! She had been worrying all night. But the trouble wasn't over, and the threats continued. When he reached his hotel room, there was a nasty letter on his bedside table, threatening him and calling him a "black nigger."[16]

Many people in the capital were Confederate sympathizers. The rebel flag was visible from the roof of the White House, flying right across the river in Alexandria, Virginia, and you could just make out the flickering fires of General Beauregard's Confederate camp. By the time of the inauguration, on March 4, 1861, seven states had already seceded from the Union: first South Carolina, on December 20, 1860, and then Mississippi, Florida, Alabama, Georgia, Louisiana, and Texas.

Shots had already been fired, though no hits had been reported. When South Carolina seceded, the rebels took possession of federal property within the state's boundaries, including two un-garrisoned forts at Charleston. They also ringed the harbor with their guns, but they did not have the resources to take Fort Sumter, which was positioned on a shoal out in the harbor. The Union flag flying there was the last vestige of federal control in South Carolina. Major Robert Anderson and his small band of men defending the fort could not hold out by themselves forever; they needed supplies and eventually reinforcements. In January, President James Buchanan sent merchant ship Star of the West with troops and supplies, but the Confederate militia opened fire, and the ship turned back.[17]

On March 4, President Abraham Lincoln was inaugurated for his first term. Held four days later, the first of the twice-weekly White House receptions was an important symbol that, in the midst of this strife, the Union was still strong. In his inauguration speech, President Lincoln had tried to reassure the southern states that he did not intend to interfere with slavery where it already existed. He argued that the Union could not be destroyed because secession was illegal. He said he did not intend to invade those states that had seceded, though he would do what he could to defend forts like Sumter that were threatened. "In your hands, my dissatisfied fellow countrymen, and not in mine, is the momentous issue of civil war. The government will not assail you. You can have no conflict, without being yourselves the aggressors..." he stated.[18]

Now that the legally elected president had taken office, the time-honored tradition of public receptions must carry on. They provided each citizen with the opportunity to speak to the President face to face. Mary also considered them a chance to show that the Union was not only politically strong, but civilized as well. She had vowed to greet as many people and shake as many hands as her husband did.[19] She was ready to play her part as First Lady, if only her dress would arrive.

For her reception gown, she had chosen a bright rose moiré antiqued cloth that would set off her fair skin, blue eyes, and brown hair with its shimmering appearance. The skirt would be bell-shaped, supported by the indispensable crinoline hoop.[20] Just after the American Revolution, women's dresses had had much simpler lines. Turn-of-the-century Empire style featured high waistlines and narrow silhouettes. Women proudly used local fabrics, celebrating self-sufficiency and the birth of a new republic. But as the country prospered, a taste for ostentatious living took over. The middle class grew rapidly, and those with plenty of money began to build ornate houses reminiscent of the French and Italian Renaissance. Everyone wanted things made in Europe.[21]

By 1818, the year of Mary Todd Lincoln's birth, women's dresses had become complicated. Straight lines and simple fabrics were replaced by fuller skirts, which got wider and wider with the passing years. By the mid-1860s, some hoop skirts measured ten feet around. Tightly corseted waists added to the bell-like effect. At first, the skirts were supported by layers and layers of petticoats, with up to six worn at a time.[22] This was bad enough in the North, where summers were mild, but in the South's oppressive heat, it's no wonder women swooned!

The crinoline brought some relief. Someone got the idea to sew rings of caning or wicker into petticoats so they would stand out by themselves, without having to wear so many layers. Women delighted over the new lightweight "skeleton skirts," made of whalebone or wicker or steel. But even with the weight removed, these skirts were not designed for easy movement. Difficult to maneuver through doorways and around the dance floor, the hoops were always in danger of getting squashed.[23]

Still, hoop skirts were considered a sign of womanhood, and girls dreamed of wearing them. Mary was only nine when she and Lizzie Humphreys decided to make their own. They went into the woods, cut several pliable willow branches, somehow snuck them into the house, then spent half the night sewing them into the hems of their straight, prim dresses. When they appeared thus arrayed for Sunday school the next morning, stepmother Betsey ridiculed them, saying, "What frights you are. Take those awful things off, dress yourself properly and go to Sunday school." Mary cried bitterly and threw a temper tantrum, but it didn't help. Betsey was still the boss. She told the story so often it became a family joke, one that humiliated her sensitive young stepdaughter.[24]

Typical for her era, Betsey believed that embarrassing and shaming a child would set her on the right path. Mary proved spiteful in return. She once seasoned her stepmother's coffee with a heavy dose of salt. For acts like these, Betsey dubbed her "a limb of Satan."[25]

By the time Mrs. Keckley arrived with the First Lady's dress, Mrs. Lincoln was getting a headache. She was full of reproach for the seamstress' tardiness. Initially, she refused to put on the new dress, though Mrs. Keckley offered to help her, coaxing her with the assurance that it would take just a few minutes to get ready. Mary petulantly replied, "No, I won't be dressed. I will stay in my room. Mr. Lincoln can go down with the other ladies."[26]

But that would never do; she knew she would regret it. She would miss her chance to make a good first impression. And what an impression she would make if she simply failed to appear! Besides, if the President went alone, she would be tortured all evening by jealousy. She saw how the ladies of Washington, those who were wives or sisters or daughters of men in power, flocked around him because of his high position. Mr. Lincoln found this amusing, but she did not.

Once, he couldn't resist teasing her about it. He came into her room while she was getting ready for some official occasion, and as he waited, pulling on his gloves, he asked her "with a merry twinkle in his eyes" which of the lady guests he would be allowed to talk to that evening. He mentioned first one name, then another, but always she found something wrong, especially with the youngest and prettiest ones. She told him heatedly that she did not approve of his "flirtations with silly women, just as if you were a beardless boy, fresh from school."[27]

While Mary Todd Lincoln sulked over the seamstress' late arrival that Friday in 1860, sister Elizabeth and cousin Lizzie Grimsley worked to soothe her ruffled feathers. Meanwhile, Mrs. Keckley went ahead and laid the new dress out on the bed, along with Mrs. Lincoln's pearls. When Mary saw the shiny white beads beside the delicate purple material, she wanted to try it all on, just to see how it looked. By the time her husband arrived to escort her to the reception a little while later, she was dressed with roses in her hair and was beginning to feel playful. Her husband was also happy. He quoted poetry and then complimented her attire, saying, "I declare, you look charming in that dress. Mrs. Keckley has met with great success."[28]

CHAPTER FOUR:

Public and Private Grief

Campbell Hospital, Washington, D.C., August 10, 1864

"I am sitting by the side of your soldier boy. He has been quite sick, but is getting well. He tells me to say to you that he is all right." Mary Lincoln wrote these words of comfort for the mother of a wounded soldier who was lying by her side.

This was not her first visit with the young Union soldier, but she had never told him her name. On these visits to the army hospitals, she was content to remain anonymous. She had her own personal reasons to be there, and she didn't need to publicize her errands of mercy. She simply perched herself on a wooden chair beside the bed—one bed in a long row, one row in a long ward, one hospital among many. Some mornings she felt such despair, she didn't believe she could go on. But these boys had to go on, without their legs, with burned faces, with gaping wounds, beaten and maimed to save the Union. She got up and did what she could.

She didn't tell the soldier who she was, but she signed the letter to his mother, "With respect for the mother of the young soldier, Mrs. Abraham Lincoln."[1]

Five weeks after the Lincoln administration formally began, rebel shots were fired directly at Fort Sumter on April 12, 1861. President Lincoln had recently announced that he would send supplies to the surrounded fort, adding that he would not land troops or munitions unless resistance was encountered. The Confederates then had a dilemma: If they did nothing, they would seem unresolved; if they attacked, a war would follow, with the Confederacy seen as the aggressor. They decided to order Major Anderson to surrender the fort, threatening to attack if he did not. He refused, and they attacked. Two days later, Anderson surrendered.

On April 17, Virginia joined the Confederacy. Now the nation's unguarded capital shared the Potomac River with its enemy. The flickering lights of Confederate campfires could be seen from across the river at night. Within a few weeks, Arkansas, Tennessee, and North Carolina also seceded. Northwestern Virginia refused to go along with the majority, breaking off and forming a separate state that was eventually admitted to the Union as West Virginia. Four remaining slave states—Maryland, Delaware, Kentucky, and Missouri—stayed in the Union.

Governors of the northern states had promised to send troops to defend Washington, but they were having trouble getting through. Around Baltimore, masked revolutionaries had sabotaged the rail lines. Some presumed loyal to the Union were resigning their commissions to join the Confederacy, and White House staff members were walking across the bridge to join Jefferson Davis. Southern rebellion was spoken publicly in the streets.

Lincoln had insisted in his March 4 inaugural address that, "We are not enemies, but friends,"[2] but by mid April, the people of Washington were preparing to be attacked. "Frontier Guards" were stationed inside the White House. Public buildings were barricaded, and women and children were urged to find someplace safer. Many left, but Mrs. Lincoln stayed on. She would not abandon her husband, and she would not run away from her role as First Lady. Her husband would need her when he couldn't sleep or when he forgot to eat. Sensible women may have been abandoning the capital, but Mary Lincoln summoned her courage and stayed.[3]

By April 25, troops from Massachusetts, Pennsylvania, and New York had finally reached Washington. "Thousands of soldiers are guarding us. If there is safety in numbers, we have every reason to feel secure. We can only hope for peace," Mary wrote to a Springfield friend.[4]

A few weeks later, in mid-May, she boarded a train headed north, to visit the fashion centers of New York, Philadelphia, and Boston. Mary had been anxious to go shopping as soon as she took up residence in the White House in March. Her first inspection on day one made it clear that presidential predecessors had let the place deteriorate. Mary believed the White House should project a sense of the state of the Union. She couldn't stave off war, but she could restore pride and present an image that the Union was alive and well. She argued for a renovation appropriation, and soon learned that Congress routinely allocated $20,000 for refurbishing the White House every four years, plus $6,000 per year for repairs. While questions remained as to how the others had spent the money, Mrs. Lincoln determined to spend hers as it was intended.[5]

While tension reigned in Washington, as the citizens waited for troops to arrive, the shopping excursion had been delayed. Now, in May, she took the first of several shopping trips during that first year of her husband's presidency. Everywhere she went, merchants showed her their finest wares. Among her purchases were a $900 carriage, several pieces of ornately carved furniture, custom-made carpets and drapes, china, crystal, leather-bound books, and tasseled bell-pulls. She ordered expenditures for cleaning, repair and modernization. She spent $6,800 for wallpaper from France (scraping, mortaring and hanging was included!)[6]

She also bought 190 pieces of royal purple and gold Limoges china from E.V. Haughwout's & Company, on Broadway Avenue in New York, for $3,200. The White House did need a new set of china. Most of the pieces had been bought during the Pierce administration and were chipped or broken, and no more than ten people could be served at one time using matching china. She was offered an irresistible bargain for a second set of china, with her own initials instead of the presidential seal in the center, for just $1,200. She also treated herself to a black point lace shawl at $650 and a camel's hair cashmere shawl for $1,000. Mary always protested that she was determined to be economical, but she spent the entire four-year allowance, plus the year's special repair budget, in less than a year. In fact, she spent $6,700 more than that.[7]

The New York correspondent of the *Philadelphia Sunday Dispatch* wrote about one shopping trip observed firsthand:

'Mrs. President Lincoln,' as the ladies call her, was shopping to a considerable extent in this city in the early part of the week. She has evidently no comprehension that Jeff. Davis will make good his threat to occupy the White House in July for she is expending thousands and thousands of dollars for articles of luxurious taste in the household way that it would be very preposterous for her to use out in her rural home in Illinois...Let me do Mrs. Lincoln the justice to say that she was dreadfully importuned to enter into extravagances of various kinds; but I heard her, myself, observe at Stewart's that she could not afford it, and was 'determined to be very economical.' One thousand dollars for a shawl was quite as high as her sense of economy would permit her to go in these excessive hard times![8]

At first, Mary dismissed criticisms about how much she had spent. She knew that public works projects often ran over budget and that the extra expenditures were routinely buried in other federal appropriations bills. In fact, this eventually happened. But first, the President was furious at his wife's extravagance. These were desperate times. Given the financial needs of the country, and the deplorable conditions for the Union soldiers, he thought her timing couldn't have been worse. Like most Americans, he thought every extra dollar should go to the troops. He declared he would pay for the overrun from his own pocket.[9]

Mary begged Commissioner Benjamin French to intercede. She was afraid to talk to the President directly. "Tell him how much it costs to refurnish he does not know much about it, he says he will pay it out of his own pocket...you know, Major, he cannot afford that...you must get me out of this difficulty," she wrote. French did talk to the President, who said:

It would stink in the nostrils of the American people to have it said that the President of the United States had approved a bill overrunning an appropriation of $20,000

for flub dubs, for this damned old house, when the soldiers
cannot have blankets...The house was furnished well
enough, better than any one we ever lived in...[10]

Despite this response, French found a way to bury the expenses in other budgets.[11] The bills were paid, but meanwhile Mrs.
Lincoln acquired a negative reputation that would follow her for
the rest of her life and beyond.

But this battle over federal appropriations paled beside the real
dangers of war. Just as she arrived back in Washington from her first
shopping trip, the war began in earnest. On Thursday, May 23, 1861,
13,000 Union soldiers were ordered to prepare three days' rations,
pack knapsacks and be ready to march across the river to
Alexandria, Virginia, directly across from the capital. When
Virginia joined the Confederacy, the rebel capital was moved from
Alabama to Richmond, and Alexandria had important rail connections to the new capital. A pre-emptive strike to capture Alexandria
was ordered. By Friday afternoon, several detachments had easily
taken control of Alexandria, which greatly relieved the residents of
Washington. One group of soldiers was sent to destroy the railroad
tracks leading south toward Richmond. Another, led by Colonel
Elmer Ephraim Ellsworth of the 11th New York regiment, went to
cut the telegraph lines.[12]

Ellsworth was a dear friend of the Lincolns from Illinois.
Originally born in Malta, New York, he grew up in Mechanicville,
New York, midway between Albany and Saratoga Springs. As a
young man, he moved first to New York City, then to Chicago, and
eventually to Springfield, where he clerked in Abraham Lincoln's
law office.[13] He had a fiancée, Miss Carrie Spafford, back home in
Rockford, Illinois. In fact, *The New York Times* reported that the
last thing Ellsworth did before marching off to Alexandria was to
write his fiancée a letter and to hold her picture to his bosom.[14]

On the way back from the telegraph office, he spied a Confederate
flag hanging over Marshall's House, a tavern in Alexandria owned by
J. W. Jackson. He went inside, saw a man in the hall, and asked him
who had put up the flag. The man said he didn't know. Ellsworth took
six men and went up to the rooftop to cut down the flag. As they
descended from the attic with their trophy, the same man was in the

hall, but this time armed with a loaded double-barrel shotgun. He was Mr. Jackson, the building's owner. He aimed at Private Francis Brownell, who led the group. Brownell struck at the gun with his musket, deflecting it, but at the same time, Jackson fired. Three wildly aimed slugs entered Ellsworth's chest, a little to the left of his breastbone, between the second and third ribs. When the bullets hit, Ellsworth was rolling up the rebel flag. He had time only to say "my God" before falling face down.[15]

Quick as lightning, Brownell turned on Jackson and fired. The ball struck Jackson on the bridge of the nose and crashed through his skull. Both Ellsworth and Jackson died instantly, and both sides had their first martyrs.[16]

The news of Ellsworth's death hit the Lincolns particularly hard. Ellsworth, their dear friend, was the first casualty for the Union cause. Mary and Abraham had treated him like family. He had read law with Mr. Lincoln in Springfield. He had been chosen to accompany the Lincolns on their inaugural journey from Springfield to Washington, as a military escort. Handsome and spirited, Elmer Ellsworth was a great favorite in the White House. Writing to her husband after Ellsworth's death, Mary's cousin Elizabeth Grimsley described him as "a great pet in the family."[17]

Ellsworth had played so closely with Willie and Tad, the two young Lincoln boys, that he once had caught their measles.[18] In the early days of the war, Mary had made her son Tad a Zouave doll, complete with the brilliant scarlet and blue uniform of Ellsworth's volunteer unit. Ellsworth had recruited these soldiers from the fire squads of New York City when President Lincoln first called for troops after the siege on Fort Sumter.[19] Tad, well known for his White House games and pranks, named the doll Jack and treasured it as representative of his gallant soldier friend, Elmer. The doll didn't prove to be as loyal as the real soldiers; Tad once put poor Jack on trial for desertion. But Tad's father encouraged his son to be forgiving, so Tad decided to give Jack a pardon. These and other games invented by Tad and Willie kept the real Zouaves amused when they were off-duty.[20]

Now Colonel Ellsworth was gone forever. His body lay in state at the White House, the Navy shipyard, and at New York's City Hall, and then he was buried in Mechanicville. During the military funeral held in the East Room of the White House, Mary placed a wreath on the young man's coffin. At the end of the service, she was given the bloodstained rebel flag that had cost poor Ellsworth his life. She was horrified and had it quickly put out of sight.[21] Mr. Lincoln was so distraught that he couldn't even speak about Ellsworth's death. When a reporter asked him about the tragedy, he said, "Excuse me, I cannot talk," then turned away and burst into tears.[22]

After several other small skirmishes, the first large-scale battle took place on July 21, 1861, two months after Colonel Ellsworth's death. The Union defeat at Bull Run was an embarrassing wakeup call. Washington officials and their wives had packed picnic baskets and taken their carriages out to some hills in Virginia some 25 miles southwest of the capital, hoping to enjoy their lunches as they watched the Union troops roundly defeat the rebels. But after several hours of hard fighting, the Union soldiers panicked and retreated back across Bull Run, a small stream running through the battlefield. Their commander, General Irvin McDowell, could not regain control, as soldiers and civilians alike high-tailed it back to Washington.

Those who had hoped the war could be won with just this one battle realized how futile their hopes had been. Mr. Lincoln spent sleepless nights trying to figure out what had gone wrong at Bull Run, and Mrs. Lincoln began to visit the wounded troops.[23]

Mary Todd Lincoln did not act as nurse to the wounded Union soldiers. She did not change bandages or give out medicines, as these jobs were reserved for doctors and nurses. What she offered was a sentimental woman's touch. Women were thought capable of healing by sheer force of their love. She read to them, wrote letters, and asked questions about their lives. She brought books and flowers. She raised $1,000 for a Christmas dinner at Douglas Hospital. When people gave her liquor, she passed this on to the troops. Out of her own pocket, she bought $1,000 worth of lemons and oranges when soldiers were in danger of developing scurvy. She visited quite often, sometimes with the President, sometimes with her sons or a woman friend, sometimes alone. But she didn't try to get publicity.

These were errands of mercy, not a public relations tour. Her White House secretary William Stoddard suggested she invite reporters along, but she never did. He wrote:

> She rarely takes outside company with her upon these errands and she thereby loses opportunities. If she were worldly wise she would carry newspaper correspondents, from two to five, of both sexes, every time she went, and she would have them take shorthand notes of what she says to the sick soldiers and of what the sick soldiers say to her. Then she would bring the writers back to the White House, and give them some cake and—coffee, as a rule, and show them the conservatory.[24]

The Civil War gave many women the opportunity to enter the field of medicine. For centuries, women had supervised childbirth and other family medical needs, but after the American Revolution, states began requiring doctors to be licensed. Since only medical school graduates could get licenses, and most medical schools didn't admit women, women were generally squeezed out of the profession. During the Civil War, though, the need for help was so great that, like it or not, doctors were forced to allow more women. The men left nursing to be soldiers, so there was an acute shortage. Over 3,000 women served as nurses during the war.[25]

Some people argued that women were too delicate to deal with the wounded bodies of strange men. But advocates countered that women were natural nurses, since they were only doing the same chores they had always done: cooking, cleaning, and caring for the sick. Nursing did not require much special training, since a nurse's tasks were mainly domestic. Gentleness, patience, perseverance, and piety—these traits were important for nurses as well as for mothers.[26]

In exchange for doing chores like those that awaited them at home, albeit in far worse conditions, women nurses of the Civil War got both adventure and economic opportunity. One woman wrote home about the chaos on her hospital ship, ending her letter with, "This is life." Another wrote that she had "really entered into the inner spirit of the times."[27]

Women also guarded morality in the soldier camps by discouraging drinking and gambling. "What, my boy, playing checkers on Sunday?" one nurse reportedly scolded a soldier, handing him a Bible.[28]

The Christmas of 1861 was dreary, as the rebellion dragged on and on. In January, Mary Todd Lincoln got the idea that a party would lift people's spirits. She sent out five hundred invitations. The guest list included generals, members of the diplomatic corps, Cabinet members, Supreme Court judges, senators and representatives, and personal friends. Some people grumbled that a party was in bad taste. Republican Senator Benjamin Wade, of Ohio, declined, saying, "Are the President and Mrs. Lincoln aware there is a Civil War? If they are not, Mr. and Mrs. Wade are and for that reason decline to participate in feasting and dancing." Others, embarrassed at having been excluded, begged for an invitation.[29]

Mary hired New York's most expensive caterer, Maillard's, and ordered wine and champagne from another New York firm, even though she and Mr. Lincoln did not drink. From Mrs. Keckley, she ordered a white satin gown, trimmed with black lace.[30]

A few days before the party, eleven-year-old Willie, the Lincolns' middle son, became sick. Mary thought she should cancel the event, but the doctor who examined Willie insisted he was getting along fine, and he told her to go ahead.[31]

On the evening of the party, February 5, Mary worried about her child while the seamstress helped her get into her dress and fix her hair. Willie was running a high fever.

Carriages started arriving around 9 p.m., met by coachmen dressed in new uniforms. The President wore his black swallowtail coat and greeted guests alongside Mrs. Lincoln in the East Room. The Marine Band played a selection of appropriate numbers, including a new piece entitled the "Mary Lincoln Polka," written especially for the evening.[32]

A magnificent buffet was unveiled at midnight, with turkey, duck, ham, terrapin, and pheasant served on the new White House china, which matched the servants' uniforms. Dinner was available until 3 a.m., and the party lasted all night. The *Washington Star* called it "the most superb affair of its kind ever seen here," a real social victory for the First Lady.[33]

But Mary barely knew it. She and the President kept breaking away from the party to watch over their son, holding his hot hand and watching his labored breathing. Tad, the youngest, became sick too, doubling the parents' worries.[34]

Once she realized how serious the illness was, Mary refused to leave her son's bedside. Willie was suffering from bilious fever, or malaria, or typhoid—accounts differ. His illness dragged on for days. The newspapers traced the course of it, reporting that Willie was "very ill," then "improved," then "out of danger," then "hopelessly ill." He brightened temporarily on February 20, 1862, but by nightfall, the struggle was over. Eleven-year-old Willie was dead.[35]

Historians have described Willie as his parents' favorite, the one most like his father in intellect and temperament. Willie was thoughtful and studious. He collected memoranda of important events, like his father's inauguration, important battles, and the deaths of famous men. One time, when Tad, the youngest, was worried over something, Willie thought about it for a few minutes, then, having arrived at a solution, he clasped his hands together and looked up smiling. "I know every step of the process by which that boy arrived at his satisfactory solution...as it is by just such slow methods I attain results," Mr. Lincoln told a guest.[36] Cousin Lizzie Grimsley called Willie "a counterpart of his father."[37] Mary had been counting on Willie to be "the hope and stay of her old age."[38] That was not to be.

After Willie's death, Mary never again entered his White House bedroom or the East Room, where his funeral was held. She stayed in her bedroom during the funeral. This was not unusual. Victorian women often stayed away from public funeral rituals because, as one etiquette book of the era explained, "Tears are not for the gaze." Women's manuals discouraged excessive displays of mourning. Good Christians were supposed to take comfort in the promise of eternal life and to submit willingly to whatever God sent their way.[39]

Mary Todd Lincoln believed devoutly in God's will, but how was she to give up her child? "If we could only realise [sic] how far happier they now are than here on earth..." she wrote to a friend after Willie's death.[40] She was so consumed with grief that she became physically ill. It was three weeks before anyone could persuade her to get out of bed and put on her clothes.[41]

Mrs. Keckley remembered that one day Mr. Lincoln led his wife to a White House window and pointed across town to the lunatic asylum on a distant hill. "Mother, do you see that large white building on the hill yonder?" he told her. "Try and control your grief or it will drive you mad and we may have to send you there." Gradually, Mary returned to her husband and her other two sons. She later told her sister, "If I had not felt the spur of necessity urging me to cheer Mr. Lincoln, whose grief was as great as my own, I could never have smiled again."[42]

Willie's father wasn't faring much better. The President shut himself up in his son's room on Thursdays and refused to see anyone.[43] But as President, he had compelling duties. He had to keep going.

Two months after Willie's death, in April 1862, Mary's half-brother Sam, a Confederate soldier, was killed at the battle of Shiloh. The night before, Mary had been talking to a minister friend in the Red Room of the White House and had declared bitterly that she didn't care if her Confederate relatives were killed or taken prisoner, because "they would kill my husband if they could, and destroy our Government — the dearest of all things to us..."[44] Mary grieved Sam's death privately, as she did when half-brother David was mortally wounded at Vicksburg the next year.

When her half-brother Alexander died in a battle near Baton Rouge in the fall of 1863, she told Mrs. Keckley that her rebel brother "made his choice long ago. He decided to fight against us and since he chose to fight against us, I see no special reason why I should bitterly mourn his death." She mourned him anyway, but she hid her grief so as to protect her husband from rumors that she supported the rebels.[45]

ॐ

While some women went to nursing during the Civil War, others served as administrators, recruiting and training nurses, or organizing vast networks of supplies. They found volunteers to make bandages, sheets, and other items. Within two weeks of the war's beginning, women in both the North and South had formed 20,000 local aid societies to supply food, clothing, medical supplies, blankets, and money.[46] But in times like these, when spies abounded and corruption was rampant, supplies didn't always get through to the troops. It helped to be a woman with top-notch connections and nerve enough to take matters into one's own hand—someone like Ann Eliza Harlan, wife of Iowa Senator James Harlan.

Like Mary Todd Lincoln, Ann Eliza Harlan was grieving the loss of a child in February 1862. That month, both Willie and six-year-old Julia Josephine Jessie Harlan died. Mrs. Lincoln and Mrs. Harlan were friends, and their husbands were political allies. Mary, the Harlans' other daughter, would one day marry Robert Todd Lincoln and become Mrs. Lincoln's daughter-in-law. Thus, Ann Eliza was the Lincoln descendants' other grandmother, and another example for them of a strong-willed and intelligent woman.

On April 6 and 7, 1862, the Union troops were almost defeated by a surprise attack at Shiloh, but reinforcements arrived just in time for General Ulysses S. Grant to pull off a narrow victory. The battle was fought in southwestern Tennessee, along the Tennessee River, just north of where the state borders Mississippi and Alabama. Two months before, Grant and Flag Officer Andrew Foote had taken two Confederate forts straight north of Shiloh, near the northern border of Tennessee. One of these was also on the Tennessee River. With these key victories, Grant and Foote cut Tennessee in two and helped Union forces gain control of the western third of the state.

But the cost was great in human lives. A thousand wounded and bloody Iowa soldiers were among the 20,000-plus casualties. Union commander General Henry Halleck issued strict orders excluding all civilians from crossing the battle lines to find survivors. People had a habit of showing up after a battle and trying to find their friends and relatives, and General Halleck didn't want a crowd. Civilian boats were stopped at Cairo, Illinois, where the

Mississippi and Ohio rivers meet. The Ohio River provided access to the Tennessee River, which was the only safe way to reach Shiloh from the north. Even the boat carrying Illinois Governor Richard Yates and staff, plus a corps of nurses headed for Shiloh, was turned back at Cairo.[47]

When she heard about the number of Iowan casualties, Mrs. Harlan and another woman, perhaps her daughter Mary, rushed across country by train from Washington to St. Louis, where they hired a steamboat. They loaded it with medicines and other supplies and raced up the Mississippi River to the mouth of the Ohio River. She knew she would be questioned at Cairo, but unlike the others, she had a magic ticket that would get her through. At Cairo, she showed it, and she was allowed to proceed. When she heard of the Illinois governor's predicament, she invited him along.[48]

At Pittsburg Landing (the Union name for Shiloh), Mrs. Harlan was presented to General Halleck, and she handed him the following letter:

WAR DEPARTMENT
Washington City, D.C.
April 10, 1862

Mrs. A. E. Harlan of Iowa, wife of the Senator of that State, has permission to pass, with a lady companion, through the lines of the United States forces, to and from Tennessee and wherever sick and wounded soldiers of the United States may be to render them care and attendance.

They will be furnished with transportation and rations by the proper officer of the Service, and all officers and persons in the Service of the United States will afford them courtesy, protection and assistance.

Edwin M. Stanton,
Secretary of War

All Quartermasters will observe and obey of course the above order.

April 11th, 1862.
M.C. Meigs,
Q.M.G. [Quartermaster General]

All agents of the Sanitary Commission are directed to give all aid and furtherance to the plans of Mrs. Harlan, which shall be in their power [and] compatible with their assigned duties.

Washington, April 11th, 1862.
Fred Law Olmstead,
General Secretary[49]

General Halleck hesitated a moment after reading the letter, but there was no doubt about its authenticity. He bowed courteously to the woman before him and replied, "Madam, you outrank me. What are your commands?" She was supplied with ambulances, bandages, transportation, and whatever other supplies he could offer.[50]

What Mrs. Harlan witnessed at Shiloh must have torn at her tender heart. "She found scores of helpless famishing men, here and there, in every direction, still lying on the naked ground in the bloody clothes in which they had been shot down...Many of these soldiers were mere lads, in thousands of cases ranging from sixteen to nineteen years of age."[51] After she'd had a chance to assess the situation, she concluded that what the wounded soldiers needed most was to go home, as soon as possible. On the battlefield, there was always a shortage of supplies and medical personnel. Many of the soldiers were suffering almost as much from homesickness as from their actual wounds. At home they would have better access to medical care, plus the added advantage of loved ones nearby to comfort them. She asked for the general's permission to transport the Iowan soldiers, and he said yes, on one condition: She must also take soldiers from Wisconsin and Minnesota. She agreed and immediately began making the arrangements.[52]

Within hours, word had gotten around that there was a way out. Suffering soldiers quickly flocked to her, some in ambulances, some carried by fellow soldiers, some crawling on their hands and knees. Mrs. Harlan's boat left with 280 sick and wounded men aboard, 60 of them from her home state. They headed for Keokuk, Iowa, approximately 150 miles north of St. Louis, on the Mississippi River.[53]

Two weeks later, they reached their destination. Some soldiers were well enough by then to ride home on their own, but seven soldiers from the 15th Iowa Regiment died soon after reaching Keokuk. A hotel there was emptied of its guests and transformed into a hospital. Following this example inspired by Mrs. Harlan, home hospitals were subsequently organized throughout the country.[54]

Her efforts at Pittsburg Landing were just the beginning. As the war continued, Mrs. Harlan worked hard to secure better food for the soldiers. She visited the Army of the Potomac in Virginia and found most of the soldiers living on nothing more than hard bread, salt meat and coffee day after day. Many suffered from diarrhea. They fought over stray onions, potatoes and turnips. She sailed back to Washington and announced that her steamboat was tied up at the Navy Yard and would return to the army the next day. She said she would gladly carry any supplies, especially fresh bread, that the people of Washington felt moved to supply. People responded generously.

Upon arrival in Virginia, she was so besieged by troops begging for a slice of bread that guards had to help her carry supplies into the field hospitals. She told her husband about the desperate situation, and he told the President, who personally issued an order that troops be supplied with bake ovens and flour wherever possible so they could have fresh bread.[55]

Mrs. Harlan also helped get more surgeons into the field, and she helped reorganize Iowa relief societies into a more efficient system. "There is little question but that Mrs. Harlan saved many soldiers' lives by her diligent work and by her determination to correct faults in the systems for the benefit of individual soldiers," a *Des Moines Register* writer concluded.[56]

Mrs. Harlan's efforts were immortalized in newspaper accounts in her own time and in historical publications later on. When she died in 1884, a former soldier who remembered her kindness made a special trip to Washington to show his eight-year-old son the face of the woman "who had been a good mother to his papa at the bat-tlefield of Shiloh."[57]

Mrs. Lincoln carried out her errands of mercy more quietly and closer to home. She had taken a break from her army hospital visits after Willie's death, but four months later, by the summer of 1862, Mrs. Lincoln had recovered enough to resume them. It took great inner strength to withstand the horrible sights and sounds she witnessed along her way. Arriving once just after an amputation, she chose to stay when several other ladies left, unable to endure the stench and the soldier's agonized groaning. She saw injuries that tore at her heart, but she did not faint at the sight of blood, despite what some people said about the general weakness of women. As one reporter explained, "The fear of contagion and the outcries of pesti-lence fall unheeded upon the ear of those whose missions are mercy."[58]

Did the press notice her quiet ministrations? During the war, some reporters knew that Mrs. Lincoln visited the troop hospitals on a regular basis. "Among the many ladies who visit the hospitals none is more indefatigable than Mrs. Lincoln," one newspaper reported.[59] Another reporter wrote, "It may not be known that Mrs. Lincoln has contributed more than any lady in Washington, from her private purse, to alleviate the sufferings of our wounded soldiers."[60]

Why was it that two years after the war, her kindness to the sol-diers was so quickly forgotten? In the fall of 1867, American newspa-pers were once again full of negative articles about Mrs. Lincoln, ridiculing her idea to sell some of her White House wardrobe to secure needed funds. It was true that in the process of setting up this sale, she had trusted some people who proved untrustworthy, but her intentions were innocent enough. The *Cleveland Herald* ran an edi-torial that fall, on October 19, 1867, criticizing Mrs. Lincoln as for-mer First Lady, stating that, "Two calls each week, with a bouquet of flowers, upon any one of the many hospitals that filled Washington, would have made her name immortal."[61] Mary Lincoln did that and more. But, as was often the case, people remembered her mistakes vividly, and all but forgot what she did well.

CHAPTER FIVE:

"A Pleasant Land Among the Mountains"

The Equinox House, Manchester, Vermont, August 25, 1863

No reporters waited at the bottom of Union Street when the 10 a.m. train approached Manchester Village in Vermont. The only observer was a uniformed footman from the Equinox House with his two-horse carriage. Mrs. Lincoln must have turned with a smile of relief to her lady companion, Mrs. General Abner Doubleday. Manchester would provide some privacy at last.

Whenever the First Lady traveled, which was often during her husband's presidency, reporters seemed to follow her every move. They were there at Long Branch, New Jersey, in the summer of 1861. They watched her during official gatherings in Washington or when she accompanied her husband to review the troops. They recounted her shopping trips to Boston and New York. Even in the White Mountains of New Hampshire, a reporter recorded her every move. But in Manchester, Vermont, no one paid much attention to her. Manchester would always provide sanctuary for the Lincolns.[1]

When the train's shrill whistle blew, the carriage driver must have reined his horses tightly, as the protesting brakes of the train squealed and the great steam engine came to a stop. The first train had rolled along these tracks just 11 years before, in 1852. Now the Western Vermont Railroad had 59 miles of tracks connecting Manchester with Troy, New York City, Chicago, Boston and beyond.[2]

The train was a great boost to those who hoped to promote Manchester as a tourist destination. These civic leaders included Franklin Orvis, proprietor of the Equinox House, the elegant hotel up the hill from the railroad tracks, at the top of Union Street. Mr. Orvis has been credited as "the 'father' of Manchester's summer business," a man of vision with "boundless energy."[3] A native of Manchester, Orvis had left for a few years to pursue businesses in Wisconsin, Illinois, and New York, but he returned when his father died in 1849. He bought the family home, renovated it, and opened it to guests as the Equinox House in 1853. Soon after that, he bought three buildings across the street; they contained what was then known as the Manchester Hotel, owned by his brother, Charles, plus a boarding house and the Straight Tavern. He connected the three buildings and dubbed the new configuration "Equinox Junior," thus adding 125 rooms to his accommodations.[4]

While Mr. Orvis worked on refurbishing his hotel and promoting its reputation, the railroads were also developing, providing important links to the nation's population centers. By 1863, Orvis could boast a long list of prominent men who had enjoyed the inn's elegance and comforts. Hereafter, that list would include the Lincolns.[5]

Manchester was ripe for tourism in the middle of the 19th century. As the Hudson River artists spread eastward into Vermont, they publicized the beauty of the Green Mountains and the Taconics by painting them. In the decade between the railroad's first arrival and Mrs. Lincoln's first visit, trains brought an ever-increasing number of visitors. They made Vermont accessible in a way that stagecoaches never had, both in the numbers of people accommodated and in the comfort of those accommodations.[6] "Manchester became a celebrated summer resort almost before she knew it. It was a logical development for a town so richly endowed by nature and so suitably located at the junction of several important stage roads," wrote local historians Edwin Bigelow and Nancy Otis.[7]

As a good Republican and a natural host, Mr. Orvis was cordial to the Lincolns. He was "by nature a sociable, authoritarian old English squire" who personally greeted each of his guests.[8] While waiting for the Lincolns to be transported the short distance uphill in the hotel carriage, he was no doubt checking in with his staff to make sure everything was ready for these distinguished visitors.

No reporters waited for the Lincolns' arrival at the bottom of Union Street, but the local press didn't miss the story. The report in the *Manchester Journal* was mercifully brief, appearing under the heading "Local Intelligence," on page two of the August 25, 1863, issue:

> DISTINGUISHED ARRIVALS—MRS. LINCOLN and son, and MRS GEN. DOUBLEDAY arrived in town on the 10 o'clock train this morning. They are stopping at the Equinox House.[9]

The conductor probably emerged first from the President's railroad car, dropping to the ground quickly to place a step stool beneath the platform. It is easy to imagine that young Tad was the next to embark. After his nine-hour confinement in the train from New York, traveling at a mere 20 miles per hour,[10] he probably could wait no longer. Bounding down the steps to solid ground, perhaps he was awed by the majestic splendor of the mountains on all sides, twirling around to take it all in at once.

Mrs. Lincoln may have paused in the railroad car's doorway, transfixed by the same sight. Mr. Orvis had not exaggerated. His hotel advertisements claimed Manchester was "unsurpassed for beauty of scenery and picturesque views,"[11] and it was indeed. She could see the two sister mountain ranges, close and roughly parallel, lining the long narrow valley. And what a blessing to find everything so lush, cool, and green!

When they had left Washington, the capital was experiencing one of the worst heat spells on record. Noah Brooks, reporting for the *Sacramento Union*, wrote on August 5, 1863, "The past three or four days have been the very hottest of the season, the mercury going up to 104 degrees in the shade in some parts of the city."[12] Like most homes, the White House had no screens to keep out mosquitoes, flies and other insects. Sewage in the nearby Potomac River produced a stench White House secretary John Hay called the odor of "ten thousand dead cats."[13] Ah, the cool, clean air of Vermont!

Mrs. Lincoln would have reached for the gloved hand of the conductor, gathered her skirt with her other hand, and stepped carefully down the narrow iron steps. Just six weeks before, she'd been severely injured in a carriage accident and had almost died. She certainly didn't want to fall again. She'd been riding alone in the President's carriage, just outside of Washington, when the vehicle rounded a sharp curve. The driver's seat fell off, and the driver with it. The horses ran wild. Mrs. Lincoln was thrown from the carriage, and her head hit a sharp rock and was split open. The wound became infected, and she lay gravely ill for three weeks.[14]

While God and the stars determined her fate, and a nurse kept constant watch by her bedside, her husband was preoccupied with the bloody three-day battle of Gettysburg. He must have agonized alternately over his wife's illness and the horrendous number of Union casualties.[15]

Upon subsequent investigation, government officials determined the "accident" was no accident. The screws used to fasten the driver's seat had been deliberately removed. The injuries Mrs. Lincoln suffered had probably been intended for the President.[16] Reporters were still asking her questions when she left for Vermont. Of course she thought there was a conspiracy to kill her husband! What an inane question! Didn't anyone remember how he had been forced to sneak into Washington on the eve of his administration?

Despite the potential dangers, Mrs. Lincoln traveled extensively during her husband's presidency. Some might have thought she was actually safer outside of Washington. She regretted not always being there for her husband, but her physical conditions sometimes required her to travel great distances for a different climate and other potential cures. Mr. Lincoln supported her in this. In September 1861, she wrote to Cousin Lizzie Grimsley that, "I have been quite sick with chills for some days...If they cannot be broken in a few days, Mr. Lincoln wants me to go North & remain until cold weather—Where so much is demanded of me—I cannot afford to be delicate, if a different climate will restore my health..."[17] In this time of war, she could not allow herself to be confined to months of bed-rest, as some Victorian women were when they felt ill. She hoped that a few weeks in the mountains would provide at least temporary relief.

The various amusements in Manchester, including intellectual conversations on art, current affairs, religion, and philosophy among the hotel guests, were a welcome distraction for Mary Todd Lincoln. Everyone was weary from the war, and on top of that she was still suffering from her most recent bereavement, the death of Willie a year before. In Washington, the pace never stopped, and the climate aggravated all of her many physical ailments—migraines, arthritis, backaches, and ague (a malarial infection causing periodic chills), to name a few. Manchester's cool mountain air was soothing, helping her relax emotionally and physically.

Mr. Orvis was pleased to have his Green Mountain resort thought of as a restorative, but not everyone in town was happy to see tourism develop. Local residents worried about the influence on their children of wealthy outsiders. In 1867, Professor Matthew H. Buckham wrote in Vermont's *Historical Gazetteer*,

> When they come with their long baggage trains of trunks and bandboxes and take possession of a country village... importing into industrious communities the habit of doing nothing and doing it elegantly, they demoralize the whole society...and convert respectable villages into the likeness of suburban Connecticut and New Jersey...[18]

Local historian Abby Hemenway also questioned the wisdom of exposing the community's youth to people whose main occupation was to "ride around in fine carriages and display themselves in fine clothing."[19]

No records exist to tell how Mrs. Lincoln and her youngest son Tad spent their days while visiting Manchester during those two weeks at the height of the Civil War, except for Bigelow and Otis' reference to frequent carriage rides.[20] Manchester had developed a surprising reputation as a cultural Mecca. This tiny southwestern Vermont community was an obscure village where most residents were simple farmers or laborers scratching out a living, so visitors were surprised at the "'cosmopolitan and exclusive' stronghold established in Manchester by the outside 'world of affairs, arts, letters, and social registers' which was to give the town 'an air of rich and cultured living.'"[21] This would have appealed to Mrs. Lincoln, and she probably participated in some of the offerings. There were also activities that would have appealed to Tad. The *Manchester Journal* reported that:

> The number of children seen daily in front of The Equinox tells plainly enough that parents think it is a real Family Hotel; and for grown-up visitors, a series of amusements have nightly been extemporized in the large Parlor. Plays, Dances, Charades, Concerts, Tableaux, Shadow-Pictures, Fancy Dress Balls, all have in their turn cheered the evening hours. Then there have been excursions to the summit of Mt. Equinox, to the cave in Skinner Hollow, to Deer Knoll, to the Marble Quarries, to Well's Pond, and to Downer's Glen. The angler has had the finest sport in Bourn and Lye Brooks, in the Battenkill, and in the Equinox Trout Pond, and the Artist and the Author have found congenial subjects for pen and pencil...[22]

Michael Doolady, a guest in 1866, further explained the arrangements for Equinox House guests who were successful anglers:

> [T]hey keep a very fair table at the hotel...the [carriage] rides about the place are quite numerous and pretty and can all be done after dinner...During the summer the guests at the hotel are privileged to try their skill and fish on the Orvis artificial pond nearby, provided their product is placed in the larder of the hotel...[23]

While the Equinox House guests relaxed and amused themselves, war concerns weighed heavily on every citizen's mind. Manchester and the surrounding communities, like towns and cities throughout the Union North, had sent their best and brightest, their strongest men, to help settle the nation's conflict. Most of the August 25, 1863, issue of the *Manchester Journal* was devoted to war news. The paper reprinted an excerpt from a New York officer's letter describing the oppressive summer heat, so hot he couldn't sleep, and a wide variety of biting insects that plagued his unit. The *Journal* also reprinted a report originally published in the *Newport News*, written by Lieutenant Tice, which detailed the "losses and present strength" of Company E, 5th Vermont, which had been on active duty for almost two years. The original company had three officers and 87 enlisted men. As of August 1, 1863, it was down to three officers and only 33 other men.[24]

The war also provided fertile ground for satire. An editorial in that issue of the *Manchester Journal* included the following passage:

> Some of the Southern journals declare that the loss of Vicksburg and Port Hudson, instead of being disasters, are really advantageous to their cause, because they will no longer have these places to defend! When they are relieved of all the places which they are at present under the painful necessity of defending, we suppose that they will be at the hight [sic] of military success.

Another small item in the same paper carried on the theme, remarking, "The rebels threatened to blow up Fort Sumter rather than have it fall into the hands of our troops. A capital way to begin, if next they will blow up Charleston, and last the rebel confederacy. Uncle Sam can sleep soundly under such threats...Go ahead!"[25]

The North could afford to be a little cocky at this point. Union forces had captured New Orleans and the mouth of the Mississippi River the year before. Now with the capture in July of Vicksburg, Mississippi, and Port Hudson, Louisiana—the last two Confederate strongholds along the Mississippi—the Union controlled the entire length of the river, which divided the eastern Confederate states from their western compatriots. On the same day that Confederates surrendered at Vicksburg, they were also retreating from the bloody battlefield at Gettysburg. The tide of the war had turned, but it would take nearly two years more to secure the ultimate victory.

In the summer of 1863, women across the country were still doing what they could to support the troops. Women's aid societies around Manchester sent reports of their activities to the local newspaper. On August 25, the *Manchester Journal* included an item from the Female Soldiers Aid Society in Peru, up the mountain from Manchester, announcing that they had just filled another box containing "11 bed quilts, 4 pillows, 9 pairs of cotton flannel drawers, 15 shirts, 7 pairs of socks, 7 sheets, 4 pairs of pillow slips, 2 towels, 8

handkerchiefs, 2 dressing gowns, dried apple, berries and hops...
nearly all new...May the recipients have as much enjoyment in
receiving them as the donors have in giving them."[26]

While Mrs. Lincoln recuperated from her carriage accident in
Manchester, she probably enjoyed sitting quietly in her suite on the
second floor at the front of the Equinox. Maybe she caught up on
her reading, or lazily watched people stroll beneath the maples that
lined the village's marble walkways, visible from her window. She
loved to shop, so she surely visited Cone and Burton's, the general
store a few doors from the Equinox, where you could get the latest
ladies' shawls and buy cotton hose for a mere 15 cents a pair.[27]

On Sunday, she went to the village's Congregational Church,
across the street from the hotel. In fact, she visited the pastor, Dr.
Cushman, and his wife at their home and continued to correspond
with them when she went back to Washington.[28]

Her presence in church signaled a recent change. During the
year following Willie's death, Mary had attended a number of
séances, sharing these experiences with at least half a dozen like-
minded friends. Her seamstress, Elizabeth Keckley, may have introduced Mrs. Lincoln to the mediums, as she had consulted them
after the death of her own son. Mary described the separation
between life and death as only a thin veil, through which, with the
help of a medium, she could communicate with Willie and Eddie,
her two dead sons. Eddie, the Lincolns' second son, had died in 1850,
just shy of his fourth birthday. Sometimes she claimed she could visit
them without the aid of a medium. She told her half-sister Emilie
Todd Helm that:

> Willie lives. He comes to me every night, and stands at the
> foot of my bed, with the same sweet adorable smile he has
> always had...little Eddie is sometimes with him and twice
> he has come with our brother Alec [Alexander]...You can-
> not dream of the comfort this gives me. When I thought of
> my little son in immensity, alone, without his mother to
> direct him, no one to hold his little hand...it nearly broke
> my heart.[29]

The conventional clergy warned against consulting mediums, characterizing them as pagans and sorcerers. In some states, a belief in spiritualism was enough proof for a woman to be declared insane.[30] By the time she arrived in Manchester, Mary Lincoln's visits to the spiritualists were on the wane, at least for the time being, and gradually, she returned to the church. Likewise, she had recently begun to wear clothing with colors other than black, colors like lavender, dark purple and gray. Etiquette manuals called for "first-degree" mourning—the wearing of only black—for six months, but Mary had waited more than a year.[31]

In Manchester, Mrs. Lincoln had the company of her two remaining sons, Robert, the oldest, and Tad, the youngest. Robert was away at school during most of the White House years, but he joined Mary and Tad for part of this first trip to Manchester. White House Secretary John Hay suggested that 20-year-old Robert came along because he sought solace for a broken heart. Hay wrote that "Bob" was with his mother in the mountains, "so shattered by the wedding" of a certain young lady that he "rushed madly off to sympathize with nature in her sternest aspects."[32]

Did Robert Todd Lincoln find comfort in the presence of the cool Green Mountains? Forty years later, high on a bluff overlooking this valley, he would purchase land to build Hildene, his beloved summer retreat. In August of 1863, he had his first introduction to Manchester.

Whether it was the scenery or the social life, Mrs. Lincoln so enjoyed her first stay in Manchester that she came back in 1864. She also made a reservation for the President and herself for the summer of 1865. But the assassination of Abraham Lincoln on April 14, 1865, prevented that. Tragically, father Abraham would never see the place his son would later call his "ancestral home."[33]

CHAPTER SIX:

Who is the Lucky Fellow?

The Patent Office, Washington, D.C., March 6, 1865

1864 was a presidential election year, and during the summer before the election, there was much public talk about the fact that, while other young male citizens were fighting the bloody war, the President's son was still in college. When Senator Ira Harris of New York questioned Mrs. Lincoln about this, she calmly took all of the blame. "Robert is making his preparations now to enter the Army, Senator Harris," she said, adding, "He is not a shirker as you seem to imply for he has been anxious to go for a long time. If fault there be, it is mine." She did not admit how terrified she was at the thought of Robert on the warfront, but she argued that education also helps men to serve their country.[1]

Robert Todd Lincoln wanted to serve like other loyal young men, but his mother held him back. The President was sensitive to the criticism that he risked the lives of other boys, but not his own. He was a father as well as a President, so he could see the situation from both sides. He asked General Grant to find Robert a place where he could be useful without getting into too much danger.[2] In the meantime, Robert enrolled at Harvard Law School that September, but he stayed for only a few months. In January 1865, the President and General Grant came up with a satisfactory position for Robert, and in February, Robert was commissioned as a captain with Grant's personal staff.

Meanwhile, President Lincoln had been re-elected. He had carried all but three states (New Jersey, Delaware, and Kentucky) and took 55 percent of the popular vote.[3] The President's second inauguration was held on March 4, 1865, and the inaugural ball two days later.

Carriages began arriving for the second inaugural ball around 9 p.m. on March 6. The scene for the elegant occasion was the Patent Office, chosen because of the size and beauty of its marble halls. A brass band at the east end of the gallery provided music for the promenade. Banners and other decorations hung on the walls, along with American flags and the flags of various army corps. The hall's frescoed ceiling added to its air of grandeur. Carriage after carriage arrived outside, and soon the ballroom was crowded. A string band furnished music for dancing on the huge blue and white marble floor, 280 feet long by 60 feet wide.[4]

At half past ten, the guests of honor arrived. An event courier cleared the way at the main entrance, and the military band played "Hail to the Chief" as President Lincoln entered, accompanied by Speaker Schuyler Colfax, then Mrs. Lincoln on the arm of Senator Charles Sumner. *The New York Times* later reported that President Lincoln "was evidently trying to throw off care for the time, but with rather ill success, and looked very old; yet he seemed pleased and gratified, as he was greeted by people."[5]

Fashion-conscious reporters, who always supplied details of what people wore to these events, were quick to notice Mrs. Lincoln's white satin dress, "very ample and rich," with a décolleté neckline and short sleeves, all covered with point appliqué, and satin ribbon trimming. She wore pearls, her hair was pulled back with trailing jasmine and violets, and she carried an ermine fan with silver spangles. Blue and gold sofas and chairs were reserved for the Lincolns and their guests on the north side of the hall. They all walked down the center of the long hall, and when they reached the far end, they turned back and proceeded to their seats.[6]

Captain Robert Todd Lincoln's date for his father's second inaugural ball was Mary Eunice Harlan, the eldest daughter of Senator and Mrs. James Harlan, of Iowa.[7] Senator Harlan had been in office since 1855 and had become friendly with the President during the first administration. In the summer of 1861, Senator Harlan had toured Iowa to gather recruits for Lincoln's army, and when the President campaigned for re-election in 1864, Harlan had traveled his home state again, making speeches on the President's behalf. Soon, the senator would be named to Lincoln's second Cabinet.[8] Mary's mother, Ann Eliza Harlan, was well-known for her efforts to help the wounded troops.

Mary Harlan was a gracious, intelligent and cultivated young woman, just the kind that Mrs. Lincoln wished to see her son marry.[9] She had been educated at Iowa Wesleyan University, which her father had helped to found, and at Madame Smith's French School in Washington, a finishing school attended by many senators' daughters. Thus, her education was similar to Mrs. Lincoln's. Mary Harlan was a good student who excelled at music. A fellow student said she played the harp "divinely."[10]

The *Times* described Robert Lincoln as "a fine-looking young man" dressed in his Union captain's uniform, but it did not name or describe his date.[11] How serious was this romance between Mary Harlan and Robert Lincoln in 1865? Neither of them recorded their feelings. But letters to Mary from her school friend Minnie Chandler between early 1866 and the fall of 1868 show some of the vagaries of the Harlan-Lincoln romance. Minnie speaks both directly and in code. And though we have only Minnie's side of the conversation, her comments prove that Mary had other suitors.[12]

Clearly, Mary Harlan wasn't the only young lady on Robert Lincoln's mind either. A week after the ball, he had returned to his post at General Grant's headquarters. During his watch one night, he wrote to White House Secretary John Hay, saying, "There have been lots of pretty girls down here lately—If you want to do a favor, send some more."[13]

Two weeks after the inauguration, General Grant invited President Lincoln to visit his headquarters, and Mrs. Lincoln and Tad came, too. They boarded the River Queen, a steam-engine paddleboat, on March 23, 1865, and paddled down the Potomac. Despite their hopes that the war was almost over, it wasn't a pleasant voyage. Many people on board were sick the first night because of contaminated drinking water, and sometime that night President Lincoln dreamed that Washington was burning. First thing the next morning, Mrs. Lincoln telegraphed a White House maid and learned that everything was fine.[14] When the boat docked at City Point, Robert came aboard to visit his family.

After a bumpy, painful trip by carriage to the place where her husband was to review the troops, Mrs. Lincoln had a migraine, and she lost her temper, creating a scene. President Lincoln had gone ahead by horseback, and when she arrived, the review was already in process. Instead of riding alongside him as she usually did, she was forced to watch from the sidelines. Another woman, the wife of Union General Edward Ord, was riding in her place. Mrs. Lincoln was jealous and berated her husband in public. Later, she was sorry and hid in her cabin all evening. A few days later, she returned to Washington, while Tad stayed with his father.[15]

On April 3, Secretary of War Edwin Stanton sent a dispatch from the War Department with the best news yet—Union forces were now in command of the Confederate capital of Richmond. According to one Union general's account, "The people [there] receive us with enthusiastic expressions of joy." Union troops had captured 4,000 prisoners, four batteries of artillery, a large train of loaded wagons, and a number of cattle in the bargain.[16]

Tad Lincoln and the President toured Richmond on April 4. Crowds of former slaves enthusiastically blockaded the President's quarters for a while, surrounding him with loud cheers.[17] Although Confederate General Robert E. Lee did not officially surrender for several days, the war was essentially over. Less than two months before, the editors of the *Richmond Examiner* had challenged Confederate President Jefferson Davis' position by arguing that the defense of the southern capital was key to their cause. They had written,

> The evacuation of Richmond would be the loss of all respect and authority toward the Confederate government, the disintegration of the army, and the abandonment of the scheme of an independent Southern Confederation...Each contestant in the war has made Richmond the central object of all its plans and all its exertions. It has become the symbol of the Confederacy.[18]

The editors turned out to be right.

Now that the war was over, Mrs. Lincoln wanted to see Richmond. She quickly organized a touring party and was back visiting Robert at City Point by April 6, this time with Senator and Mrs. Harlan and their daughter Mary, plus a French marquis, Senator Sumner, and Elizabeth Keckley (she had once been a slave and wanted to see the Confederate capital in ruins). Together, the group toured the blackened city; most of the central business area had been destroyed by fire from the battle. One *New York Times* reporter estimated the capital's damage in the "tens of millions of dollars" and described the business district as "a heap of smouldering [sic] ruins."[19] After three days, on April 9, they returned to Washington.

That same day, Captain Lincoln attended the Confederate surrender at the Appomattox courthouse. He stood guard outside the door while Confederate General Robert E. Lee and Union General Ulysses S. Grant signed the official surrender. Later, the President's son was introduced to General Lee. Then he headed to Washington with General Grant's staff, arriving five days later, in time to have breakfast with his father at the White House on April 14. Tradition says he showed his father a recent picture of General Lee, and the President said he looked like a "noble, noble, brave man." The President told his son how happy he was to see the war over, adding, "I trust that an era of good feeling has returned and that henceforth we shall live in harmony together."[20] That night, the President's dreams were ended by an assassin's bullet.

Suddenly, 21-year-old Robert, as the eldest son, was head of the Lincoln family. It was he who appointed Judge David Davis as executor of his father's estate, he who served as the family's only representative at his father's funeral, he who accompanied the body on its two-week procession back to Springfield. Senator Harlan was also in this procession.[21]

Mary Lincoln was so undone by her husband's death that she could scarcely come out of her room, let alone vacate the White House. On April 25, Robert was still apologizing to President Andrew Johnson about the delay, saying his mother needed at least two and a half more weeks, but in fact, it was May 22 before she finally departed.[22]

Mrs. Lincoln, with Tad and Mrs. Keckley, moved to Chicago. Robert was already worried about his mother's mental state. She had good reason to be distraught over her husband's death, but Robert saw something else as well. "It is very hard to deal with one who is sane on all subjects but one," he wrote to Mary Harlan around the same time. That subject was money.[23]

As early as the summer of 1865, the newspapers carried rumors that Robert Lincoln and Mary Harlan were engaged,[24] but for several years, it was just speculation. Minnie Chandler's letters over the next year and a half prove that both "Bob" and Mary were still considering their options.

Robert Todd Lincoln was a worthy contender for Mary Harlan's hand. Educated at Harvard (he received his undergraduate degree in 1864), at the University of Chicago Law School, and in the law offices of Scammon, McCagg and Fuller in Chicago, he was preparing to practice on his own. Because of his name and his talents, he seemed destined to a bright future. By habit, he was practical and precise, so much so that some people thought him to be cold and aloof. Those who knew him best liked his warmth, humor, intelligence, and generosity. He had been popular with college classmates and fellow soldiers alike; he was known as one unwilling to shirk his duty. One of Grant's officers said, "He was always ready to perform his share of hard work, and never expected to be treated differently...on account of his being the son of the Chief Executive."[25]

Mary Harlan was equally worthy. As a Harlan, she was descended from a family of sturdy, principled, colonial Quakers. Two brothers, George and Michael "Harland," moved with their families from England to Ireland and finally to William Penn's colony, where they found freedom to practice their religion. The brothers arrived in New Castle, Delaware, in 1687, and settled near Centerville. Later they moved to Chester County, Pennsylvania. They established farms and formed Quaker meetings, some of which still exist today.[26]

As Quakers, the Harlans were independent thinkers. They believed that spiritual authority lies within, not with leaders, and they had no clergy. Worship consisted of sitting silently until someone felt divinely inspired, and if no one spoke, the whole service would be a time of silence. The Quakers were also pacifists. Harlans were among the worshippers one morning during the Revolutionary War at Old Kennett Meeting House in Kennett Square, Pennsylvania. As the Quakers said their prayers, a skirmish took place just outside their door, in the meeting house's graveyard. One worshipper later recorded that, "While there was much noise and confusion without, all was quiet and peaceful within."[27]

Eventually, many Harlans headed west, settling particularly in the Midwest. Somewhere along the way, most of them dropped the final "d" from their name. Mary Todd Lincoln had a distant connection to some of these early Harlan pioneers. Silas and James Harlan, two brothers, went by canoe with a group in 1774, traveling down the Ohio River and up the Salt River to a place they named Harrodsburgh, now part of Kentucky (and not far from Lincoln's birthplace). It was reportedly the first permanent white settlement west of the Appalachians. While James farmed, his brother Silas helped to fight Indians and the British. Silas was a major under George Rogers Clark and died in the battle of Blue Lick Springs in 1782. Mary Todd's great-uncle John was also there, and her brother would be named for the battle's commander.[28]

Senator James Harlan, Mary Harlan's father, was a distant cousin of the Silas Harlan who had died fighting in Kentucky. Mary's father was born in Clark County, Illinois, on or around April 26, 1820 (accounts differ), the son of another Silas Harlan and his wife, Mary. When James was four, the family moved to Parke County, Indiana, and settled between the Big and Little Raccoon Creeks, about 50 miles west of Indianapolis. They lived in a small community called New Discovery, where his father was known as the "governor." New Discovery had no church, but a Methodist circuit-riding preacher conducted services in the Harlan home. Sporadic education was offered in a small log building about a mile away, with sessions lasting for three months at a time. James Harlan attended until he was 13 or 14, but he credited his mother with teaching him to read, using the family's three books—the Bible, an almanac, and *Harvey's Evening Meditations*. When the Harlans moved to Indiana, Abraham Lincoln, who was eleven years older than James, was growing up under similar circumstances some 100 miles straight south, in Warrick County, Indiana, near the Ohio River.[29]

Young James' father could see that his son had ambitions for more than farming, so he collected what little money he could and sent James to Indiana Asbury College, now DePauw University, in nearby Greencastle. There, James excelled at debate and was active in Methodist student organizations. He also had a list of 15-20 young ladies whom he visited. Eventually, he came to a "definite understanding" with one of them, Miss Ann Eliza Peck.[30]

Ann Eliza was born in Maysville, Kentucky, the third child of James and Eunice Knight Peck. In 1832, when she was eight, both her parents died of cholera, leaving Ann Eliza, her brother and five sisters. The older children took care of the younger ones. A few years later, Ann Eliza moved in with a married sister and entered school in Greencastle, Indiana, where she met James.[31]

James valued education in general and supported education for women. This is clear from the importance he gave it when choosing a wife. He met with Ann Eliza two or three times a week to hear her recite lessons in academic subjects not available at Mrs. Larabee's School for young ladies, where she was a student. He recorded in his diary that, "I gave her an examination on her preceding lessons in Upham's mental philosophy; and formed a very flattering opinion of her capacity."[32] James graduated in 1845, and they married on November 9, 1845, when she was 21 and he was 25.

They soon moved to Iowa City, where Mr. Harlan would become president of Iowa City College, an institution sponsored by the Methodist Episcopal Church. Mary Eunice Harlan was born there on September 25, 1846, followed by Silas (born in 1850, he only lived a day); William Aaron (born in 1852); and Julia Josephine Jessie (1856-1862).

In Iowa, two colleges were rivals for the financial support of the Methodist Church:[33] Iowa City College, where Harlan was president; and Mount Pleasant Collegiate Institute, in Mount Pleasant, a small town in southeastern Iowa. In 1847, Iowa City College closed—Mount Pleasant had won. The Harlans stayed in Iowa City while Mr. Harlan finished studying law. He was admitted to the Iowa Bar that year and opened a law office. In 1847 and 1848, he ran unsuccessfully for the position of Iowa Superintendent of Public Instruction.[34]

Five years later, in April 1853, he was offered the presidency of the Mount Pleasant Collegiate Institute. The seven-year-old school was in bad financial shape, despite the church's backing. He took the job only after the trustees accepted his three-point plan: He would raise money for a second building, develop a baccalaureate program like his alma mater's, and change the school's name to Iowa Wesleyan University.[35]

The new building, known officially as "the main edifice," but popularly called "Old Main," was constructed in 1855. The school now had two buildings on the flat Iowa prairie. That same year the school became a university. (In 1912, the name was changed to Iowa Wesleyan College.) The new baccalaureate program focused on classical languages, math, science, modern languages, and music.[36]

Mary's parents enrolled her in the college's "primary" (prep school) department in 1854. She attended sporadically for the next eight years, also attending school in Washington. In 1862, at age sixteen, she finished her preparatory work, and the next year, she enrolled as a first-year university student. Her schooling continued to be sporadic, and she did not graduate.[37] On January 15, 1866, schoolmate Minnie Chandler wrote to Mary that she was:

> delighted to receive your very interesting letter this morning & especially as it informed me that you are to come back, which I was by no means sure of before. By the by Mrs. Hoffman & I had a little talk about you the other day a part of said conversation I will relate to you, she asked me when you were coming back, that she had not heard from you, had refused two young females your place & wanted to know about it, she had not heard from you as she expected to, I told her that you were not coming back until February certainly & perhaps not at all indeed the latter was my opinion, for when you went away you said you

would miss so much that you didn't think you would be able to keep up with the classes...I am so glad you are coming back, I have positively been good natured all day. I found your Grecian History some time ago & am keeping it for you; we are as far as Louis xiv in French history...[38]

In the January 15 letter, Minnie also passed on a rumor heard by a mutual friend that Mary and Bob Lincoln were engaged: "[T]hat young lady heard positively that you were engaged to Bob Lincoln & she denied it as you asked her to ..." Mary's other suitors were also mentioned. Later in the same letter, Minnie wrote, "How is Gen. Warmouth or whatever his name is? You are not at all fickle dear are you? Now that you have received a letter from B.L. you like him as well as ever."

Five young men that Mary was considering were discussed cryptically in an undated letter Minnie marked "Confidential." The nickname "Prince Bob" must have referred to Robert Todd Lincoln, as he had been dubbed the "Prince of Rails" during his father's first election campaign:

> My dear darling Mary, I am so glad to hear that you [are] so truly happy. I hope that you may live a long time to enjoy your happiness, if I may say so, but who is the happy gentleman? My curiosity is raised to the highest pitch, you say I will be surprised, is it Edgar Welles, Daddy Henderson, Mr. Denaise, Prince Bob, or Mr. New Orleans...[If I knew which one] I could congratulate the gentleman & tell him that he had picked out one of the dearest sweetest, best girls that ever lived & one that I think will make him a good, true wife.

During the summer of 1866, things were still far from settled. On July 13, Minnie asked, "How many are you engaged to now? Ten or a dozen?" On August 4, in response to a published rumor that their engagement was broken, she wrote, "When that piece came out in the paper about you and Bob Lincoln, I said that I didn't believe a word of it, if you had ever been engaged to him you were now, but that I thought you were a great flirt, that you had quantities of beaux..." Later in that letter, she wrote, "You dear little soul. So happy that you are free from all the gentlemen, you only have an understanding with one and three or four very attentive, I'm glad I'm not a gentleman and one of your lovers; where do you keep your heart, or has Bob got it so entirely."

That fall, rumors circulated again that the Harlan-Lincoln engagement was off. On October 3, Minnie described herself and Mary Lincoln as two old maids forever sworn off men:

> I have almost decided to return [to school]. I wish to be fitted for my station as 'Old Maid,' as one must have something to think of while knitting in a large armchair, by a cosy [sic] little fire, with a dear old cat in their lap, don't I present a cheerful picture? You are to be in the same room, of course, with a parrot on your shoulder, instead of a cat in your lap. Now Mary my love as we have determined to lead a life of single blessedness, of course we give up all thoughts of the male portion who live in this degenerate 19th Century; so that we shall not want any 'Old Bach' neighbors, not even the would be admirer...

But Minnie betrayed her happy old-maid pose by complaining later in the same letter that the "epidemic" of young women getting engaged was leaving behind a corresponding "derth [sic] of young gentlemen." Why would a happy old maid care?

On December 16, Minnie dug for information: "How is Bob Lincoln? I have been asked several times this year if you were engaged to him, I say I don't know and then they insist upon it that I must know, but beg pardon for having asked." Mary and Minnie visited in person over the Christmas holidays, so the next developments in the story were probably discussed privately, leaving no paper record.

By early spring, the fate of the romance was still not clear. Minnie wrote on March 17, 1867, that, "I consider it very dangerous my dear Mary to have such very charming gentlemen friends as the one you spoke of. What about Judge Warmouth? Have you seen him or heard from him?" Later she added, "So B.L. did write, did he. I wish I could see the letter, I have no doubt it is a very funny one."

Minnie's letters did include news of other subjects as well. They were filled with lively opinions about others in their social circle, with details of the latest fashions, of parlor concerts, of music lessons, books and school. On April 28, Minnie wrote about a rift between Mary and another girl. Mary, it seemed, wanted some kind of revenge by a waterfall, but Minnie warned that it "wouldn't be much of a satisfaction." Minnie also talked about her own romantic fantasies. She was soon to depart on a trip to the West with her family:

> Just think of it Mary, perhaps I shall have the exquisite felicity of seeing 'our Spanish friend' when I 'depart for the land of the red man,' how romantic it would be if he should save me from the 'Injins,' perhaps just as I was about to be scalped. Our friend 'eyes' too, isn't he going out West somewhere? I have no doubt he would be glad to talk about you to me, and tell me of the numerous little incidents that must have occured [sic] during your long walks....I know there has been some trouble with Judge Walworth (is that the name) and I take enough interest in you, you dreadful flirt, to want to know what it is. I wrote to Frank Sharp and asked if R.L. was really engaged to Mary Arthur, she says she doesn't know but that he has been very attentive indeed.

Minnie writes again on August 9, but says nothing definitive about Mary and Robert's relationship. Her other letters are undated.

Finally, there is one very poignant letter from Minnie, perhaps the last of the series, most likely written the third week of September 1868. It is full of a young woman's agony: Minnie had apparently been left off the invitation list for Mary's wedding. Unlike the other letters, which start with the salutations "My dear Mary" and "My darling Mary," this one begins curtly.

> Miss Harlan, Sunday though it be, the peculiar circumstances indeed which I am about to relate I will say fact, must excuse me. My instincts seldom mislead me Miss Harlan & it is with deep grief that I this morning heard of your perfidy. There I was, obliged to smile sweetly upon a

gentleman while he told me that Miss Harlan was to be married this week...Words fail to describe my astonishment and I just stated that I was to be bridesmaid and my dress was not made and in short I covered my agitated feelings with a dress.

The Harlan home, Washington, D.C., September 24, 1868

As she waited for Robert and Mary's wedding ceremony to begin, Robert's mother Mary Todd Lincoln must have been thinking back to her own wedding day. She was happy to see the two of them marry, and she certainly hoped their lives would be less tragic than hers.

The couple gave their parents more notice than Mary Todd had given when she married Abraham Lincoln. By late summer of 1868, Robert Lincoln and Mary Harlan were announcing their engagement. The ceremony was originally planned for late autumn, but it actually took place on September 24, the day before Mary Harlan's 22nd birthday. There are at least two theories as to why the ceremony was moved up. A biography of Senator Harlan reports that he rushed back to Washington that September for a special session of Congress and the marriage of his daughter, suggesting that the date was changed to coincide with this trip. The *Washington Star* said the date was changed to accommodate the President's widow, who was anxious to sail for Europe.[39]

Apparently, Mary Harlan had promised that Minnie would be her bridesmaid. Perhaps the date change prevented Mary from notifying her friend in time, but whatever the reason for her being left out, Minnie was clearly hurt. The *Washington Star* listed every wedding guest by name and described the apparel of every woman present, and Minnie wasn't on the list.[40]

The *Washington Express* named Edwin Stanton, Jr., and Edgar Welles, two of Robert's friends, as the "bridesmaids." Only 33 people, including the bride, the groom and the minister, attended the ceremony, held Thursday evening, September 24, 1868, in the Harlans' Washington, D.C., home.[41]

The *Washington Star* reported that:

> The guests commenced to assemble about 7 o'clock. The spacious parlors of Senator Harlan were tastefully and elegantly decorated with rare flowers, formed in pyramids and bouquets, furnished by the friends of the bride. On the wall, directly opposite the spot where the bridal party stood, was a curiously arranged monogram of roses, forming the letters 'M. R.'...The bride and bridegroom entered the parlors from the rear shortly after 8 o'clock. As they advanced to the centre, they were met by Bishop Simpson...who commenced the ceremony....[42]

Evidence of the importance of fashion, manners, and the adulation of one's peers came in the *Washington Express* report, which began:

> The fashionable belles and beaus have been all a flutter for some weeks past in anticipation of the marriage of Capt. Robert S. [sic] Lincoln, son of the late president, with Miss Mary Harlan, daughter of Senator Harlan. How the bride was to be dressed, and how 'Bob' would look, were matters of all-important interest to the many divinities in this vicinity, who, for the time being, had nothing else to think of or gossip about. At last the curiosity of the ladies and the wonders of the men have been gratified. The nuptials took place last evening...[43]

The *Washington Star* also carried full descriptions of all the ladies' dresses, starting with that of the bride [PLATE 10]:

> The bride was dressed in a rich white silk, elegantly trimmed with white satin and blond, made with high corsage and long sleeves, with illusion and satin folds, with train and overskirt and belt, and fan-shaped bow behind. She wore a handsome pointed illusion white veil, very full, fastened under the back hair with a small wreath of orange blossoms. Her ornaments were rich pearls. The hair was tastefully arranged, plaited and puffed. The entire dress,

though plain, was exceedingly tasteful and rich, aiding, though not adding, to the beauty of the bride.

The *Star* described Mrs. Lincoln as "attired in deep mourning, without any jewelry or ornaments whatever," while Mrs. Harlan wore:

> ...a wine-colored silk dress, made with high corsage and long sleeves, with a lower skirt trimmed with a deep flounce and folds of the same. The upper skirt was looped up with flat bows and trimmed with a deep fringe of the same color as the dress. She wore a point lace collar. Her ornaments were pearls.

The *Washington Express* described Robert as "very properly attired in a suit of black broadcloth, with a *solitaire* adorning his necktie, and white gloves completing his toilet." The happy young gentleman looked the "very impersonification of joy" and received his friends' and relatives' congratulations "with becoming modesty."

After a wedding supper, by the celebrated Washington caterer J.H. Wormley, and some accompanying vocal music, the event concluded. The next day, the newlyweds, plus Stanton, Welles, Robert's mother, and brother Tad all rode in a special train car to New York, enjoying a wedding lunch along the way, also prepared by Wormley.[44]

Somehow, the hard feelings between Minnie and Mary eventually resolved, because letters dated after Mary's wedding exist. By then, they were both married, and apparently the letters were more sporadic, full of everyday news of husband and children.

Likewise, for the next 58 years, the center of Mary Harlan Lincoln's life was her husband and her family. Her influence was strong at home, but publicly she held no positions of leadership in civic, philanthropic or church organizations, and she championed no causes. Iowa Wesleyan historian Louis Haselmayer described her:

> The life of Mary Harlan Lincoln is one of complete involvement in family affairs...She had almost no public life of her own except as a social hostess for her father...[and] for her husband...dictated by the needs of her husband's position and her children's interests. She performed this gracefully and graciously but she did not aspire to nor attempt to be 'a

leader of society'...As a result, her life is shadowy and almost without any independence of its own.[45]

Still, the historical records hint at something more. Mary Harlan Lincoln did not seek to be the center of attention, as Mary Todd Lincoln often had, but the family files contain invitations to see the Queen of England, the Prince of Wales, and the Shah of Persia, proving that there was also a glittery side to her life. She and her husband were members of an elite social circle in Chicago during their young married years, and she had occasion to meet many influential people throughout her life.

Occasionally, Mary Harlan Lincoln could prove herself to be a rebel. For example, she followed her daughter's lead and joined the First Church of Christ, Scientist in 1898. In the Victorian era, the choice to follow a woman prophet who spoke of God as the divine Father-Mother was in itself a small act of revolution. Mary Harlan Lincoln was a member of the church for the rest of her life and left the church a large part of her estate when she died. And while her life was centered in her home, she was a strong-willed woman who wielded lasting influences on her children and grandchildren.[46]

PLATES 1 AND 2 The earliest known pictures (daguerreotypes)
of Mary and Abraham Lincoln, taken in Springfield, Illinois, around 1846,
just after he was elected to Congress.

PLATE 3 Mary Todd Lincoln as the elegantly dressed First Lady,
photographed by Mathew Brady, circa 1860-61.

PLATE 4 An engraving by J.C. Buttre of the Lincoln family
in the White House (L to R: Mary, Willie, Robert, Tad, and Abraham).

PLATE 5 Mary Todd Lincoln in mourning attire, 1860s.
She always dressed in black after Abraham Lincoln's death.

PLATE 6 The Lincoln Memorial. Robert Todd Lincoln and his wife Mary attended the dedication on May 30, 1922.

PLATE 7 Ann Eliza Peck Harlan, Mary Harlan's mother, as a young woman.

PLATE 8 Senator James Harlan, Mary Harlan's father, as an elder statesman.

PLATE 9   The home of Ann Eliza and James Harlan in Mount Pleasant, Iowa,
across the street from Iowa Wesleyan College.

PLATE 10 Mary Harlan Lincoln's wedding portrait.
She and Robert Todd Lincoln were married September 24, 1868.

PLATE 11 Photograph of Robert Todd Lincoln, taken in the 1870s.

PLATE 12 Mary Harlan Lincoln photograph, circa 1868.

PLATE 13 Robert and Mary Harlan Lincoln's young children
(from lower left): Jessie, Abraham II (Jack), and Mary (Mamie).

PLATE 14 Mary (Mamie) Lincoln (far left) poses with Clara Cole and Frances
Wheeler for a statue for the Iowa Statehouse.
Sculptor Harriet Ketcham died before the work could be completed.

PLATE 15 Abraham Lincoln II (Jack) on his deathbed in London, 1889-90.

PLATE 16 The two Lincoln sisters, Mary (Mamie) and Jessie.

PLATE 17 Lincoln Isham and his father Charles on the
terrace at Hildene, circa 1905-06.

A Question of Sanity

The Harlan home, Mount Pleasant, Iowa, Summer 1884

Mary Harlan Lincoln was busy the summer of 1884, when her cousin Florence Snow came to visit the Harlan family home in Mount Pleasant. Mary and the children, Mamie, Jack and Jessie, were staying at her parents' house next to the college. Mary did what she could to take care of the household while her mother convalesced, probably at the Hygeia Hotel, a popular spa and resort in Old Point Comfort, Virginia. Mrs. Harlan had not recovered from a serious accident the year before, when her carriage was crushed by a runaway team of horses. She was thrown onto the frozen ground, causing internal injuries from which she never would recover. She died at the end of that summer, on September 4, 1884, in Old Point Comfort.[1] Perhaps it was a blessing for Mary to be busy during her mother's final illness.

Mary Harlan Lincoln was also fully engaged that summer in a huge project that fell to her as the daughter-in-law of the late Mary Todd Lincoln. The President's widow had died two years before. Mary Harlan Lincoln was completing an inventory of the contents of her 64 trunks[2] and trying to figure out how to distribute the many items to family members, friends, historical collections, and museums. Understanding that these items had great historical as well as sentimental value, she approached her task with great care.[3]

Mary worried that her work required so much of her attention that she was neglecting her Kansas cousin. When she apologized for this, Florence protested that she was not bored and that she needed no special amusements when "there was such a world of vital thought in everything about, and I had my eyes to see."[4]

Florence, who had just graduated from college, marveled at her uncle's vast library and loved to browse through the collection. She had always admired her uncle and had been inspired by his example. Ever since she was six or seven, he had been writing her letters, telling her among other things about his early life in pioneer Indiana. As a boy, his family had had only three books. Now he had a whole library. Florence marveled at them, noting that there were "books, books and still more books, ready to satisfy one's hunger through the longest life."[5]

In her uncle's library she chanced to meet Robert Todd Lincoln, her cousin-in-law, when he came in to borrow a law book one day. They ended up talking, and the encounter created a strong and lasting impression. Florence wrote that:

> I liked him immediately...In our slight opportunity for acquaintance during his short stay, his appearance and manner and evident character impressed me more and more, measured with my notion of what such a man should be. One could well believe that he had wrought out his gift of individual life with no undue regard to parental attainment, and was happy with his success.[6]

Florence also kept busy in Mount Pleasant playing with her second cousins, fifteen-year-old Mamie, eleven-year-old Jack, and nine-year-old Jessie. Florence recalled that the girls "did all sorts of nice things for me and made me lonesome for the younger sisters I might have had." She and Mamie were near enough in age to be natural companions. Senator Harlan took them to Chicago, where they admired the vastness of Lake Michigan, wandered through the city's Art Institute, saw a Shakespearean play, and visited a cyclorama about the battle of Gettysburg, with its "triumph of realism." They marveled at the abundant skyscrapers and at the crowds of people. "What magic there was in the enormous buildings and the limitless life and color of the crowded streets. How beautiful the lake...only a little less wonderful than the ocean must be," Florence later wrote.[7]

She was also fascinated by cousin Mary Harlan's sorting project, and she was glad to be invited upstairs to take a look. How amazing it was to see all the First Lady's things up close. What a vast and varied array! In a large empty bedroom, Mary had removed the furniture and circled the room with trestle tables. Against one wall was a pile of trunks. She spread everything out on the tables, sorting them according to final destination, for example: "Springfield," "Chicago," "Smithsonian," her children, a nephew or niece, a friend.[8]

Mary showed Florence some of the First Lady's gowns that she had set aside for Mamie and Jessie. Florence also saw stacks and stacks of children's clothes, things now too small for Mamie, Jessie and Jack. Florence explained:

> ...Grandmother Lincoln had bought lot after lot of children's clothing, dresses and coats, hats and shoes, and all sorts of trinkets that might be nice for Mary or Jessie or Jack, or maybe for the children of friends or servants. Then they were packed away to be ready when the time came and were forgotten.[9]

Mary Todd Lincoln's lifelong habit of acquiring things continued in her later days. In the last seven years of her life, when she didn't have a permanent home to store them in, she more than tripled the number of trunks it took to store her possessions. The letters she wrote to Mary Harlan Lincoln during her last sojourn to Europe were full of reports about things being shipped home for her daughter-in-law or the children. The letters were also full of advice about fashions in Europe, about who her daughter-in-law should hire to sew her dresses, or about what laces and fabrics and complimentary items she should take from her mother-in-law's trunks and put to use.[10] "[D]o oblige me by considering me as a mother—for you are very dear to me, as a daughter," she wrote. "*Any thing & every thing* is yours—if you will consider them worth an acceptance...It will be such a relief to me to know, that articles, that were costly, can be used & enjoyed by you..."[11]

Mary Todd Lincoln had been very generous with gifts, so much so that Mary Harlan Lincoln was sometimes overwhelmed. Robert Lincoln kept one letter, written by his mother, in which she told his wife, "...Robert writes that you were quite frightened, about the baby clothes—Certainly they were made of the simplest materials & if they were a little trimmed there was certainly nothing out of the way...certainly a simple embroidered cloak—is not too much, for people in our station in life..."[12]

The habit of buying things, storing them away and forgetting them was typical of Mary Todd Lincoln in her later years. She admits this in some of the letters from Europe, noting that she couldn't remember everything she had shipped home, nor could she remember all the things she had stored in Chicago before she left. This confusion later would lead her to accuse her son and his wife of stealing things from her.

Mary Todd Lincoln's shopping habits were widely documented and had often been publicly criticized from the beginning of her husband's first term as president. Mary Harlan Lincoln knew all about that. This project of sorting through her mother-in-law's many trunks no doubt conjured up all sorts of painful memories. First her mother-in-law had been overly generous, then openly hostile, then distant and unforgiving.

But personal feelings aside, Mary would do her duty. She would not have all these things wasted, even though, as she told Florence, they "only indicated a kind of collector's mania that might have been immensely more attractive."[13]

In the beginning, Mary Harlan and Mary Todd Lincoln got along splendidly. The presidential couple had known Mary Harlan since she was a child, their families had long been close friends, and the President had "loved and admired" Mary Harlan since she was a young girl, according to Mary Todd Lincoln. Both women came from similar backgrounds and had similar educations. They enjoyed conversing in French, they knew the important politicians of the day, they could talk about current events, and they enjoyed the latest fashions. Mary Harlan Lincoln was wonderful in her mother-in-law's eyes, the dear daughter Mrs. Lincoln never had.[14]

On October 1, 1868, a week after Robert and Mary's wedding, Mrs. Lincoln and Tad boarded the City of Baltimore steamer and sailed to Bremen, Germany. Mrs. Lincoln gave two reasons for rushing off to Europe: first, her conviction that she would find helpful cures, and second, her wish to enroll Tad in school. Historians have speculated that Mrs. Lincoln was also anxious to put distance between herself and the United States because of the negative publicity she had endured during the previous year, when she had proposed selling her old White House wardrobe. She was probably also still suffering from an exposé published in the spring of 1868 about her years as First Lady, written by her seamstress and supposed confidante, Elizabeth Keckley.[15]

Secondhand stores on Seventh Avenue in New York offered the used finery of the upper class for sale, and European royalty who needed money routinely sold off their used clothes. But Mary Todd Lincoln's plan to sell the gowns she no longer needed became an object of public ridicule. When the clothes went on display at a Broadway Avenue shop in October 1867, many people complained that she didn't need the money. She made matters worse by sending letters, pressuring and pleading when sales did not go well and criticizing those who did not buy.[16]

The Democrats saw in this a great political opportunity. While campaigning for the upcoming elections, they alternately charged that Republicans had given some of these clothes to the First Lady as bribes, or that the Republicans had been so stingy toward the President's widow that she had been reduced to selling her clothes in order to get by. Questions surfaced once again about how she had handled money as First Lady. For weeks, the newspapers carried stories and accusations, the kindest among them saying only that her sale was "vulgar" or she was "greedy."[17]

One newspaper, the *Chicago Journal*, went so far as to suggest that, "The most charitable construction that Mary Lincoln's friends can put on her strange course is that she is insane." Of course, as biographer Jean Baker points out, "In the rigid Victorian codes of female respectability, eccentricity was easily transformed into lunacy."[18]

Robert was certainly embarrassed by his mother's actions. He had long known that his mother could be irrational about money. Around this time, he told his future wife that, "I have no doubt that a great many good and amiable people wonder why I do not take charge of her affairs and keep them straight...I am likely to have a good deal of trouble in the future..."[19]

Mary Todd Lincoln suspected that her son's embarrassment had something to do with the sudden announcement in November that, two and a half years after his death, her husband's estate was finally ready for settlement. She told Mrs. Keckley that she believed her son had pressured the executor and family friend, David Davis, to speed things up. Still, she had to wait until the following July for all of the money to be distributed.[20]

While she was waiting to receive her full portion of the settlement, in the spring of 1868, Mrs. Keckley's unexpected memoir about the White House years came out. Although it was labeled a novel, no one took it that way, and it included private details about her former employer. It was Mrs. Keckley, for example, who told the story about President Lincoln showing his wife a Washington mental hospital from the White House window. Keckley said the President pleaded with Mary to recover from her extreme grief over Willie's death, so they wouldn't have to send her there.[21]

Wishing to leave these troubled associations behind, Mary Todd Lincoln made plans to go to Europe as soon as possible. Some have even suggested that the date of Robert and Mary's wedding was pushed up to accommodate her.[22]

During this first long stay in Europe, the two Mary Lincolns kept in touch by letters. In her epistles written over the next two and a half years, Mrs. Lincoln wrote colorful descriptions of the sights, told about visiting with other traveling Americans, and detailed her various ailments as well as her search for cures. She gave motherly advice and worried about her daughter-in-law's health. Her March 22, 1869, letter was perhaps written in response to an announcement that young Mary was newly pregnant, since the letter was dated almost seven months before the birth of Robert and Mary's first child:

> It pains me beyond expression, to learn of your recent illness & I deeply deplore—that I was not with you, to wait upon you. Let me urge upon you, my dear child, to take good care of your precious health—*even* the *thought* of you,

at this great distance, is a great alleviation, to the sorrow, I am enduring...My thoughts have been constantly with you, for months past—and oh how I have wished day by day, that you could be with me & enjoy the air and the sunshine, of the lovely climate I have just left...go to the sea side—and *rest quietly for a month*—no less time. Let me beseech you, dear Mary, to take care of your health—My headache now aches [sic] for the tears I have shed, this morning, in thinking of you, & you [sic] sickness...I shall, dear Mary, await most anxiously, news from you—If I do not hear soon I shall imagine every trouble...[23]

On October 23, 1869, Mrs. Lincoln was worried about her daughter-in-law giving birth. Her own mother had died in childbirth, as had Abraham's sister and many other women. She wrote to her friend Sally Orne that:

I am feeling so anxious *all* the time about that very precious little Mary in A[merica?] for her time of trouble has surely now come—and I do not know why, but I am fearing a suffering time for her—She is so innocent & lovely in character, my son is greatly blessed in so sweet a young wife—and she writes me that she never imagined *such* devotion, as she receives from him...[24]

A week or so after writing the above letter, Mrs. Lincoln received one from Robert, announcing that she was a grandmother and assuring her that her first granddaughter had been born safely, on October 15, 1869. The birth had not been easy, but there was no reason to worry. Mrs. Lincoln passed the news on to Sally, along with speculation about what the baby would be named:

A week ago, I received the welcome news from my son that on the 15th of October our dear Mary—became the mother of a sweet little daughter—after great suffering of eight hours & she was doing *well*—Heaven be praised, for *that* mercy... as *the other* GRANDMA PRESIDED with the Dr & nurse over the advent of the darling child perhaps *she* may consider *herself* entitled to the name—surely—myself, as *one Grandmother* (how very queer that sounds to *me*) being named Mary, the mother of the child *Mary*, the child being called so too, would be rather too much in the beginning..."[25]

But the child was named Mary after all, making her the third Mary Lincoln in a row. Grandmother Lincoln adored her from afar and nicknamed her "Little Mamie."[26]

Was Mrs. Lincoln feeling old in December 1869, when she lied to Sally about her age? Her birthday was the next day, and she wrote that she would be 46, when really she would be 51. "I feel 86," she added.[27] Was this simple feminine vanity, or was her feeling of being old the natural consequence of becoming a grandmother? Mary Todd Lincoln certainly did feel old that winter as she suffered through one painful illness after another. First, she complained to Sally about arthritis and neuralgic headaches,[28] exacerbated by an infected index finger she had pricked with a needle.[29] Then in December she was furious about a false rumor printed in a London newspaper that she was planning to marry a German count.[30] In January, her back ached, along with her head.[31] In February, she had a cold that confined her to bed.[32]

By April, she said she wished she were dead. To Sally, she wrote, "[T]here are moments of each day, when I feel the greatest repugnance—to return to the *fearful battle of life*—which has broken my heart. I must accept my terrible fate—to undergo *daily crucifixion* —knowing that in *God's Own Time*—the weary & heavy laden— will be loosed from the bonds of earth."[33]

Adding to her physical woes was her emotional suffering over the delays in her protracted campaign for a government pension. The petition was first submitted in January 1869,[34] but it had languished in committee and unresolved debate. Her precedent-setting request seemed extravagant to some senators — $5,000 a year was twice the income of most American households (but equal to the yearly income of a congressman).[35]

Of course, this debate also brought up all the old criticisms about Mrs. Lincoln and money. Anxious for news about the pension, Mrs. Lincoln frequented places where she could read American newspapers, and therefore she read these criticisms as they were published.[36]

In May 1870, she collapsed in the English Reading Room in Frankfurt, Germany, after seeing an article announcing that her request was being tabled indefinitely in the Senate. No one had bothered to telegraph her before printing the news. The committee cited lack of precedent; no president's wife had ever requested a widow's pension before. They also cited insufficient need. The government had given her the rest of her husband's yearly salary when he died, to compensate for her immediate loss of income. With this $22,000, she had bought a house in Chicago. By now, she had also received her portion of her husband's estate, more than $36,000, another fact that had been made public. Some senators believed that she was living in royal style, maybe even with items stolen from the White House.[37]

Mrs. Lincoln had already denied these unfounded rumors about taking things that did not belong to her. She now reminded her friends and supporters that she was living on the interest from her inheritance, not the estate itself. Her annual income was only about $2,500. She also argued that her situation was different than other presidential widows because her husband had died while in office, and therefore while still on duty. Widows of soldiers who fell in battle got pensions, and she argued that as the widow of the commander-in-chief, she deserved no less.[38]

The question of money for Mrs. Lincoln once again got people talking about her mental state. Sally Orne made a point of defending Mary's sanity in a letter written to Senator Charles Sumner on September 12, 1869. Sumner was championing Mary's cause in the Senate. Mrs. Orne's letter, written more than five years before Mrs. Lincoln's insanity trial, said:

> As it has been suggested by some that Mrs. Lincoln is partially deranged, having seen her so recently it may be proper for me to say to you that I have watched her closely by day and night for weeks and fail to discover any evidence of aberration of mind in her, and I believe her mind to be as clear now as it was in the days of her greatest prosperity and I do believe it is unusually prolonged grief that has given rise to such a report.[39]

Mrs. Orne also argued against the accusations that Mrs. Lincoln was living grandly in Europe. She had visited Mrs. Lincoln in Frankfurt and had seen her humble room on the fourth floor of a "second-rate hotel." She described Mrs. Lincoln as a sad picture, weighed down by immense grief.[40]

By May of 1870, the House of Representatives had already approved a bill allowing Mrs. Lincoln a $3,000 pension,[41] but the Senate still stood in the way. After her collapse in the reading room, Mary Lincoln's doctors suggested she go to the spa at Marienbad. She regained her strength there, and then renewed her campaign for a pension. She wrote letters to let people know that the figures in the news were deceiving, urging them to act on her behalf.

In June, the pension bill was finally brought before the full Senate, but the debate continued. Senator Richard Yates, arguing against it, insinuated that Mrs. Lincoln had been unfaithful to her late husband and had sympathized with the Rebellion. (Sen. Yates was the Illinois governor taken via Ann Eliza Harlan's boat to Shiloh in 1862.[42]) Others believed Mrs. Lincoln deserved her poverty, citing how she sometimes mishandled money. Vermont Senator Justin Morrill argued that the President had died in a theater, not on a battlefield. Still others argued that the government had already given her enough.[43]

Mrs. Lincoln's supporters in the Senate were lukewarm in her defense until 24 hours before the close of the session. Finally, on July 14, 1870, Senator Simon Cameron of Pennsylvania spoke movingly on her behalf. He reminded his fellow senators that Mrs. Lincoln had been slandered in Washington from the very beginning: "The ladies, and even the gentlemen, the gossips of the town, did all they could to make a bad reputation for Mrs. Lincoln... They could not destroy [the President], but they did...destroy the social position of his wife. I do not want to talk, and I say, let us vote." Mary Lincoln got her pension of $3,000 a year, with a vote of 28 to 20 (24 senators were absent).[44]

For the rest of the year, Mary Lincoln's financial worries were eased somewhat, but not her health concerns. She suffered constantly from coughs and colds and headaches. Both she and Tad were homesick. In November 1870, she wrote longingly to her daughter-in-law about the grandchild she had not yet seen: "That blessed baby, how dearly I would love to look upon its sweet young face, if my boy Taddie and myself are wanderers in a strange land, our thoughts are continually with you..."[45]

She considered sending Tad back to Chicago ahead of her, to stay with Robert, but she couldn't stand the thought of being alone for the winter. She booked him passage on a Cunard liner, but then wouldn't let him go. "His presence has become so necessary, even to my life," she had earlier confided to her daughter-in-law.[46]

Finally, in the spring of 1871, the two of them returned together. The bone-chilling climate that winter had aggravated Tad's weak lungs, as did the bad weather during their sea passage. In May, when the two finally arrived, he already had a cold. They had a happy reunion with Robert and his family for a few days. Then daughter-in-law Mary rushed off to tend her sick mother, and Mary and Tad moved to the Clifton House, where Tad got sicker and sicker. The doctors determined that he had pleurisy, a bacterial infection, and for his last six weeks, his lungs slowly filled with fluid. Finally he could not breathe lying down, so he had to sleep in a chair. On July 15, 1871, after weeks of nearly endless agony, 18-year-old Thomas "Tad" Lincoln died.[47]

Robert, now the only surviving brother, went off to the Rocky Mountains for a month, saying he was "all used up" by Tad's death.[48] And Mary, their mother, stepped closer to the brink of madness.[49]

Robert and Mary tried taking his mother into their home. Mary Harlan Lincoln did what she could to comfort her mother-in-law, but nothing helped. Mrs. Lincoln was either deeply depressed, craving absolute silence and solitude, or she was angry, trying her daughter-in-law's patience with her hostile outbursts in front of servants and the children. Sometime in October, Mary Harlan Lincoln packed up the children and took the train to her parents' home in Mount Pleasant. Her mother was still suffering from the first of two serious carriage accidents. It is unclear if this accident, or trouble with her mother-in-law, was the reason for her trip to Iowa, but Robert later told his aunt that he and his wife had to "break up housekeeping to end the trouble," a Victorian euphemism for marital separation.[50]

Mrs. Lincoln eventually moved out of her son's house, but she was still there on the night of the Great Chicago Fire, October 8, 1871. For at least some part of that fall, she lived with a spiritualist community outside of Chicago. By the winter of 1871–72, she was back in Chicago. She spent the summer of 1872 in Waukesha, Wisconsin, "taking the waters."[51]

Sometime before the summer of 1872, Robert dissolved his law firm and traveled in Europe for several months with his wife and their children.[52] In November, they were back in Mount Pleasant.[53] Over the next year, the relationship between the two Mary Lincolns dissolved further. Did Mrs. Lincoln criticize her daughter-in-law with unwelcome truths (biographer Jean Baker refers to "circumstantial" evidence that Mary Harlan Lincoln had an alcohol problem[54]), or was the mother-in-law just unfair and overbearing? At times, Mary Todd Lincoln became "violently angry." The two women avoided each other, but despite the strain, Robert and Mary arranged visits between Mrs. Lincoln and her granddaughter Mamie, whom she genuinely adored. Robert also hired a nurse to travel with his mother.[55]

Mary Harlan Lincoln spent the summer of 1873 with her parents, visiting her ailing brother William in Colorado.[56] On August 14, 1873, she gave birth to a son. They named him Abraham Lincoln II, a tribute to Robert's father, but they always called him Jack. No record of Mrs. Lincoln's reaction to the birth of her first grandson remains. She was in Canada that summer, presumably fleeing from gossip that accompanied a recent biography of her husband, insinuating that Abraham Lincoln was without religion and was an illegitimate child (neither of which proved true).[57]

When she headed to Florida for the winter of 1874–75, the newspapers noted that she was ending a nine-month seclusion, due to "nervous exhaustion." Her nurse traveled with her. In Jacksonville, she moved into Mrs. J. T. Stockton's boardinghouse and avoided publicity by keeping her shades closed. She spent the winter in her darkened room, lit only with candles.[58]

On March 12, 1875, she was seized with the conviction that her last remaining son was dying. She rushed to the telegraph office and sent a message to Robert's law partner, Edward Swift Isham, saying: "My Belief is my son is ill telegraph me at once without a moments delay—on Receipt of this I start for Chicago when your message is received[.]" She also sent a message to her son: "My dearly beloved Son Robert T. Lincoln rouse yourself—and live for my sake[.] All I have is yours from this hour. I am praying every moment for your life to be spared to your mother[.]"[59]

Robert was fine. When he learned about his mother's unfounded fears, he asked the Western Union official in Chicago to contact his Jacksonville counterpart and discreetly check on his mother's mental state. When she returned to the telegraph office the next day, wanting to send another message, the Jacksonville telegraph operator tried to convince her that her son was fine, but she didn't believe him. The agent was forced to send Robert a telegram saying that Mrs. Lincoln was on her way to Chicago.[60]

When Robert met her at the train station, she expressed surprise at his robust health. She then proceeded to tell him that someone was following her and that someone had tried to poison her on the train. She added that a wandering Jew had stolen her pocketbook but would probably return it the next day. Robert urged his mother to come to stay at his home, but she refused, so he booked two rooms at the Grand Pacific Hotel, one for her and another next door for himself.[61]

Even from that close, he couldn't keep her from walking the halls in her nightdress. On April 1, a few days short of the tenth anniversary of her husband's assassination, Mrs. Lincoln, half-clad, tried to take the elevator to the hotel lobby. When Robert tried to stop her, she cried out, "You are going to murder me!" She was terrified that something was about to happen to her son, or that Chicago would again be consumed by fire, or that someone was going to kill her. She told the hotel manager that she was hearing voices and receiving requests to visit people in nonexistent rooms. Servants worried as they watched her mix her various medicines. She once insisted on being taken to the hotel dining room so she could see the tallest man there, but she apparently did not explain this need.[62]

In late April or early May, Robert learned his mother was carrying around government securities worth $57,000, sewn into her petticoats, and that she was contemplating traveling again, perhaps to California or Europe. Robert had already hired Pinkerton detectives to follow her and keep her out of trouble. He now consulted several physicians, and he hired a lawyer. He thought she needed someone to watch over her and to control her finances.[63]

Cook County Courthouse, Chicago, Illinois, May 19, 1875

When Robert Todd Lincoln walked into the Cook County courtroom on a Wednesday afternoon in May 1875, reporters stationed there probably took note, but they may not have immediately become suspicious. Judge Marion Wallace had set aside his usual docket of cases for a jury trial that afternoon, but the appearance of Mr. Lincoln and the other attorneys gathering for the case could have suggested it involved some contractual dispute, perhaps for a bank or an insurance company. Both members of the Isham & Lincoln firm were present, as was B.F. Ayer, of the prestigious Chicago firm of Ayer & Kales. But what was their connection to Isaac Arnold, who had been an Illinois congressman during the war and was now a lecturer and writer about President Lincoln? Others in the courtroom included several merchants, a cashier at Merchants Loan and Trust, and several doctors.[64]

The rest of the men probably consulted with each other, occasionally glancing toward the door and at their pocket watches, but Robert Lincoln may have stayed apart, trying not to attract attention as he studied some papers before him on the table. He hated publicity. He knew how newspapers love scandals, and he hated what was about to happen. In this era, open discussion about mental illness was not welcome. Instead, the existence of mental illness in a family was most often cause for great shame. The Lincolns were not reclusive, as some people thought, but as much as possible Robert Lincoln had tried to keep his name out of the papers. When the *Chicago Tribune* once asked for a photograph of him, he refused, replying, "I read the *Tribune* daily and it is one of the minor pleasures of life left to me that I can open the paper feeling sure that I am not to be confronted by a portrait of myself." He knew that the newspapers would relish this story, and he dreaded it, but he believed he was doing what had to be done.[65]

Mental illness was not so well understood in the 1870s, and Robert was perhaps less inclined to understand it than others. He had been conditioned by education and by his father's example to use mind and logic to build success. In addition, as the eldest son of President Lincoln, he had determined not to buck convention or to act in any way that would put his father's name to shame. But his mother's behavior was erratic, embarrassing, and potentially dangerous. He believed she needed some kind of legal restraint for her own protection.

Robert had been worrying about his mother for so long. She had never been right after his father's death, and doubly so after Tad's. She had been constantly under a physician's care for the past year and a half. Dr. Willis Danforth first saw her in November 1873 for "nervous derangement and fever in her head." She had complained that an Indian spirit was pulling wires through her eyes and that he occasionally lifted off her scalp. At this point, Dr. Danforth believed her hallucinations were due to a physical cause. Gradually, she got better and he stopped seeing her.[66]

From March until September 1874, he saw Mrs. Lincoln again, almost daily. She had similar complaints. In addition, she said her dead husband had informed her that she would die in a few days. At this point, Dr. Danforth concluded that her "debility of the nervous system" was not due to a physical condition. She spent most of this year confined to her hotel room, and then she went to Florida that November. She came back only because she thought her son was seriously ill.[67]

During her first few months back from Florida, it was her daily habit to go out shopping, sometimes more than once. She worried about money, but she still bought all kinds of things she didn't need, and she often bought them in large quantities. She bought a dozen pair of curtains but had no home to hang them in (she had turned her Chicago house over to her son the year before); she bought expensive jewelry even though she never wore it anymore; she bought gloves and handkerchiefs, a dozen pair or more at a time. She bought a bolt of silk material and five yards of red ribbon, even though she wore only widow's clothes. Her closet at the Grand Pacific Hotel was piled with packages she had never opened after they were delivered.[68]

Robert consulted with doctors and lawyers and began to put together a case for having his mother committed to an asylum and to have a conservator appointed to handle her finances. By law, a conservator could not be imposed without first proving she was insane. Robert first talked with his own physician, Dr. Ralph Isham, who was also his law partner's nephew. Dr. Isham had no expertise in mental medicine, so he referred Robert to Dr. Robert T. Patterson, owner and lead doctor at Bellevue Place, a small and exclusive mental hospital outside of Chicago.[69]

Robert Lincoln's lawyers, of the Ayer & Kales firm, brought in attorney Leonard Swett, one of the best trial lawyers in Illinois and a former friend of Abraham Lincoln's. Swett gathered five other doctors. Two had treated Tad during his final illness and knew the family, two were specialists on mental illness, and the other was Willis Danforth, Mrs. Lincoln's doctor. Dr. Danforth visited with Mrs. Lincoln at the Grand Pacific Hotel on May 8. He reported that in general, she conversed rationally, but she repeated to him the story of having been poisoned on the way back from Florida. She said she knew there was poison in her coffee, but she drank it anyway, and then had a second cup, hoping to make herself vomit. Dr. Danforth did not discover any evidence that she had been poisoned, and he believed she was insane.[70]

On May 16, all of the doctors met with Robert and discussed his mother's condition. After hearing from Robert and Dr. Danforth, they all agreed that she should be institutionalized. Robert also consulted with his close friend, Judge David Davis, and his mother's favorite cousin, John Todd Stuart. They agreed that some type of restraint was necessary, and Judge Davis urged Robert to act quickly because of the rumor that Mrs. Lincoln was planning to travel again soon. Davis said, "[A]n unfavorable verdict would be disastrous in the extreme, but this must be risked." He added that he did not see "how Robert can get along at all, unless he has the authority to subject his mother to treatment."[71]

On the morning of May 19, 1875, Robert filed an "Application to Try the Question of Insanity," as the petition form was titled. Later, Robert told his friend John Hay that, "I knew that the next day after my action the whole country would be flooded with criticisms, kind or unkind as might happen, but all based on a short press dispatch, which could not sufficiently give the facts. Yet I could not wait any longer."[72] He told his mother's friend Sally Orne, "Six physicians informed me that by longer delay I was making myself morally responsible for some very probable tragedy..."[73]

Across town, around one o'clock in the afternoon, someone knocked on the door of Mary Todd Lincoln's Grand Pacific Hotel room. She supposed it was the delivery boy from Gossage's, where she'd been shopping that morning. Indeed, the boy was there, but so was Leonard Swett, one of her husband's former colleagues from Illinois, a man who had ridden the Illinois legal circuit with her husband and nominated him for President in 1860. Why was he here? Mrs. Lincoln welcomed him, even though she was surprised to see him. She told the delivery boy to put the bundle in her closet. Then she turned to Mr. Swett to learn the purpose of his visit.[74]

Mr. Swett looked nervous. He held a sheet of paper in his hand. "Mrs. Lincoln, I have some bad news," he said, inviting her to sit down.

Mary Todd Lincoln's mind raced. "What's happened to Robert?" she cried out.

"It's not Robert. It's you. You have been ordered to appear in court."

"Whatever for? What have I done? Have I forgotten to pay a sales clerk? I'll get my pocketbook right away." Mrs. Lincoln started to cross the room, but Mr. Swett stopped her.

"It's not just the shopping. It's other things as well. Mr. Turner says you hear voices in the walls. You've said that someone is trying to poison you. You won't keep your money in the hotel safe. Your family and friends are worried about you. They have concluded that your many troubles have led to a mental disease. The issue before the court is the question of your sanity."

When Mr. Swett opened the great mahogany door of the Cook County courtroom, the noise at the back of the room must have caused the reporters and spectators to turn.[75] The President's widow, veiled and dressed in black, entered behind him, followed at a discreet distance by two policemen. Mr. Swett led Mrs. Lincoln to a table and Robert helped her into her chair. The reporters noted that she barely gave her son a glance as she sat down.[76] Were the reporters prepared for what was to happen next?

Mr. Swett went to confer with Robert and with Isaac Arnold, the man they had hired to serve as Mrs. Lincoln's attorney. He was getting cold feet about representing her because he too believed that Mrs. Lincoln was insane. Swett angrily replied that Arnold must do his duty and defend her.[77]

The judge entered the room, called for order, and began to read the paper before him: "The matter before us is a hearing into the sanity of Mary Lincoln, widow of Abraham Lincoln, deceased."[78]

The reporters began to scribble furiously.

Robert Lincoln's "Application to Try the Question of Insanity" was a request to find Mary Lincoln insane and to appoint a conservator to control her estate. Because Mrs. Lincoln was given no warning, and thus no time to prepare a defense, Robert has been accused of trying to steal her money. But Mrs. Lincoln got the defense she was entitled to by law, and fortunately for her, the state of Illinois offered her more protection than some states. At this point in history, women could sometimes be locked up for charges of insanity simply on a husband's word. Mrs. Lincoln was more fortunate than most American women accused of insanity because she had the right to a jury trial. A six-year-old Illinois law guaranteed her that right.[79]

"Robert was forced to comply with the country's—perhaps the world's—strictest legal standards for commitment of the insane," concluded Mark E. Neely, Jr., and R. Gerald McMurtry, who studied the case extensively and wrote *The Insanity File: The Case of*

Mary Todd Lincoln. Unlike others who had previously written about this case, they had access to the "MTL Insanity File," Robert's secret papers, which included a number of letters written by Mary Todd Lincoln that Robert believed helped prove his case. Neely and McMurtry also extensively studied the legal and mental health systems of that era and other literature about the trial.[80]

By law, those charged with insanity had to be informed so that they could be present to answer the charges. They also had to be allowed representation. But the law did not specify how much notice a defendant must be given. "The Illinois Supreme Court... had said nothing of time to prepare a defense and engage counsel: the accused must only 'have notice and be allowed to make manifest his sanity...'" Neely and McMurtry wrote.[81]

Those who argue against Neely and McMurtry's assessment may point out that Mr. Arnold did not make much effort to defend his client. He did not even call Mrs. Lincoln to the stand. Some also argue that the law was prejudiced against women, pointing to the case of Elizabeth Packard, who in 1860 was committed to the Illinois State Hospital solely on her husband's word. Her husband was a conservative Congregational minister, and her spiritual views were too experimental for him. She was attracted to spiritualism and Swedenborgianism, a philosophy that combines science, mysticism and theology. Reverend Packard considered his wife's theological opinions as proof of her insanity. He brought the sheriff and two doctors to his home. The doctors took his wife's pulse, declared her insane, and she was taken to the institution. She was finally released in 1863. In 1867, she testified before the Illinois legislature, and the result was a law requiring a jury trial for those accused of insanity.[82]

The twelve-man jury who weighed the evidence at Mrs. Lincoln's trial listened to a variety of witnesses testifying to Mrs. Lincoln's odd behavior in the last two years, behavior that Robert argued was dangerous to his mother's safety. When Robert took the stand, his testimony about the events of the past few months brought tears to his eyes. Mrs. Lincoln's doctor detailed the recent indications of mental illness. The hotel manager told how she had walked the halls partially undressed, heard voices, and complained that someone was trying to murder her, among other things. Hotel employees also testified to her odd behavior. Robert later said that some evidence that could have been used was withheld at his request.[83]

After three hours of testimony, the jury retired briefly. During the recess, Robert tried to talk with his mother, taking her hand gently, but she reproached him by saying, "O Robert, to think that my son would ever have done this." The jury soon returned with the verdict that Mrs. Lincoln was "insane and fit for commitment in an asylum." They included in their judgment the assessment that she was not homicidal or suicidal. She had sat through the proceedings with an outward calm, but inside she was desperate, angry, and afraid.[84]

That night, feeling completely alone in the world, betrayed by her only remaining son, she was inspired to commit a desperate act. Somehow, she evaded her guards, went to the hotel pharmacy, and ordered a deadly dose of laudanum and camphor. She told the druggist it was for her shoulder. Thankfully, the druggist recognized her and stalled for time, telling her it would take 30 minutes to make the mixture. She left immediately and went to another pharmacy a block away.[85]

The hotel druggist and the Pinkerton guard were hot on her trail, helping prevent her errand at the second drugstore and also at a third. Finally, she returned to the hotel pharmacy, where the druggist gave her a harmless mixture of burnt sugar water. When she took it and it did not work as she expected, she evaded her guards once again and went back to the hotel druggist. Once again, he managed to trick her with sugar water.[86]

Earlier, the druggist had called for Robert, who finally arrived. He and Mr. Swett watched Mrs. Lincoln for the rest of the night. She had lost everything: her dignity, her freedom, and now even control over her own life. She would never, ever forgive Robert. But she was smart enough to hide her anger from him as she began plotting against the court's decision.[87]

Robert did not want to send his mother to a public asylum. The place he chose for her was Dr. Patterson's Bellevue Place, the private sanitarium in Batavia, about 40 miles from Chicago. Reform-minded doctors in the mid-1870s believed they could cure their mental patients with a regimen called "moral treatment," which included rest, proper diet, frequent baths, fresh air, and pleasant occupations—in short, no responsibilities or obligations. Few records exist on the specifics of Mary Lincoln's treatment, but Bellevue patients were sometimes given "quinine, morphia, marijuana, cod-liver oil, beer or ale" as medications. They were made comfortable, their interests aroused, and discussions of their troubles encouraged. For amusement and relaxation, they could play croquet, take walks around the grounds, go for carriage rides, or play the piano.[88]

Moral treatment depended on a low doctor-patient ratio. It was not very effective in huge public hospitals, but at Bellevue, Mrs. Lincoln was more privileged than most. She lived with Dr. Patterson and his family in her own private quarters, away from the other patients.[89]

Robert visited his mother every week,[90] but he had other pressing matters to attend to as well. He was putting in long hours at work, building up his legal practice with his partners, Edward Isham and William Beale. At first, much of their business came from Chicago and surrounding Cook County, but after 1874, more and more came from out of state. Among the firm's best-known clients were the Pullman Company, Commonwealth Edison, Chicago Elevated Railways and Marshall Field and Company. They handled wills for the rich and famous, including Walter Newberry, Marshall Field, and Joseph Medill, owner of the *Chicago Tribune.*[91]

At home, Robert was busy being a parent. In June 1875, he wrote John Hay that his two children were "small steam engines and such a circus as we have every night, you never see."[92] That sounded like his own childhood. Both of Robert's parents had been indulgent, enjoying their children's antics. On Sundays while Mary Lincoln was at church, Abraham Lincoln took the children to his office, a habit that his law partner dreaded, for he knew that pen points would be smashed, books would be scattered, and ink would be spilled on important papers.[93]

Critics and friends alike noted the Lincolns' deep involvement with their children. Springfield neighbor James Gurley recalled that, "Lincoln would take his children and would walk out on the rail way out in the country—would talk to them—explain things carefully—particularly. He was kind—tender and affectionate to his children—very—very." [94]

Mrs. Lincoln loved the spirit and drama of her children's games, and she could play along, even when warning them to be careful. One day, young Bobbie and a friend were acting out a scene from Sir Walter Scott, using fence posts as lances. Mary looked out the window and saw the boys brandishing their sharp-pointed weapons. To yell out a simple warning would have spoiled the spirit of the game, so instead, she got in character and cried, "Gramercy, brave knights. Pray be more merciful than you are brawny!" [95]

And now, Robert had charged his mother with insanity. He believed he had no other choice. He was embarrassed by his mother's behavior and probably could not understand it. He was such a perfectionist, careful in all of his habits. How could he understand such irrational behavior, when he always tried to behave in a manner above reproach? One of his contemporaries once described him as a person who "inspires one immediately with perfect faith in his uprightness and honesty...He is not only scrupulously accurate and just in all his doings and statements, but his whole moral sense is so keen that the slightest irregularity on the part of others meets with the severest condemnation." [96]

This rift in the mother-son relationship would never be entirely resolved. [97] Robert's mother felt completely betrayed and abandoned. She maintained cordial relations during Robert's frequent visits, but immediately she began searching for a way out. Despite the distance that had evolved between Mary and her oldest sister and husband, Elizabeth and Ninian Edwards, in August she received an invitation to visit them in Springfield. At first, this seemed to be an invitation for a short visit, but in time, the scheme evolved into plans for an extended stay.

Two activist friends from Chicago, Myra and James Bradwell, who believed Mary Todd Lincoln had been wrongly committed, helped her campaign for her release. They described their observations of Mrs. Lincoln's condition to the Edwards couple and said she could converse quite sanely on a wide variety of topics. Robert

Lincoln resisted the idea of an extended visit, but the Bradwells and his mother continued to pressure him.[98]

On August 7, the Bradwells brought a reporter, Franc Wilkie, with them on a visit with Mrs. Lincoln. He questioned her on a variety of subjects and decided she was sane. His *Chicago Times* story carried the headline, "Mrs. Lincoln. Her Physicians Pronounce Her Entirely Sane." The proclamation was based on his own observations, not on interviews with the doctors. When he saw the story, Dr. Patterson wrote to the *Chicago Tribune* denying it. "She is certainly much improved, both mentally and physically; but I have not at any time regarded her as a person of sound mind... I believe her to be now insane," he wrote.[99]

Mrs. Lincoln and the Bradwells continued to pressure Robert for a compromise. Rather than confinement at the institution, they argued that Mary Todd Lincoln should be released to her sister's home. Using the media and direct appeals, Mrs. Lincoln, the Bradwells, and Mr. Wilkie continued to lobby for this arrangement. Everyone involved, except perhaps Dr. Patterson, believed that Mrs. Lincoln was sane on all subjects except money, and by law she was required to have a conservator for her finances for at least a year after the original judgment against her. Robert consulted with Dr. Patterson and the other doctors, and even though he doubted the wisdom of the arrangement, he finally agreed to let his mother spend the rest of the year in Springfield. On September 11, 1875, he accompanied his mother to her sister's home.[100]

A month before Mrs. Lincoln's release, Elizabeth had told her nephew that the "peculiarities" of her sister's "whole life have been so marked and well understood by me that I have not indulged in faintest hope, of a permanent cure," but in early November, she pronounced that she had "no hesitation, in pronouncing her [sister] sane, and far more reasonable, and gentle, than in former years."[101]

On November 6, 1875, Robert and Mary's third child, another daughter, was born. They named her Jessie, after Mary Harlan Lincoln's younger sister, who had died in her sixth year. For once, the family had to choose a name besides "Mary" for a female Lincoln; this generation already had the Mary nicknamed Mamie, Jessie's older sister. Robert was pleased to have a second daughter. A few years later, writing to his friend John Nicolay about the birth of John Hay's daughter, he commented that, "My experience with girl babies makes me envy him. They are very nice."[102]

Soon after Jessie's birth, her mother went West several times with her mother to visit William, her ailing brother. On their last trip, they arrived just in time to say good-bye. William died in San Francisco in January 1876, at the age of 23. Mary spent the next month with her parents in Mount Pleasant.[103]

That same month, Robert received a letter from Elizabeth's husband, Uncle Ninian, that his mother was carrying a pistol and had said she was plotting to kill Robert. Both Ninian and Elizabeth wrote letters on that subject the next day as well. Soon after she arrived at her sister's house, Mary had become fixated on regaining control of her estate. Robert had been exploring several options to allow her at least some partial control, but he had thought he could afford to stall because the law would not allow him to be released as conservator for at least a year. His mother apparently thought he was just being an obstructionist, and this angered her and made her impatient. He didn't take the threat of the pistol very seriously, but he worked harder to find a compromise that would release him as conservator but retain some kind of oversight for her finances.[104]

Meanwhile, when Judge Wallace, who had presided over her trial, refused to entertain any changes until the year had passed, Mary Todd Lincoln seemed finally to accept that she would have to wait until summer for anything to happen. Once again, she distracted herself with shopping, and Elizabeth worried about where to store all of her sister's many possessions.[105]

When the year was finally over, after much wrangling and negotiating and discussing between Robert, his aunt and uncle, friends, doctors, and lawyers, Mary Todd Lincoln agreed that if her estate was restored to her, she would deposit it with a Springfield banker she trusted and she would let him send her monthly checks to live on. In order to release Robert as conservator, the parties had to petition the court for a reversal of the insanity judgment, which was done and granted on June 15, 1876.[106]

By this time, Robert was sorry he had ever had his mother committed. "If I could have foreseen my own experience in the matter, no consideration would have induced me to go through with it...the ordinary troubles and distresses of life are enough without such as that..." he later told his aunt. What he really had wanted all along was a way to restrain his mother financially, but the law had allowed only one avenue for that. He worried that the government could vote to end her pension, and if that happened after she had spent her whole estate, she would have nothing to live on. He agreed with those who said she often seemed perfectly sane on subjects except matters of money, and he did not expect that to change. Aunt Elizabeth agreed that it is "utterly hopeless" to imagine Mary Todd Lincoln recovering from her "buying mania."[107]

Once she regained her legal rights, Mary Todd Lincoln immediately unleashed the fullness of her fury on her son and his wife. Directly contradicting earlier letters in which she had generously offered Robert and Mary free access to many of her possessions,[108] she wrote the following curt demand four days after regaining her rights:

Springfield, Illinois
June 19th - 1876
Robert T. Lincoln

Do not fail to send me without *the least* delay, *all* my paintings, Moses in the bullrushes included—also the fruit picture, which hung in your dining room—my silver set with large silver waiter presented me by New York friends, my silver tete-a-tete set also other articles your wife appropriated & which are well known to you, must be sent, without a day's delay. Two lawyers and myself, have just been together and their list, coincides with my own & will be published in a few days...Send me my laces, my diamonds, my jewelry—My unmade silks, white lace dress—double lace shawl & flounce, lace scarf—2 blk lace shawls—one blk lace deep flounce, white lace sets one-half yd in width & eleven yards in length. I am now in constant receipt of letters, from my friends denouncing you in the bitterest terms, six letters from prominent, *respectable*, Chicago people such as you do not associate with...As to Mr Harlan—

you are not worthy to wipe the dust, from his feet. Two prominent clergy men, have written me, since I saw you—and mention in their letters, that they think it advisable to offer up prayers for you in Church, on account of your wickedness against me and High Heaven. In reference to Chicago you have the enemies, & I chance to have the friends there. Send me all that I have written for, you have tried your game of robbery long enough...You have injured yourself, not me, by your wicked conduct.

Mrs. A. Lincoln

My engravings too send me. M.L. Send me Whittier Pope, Agnes Strickland's Queens of England, other books, you have of mine—[109]

Mary Lincoln grew stronger in the months that followed, as she continued to recuperate at her sister's house. But she lied when she wrote that she was not injured. She was in fact embarrassed to associate with former friends, who she said "never cease to regard me as a lunatic. I feel it in their soothing manner. If I should say the moon is made of green cheese they would heartily and smilingly agree with me."[110] The best solution seemed to be self-exile again, so back to Europe she went.

In September 1876, she sailed for France, settling at Pau, a popular health spa at the foot of the Pyrenees. She traveled in France and Italy over the next four years, but she always returned to Pau.[111] She kept close track of her money by writing frequent letters to her banker. She was still afraid of the poorhouse.[112] She wrote extensively to her nephew Lewis Baker, she sent presents to her grandchildren, but she had little contact with her son and his wife.[113]

In December 1879, she was hanging a picture when she fell and seriously injured her back. She was put in plaster, and she was also in agony. The following June, she fell again, this time on the stairs. In October 16, 1880, she sailed back to the States, returning to her sister's home in Springfield. She kept her shades closed, lit her room only with a candle, and quarreled often with her sister. According to a great-niece, she wore a money belt at all times, even under her nightdress, and spent hours looking through the treasures stored in her 64 trunks.[114]

"Grandmother said it was funny, if Aunt Mary was so sick, that she was able to be up all day bending over her trunks," Mrs. Lincoln's great-niece, Mary Edwards, said.[115]

In May of 1881, Mary Todd Lincoln had a surprise visit from her son and her granddaughter Mamie. That fall, she traveled to New York to consult with an orthopedic surgeon, and Robert and his wife visited her several times. On July 15, 1882, Mary Todd Lincoln died.[116] Biographer Ruth Painter Randall poetically described her life before this moment of release:

> But the distilled essence of the great agony which was surging over the country [when President Lincoln died] was in the heart of the sick and broken widow. She too had received a wound that was fatal, though it would be long years before she could die. Two lives had crashed that day. Lincoln's struggle was soon over; his mystic ship was safe in harbor; it was Mary's ship, crippled, that must sail on and on...[117]

Two years later, Mary Todd Lincoln's many possessions, the 64 trunks that Robert had inherited, were in Mount Pleasant, awaiting Mary Harlan Lincoln's directions. Robert was too bitter to deal with this project, so his wife took it on.[118] Even for her, it was hard work. Mary's cousin Florence wrote that Mary was obviously "heavily burdened in the immense work" of distributing these possessions, but when Florence expressed her admiration at her cousin's care and dedication, Mary shrugged it off.[119]

"Here am I," she told Florence that summer of 1884, "deciding what to do with this unconscionable accumulation." But she added that she "would accomplish it like the Harlan she was and the Lincoln she had become."[120]

CHAPTER EIGHT:

"So Restful for the Children"

Harlan home, Mount Pleasant, Iowa, 1883-1887

During a visit to the Harlan home in Iowa, Mary's cousin, Florence Snow, commented to Mamie Lincoln that it must feel special being related to Abraham Lincoln. People were always saying that. Grandfather Lincoln had been dead four years when Mamie was born, and Mamie's father didn't talk much about his parents, so what she knew about the President was mostly gained from textbooks, like everyone else. She felt as far from him as anyone. She could remember Grandmother Lincoln as an old woman, but she could hardly imagine her as the elegant lady in the Mathew Brady photographs.

On the other hand, she knew Grandfather Harlan quite well. He took her places, and he walked with her around the Iowa Wesleyan campus, inquiring about her opinions, listening to her stories, and asking what she was reading. Mamie admired his brisk walking pace, his stately posture, his gracious manners, and the way he treated everyone respectfully, even if he disagreed with them. Someday, she hoped to marry a fine scholarly gentleman just like him.

So Mamie's response to her cousin's admiring comment about her Lincoln heritage was, "Yes, but it means so much to live with Grandfather Harlan!"[1]

Florence also admired Mamie's grandfather Harlan, who was her Uncle James. She later wrote in her memoirs that, "This storybook brother of Mother's, and Father's heart-friend, who had written me since I was six or seven of his rich life wrought out of the Indiana pioneer conditions, had been my constant inspiration." She and her mother and father were all proud of James Harlan for his character, his career, and his close connection to Abraham Lincoln, whom they also admired. Florence said that her Uncle James "could never fail to be as genial as he was deep and calm … Uncle Harlan in his dress and manner, his more musical voice and distinctive English, was the type of leader that all sorts and conditions of Americans love to elevate and honor." She added that her mother thought Mamie "was a good deal like him."[2]

Like grandfathers everywhere, Senator Harlan was proud of his grandchildren and continually amazed at how much they grew between visits. In September 1883, he recorded the evidence. On a narrow white closet door upstairs in his house, he drew three ovals with a pencil and put the name of a grandchild in each one. He called Mamie and Jack to join him one day, and Jessie a few days later, and he had each grandchild stand with his or her back to the door while he measured them. Inside the circles, he wrote the following inscriptions:

1883
Mamie Lincoln Sept. 4
5 ft. 4 inches

Jack Lincoln Sept. 4
4 ft. 5 inches

Jessie Lincoln Sept. 7
3 ft. 10 inches[3]

A decade before, Senator Harlan had been defeated for re-election as senator after a "brilliant but stormy career in post-Civil War politics."[4] He and his wife returned to Mount Pleasant, a young town not yet 40 years old. He left the bustle of Washington for the quiet serenity of this cosmopolitan university town.

Mount Pleasant's first white settler, Presley Saunders, arrived in 1835, after serving in the same regiment as his friend Abraham Lincoln during the Black Hawk War. Saunders chose to homestead in southeastern Iowa because of the area's fertile soil, gently rolling hills, and abundant supply of clean water. In fact, he liked the place so well he named it Mount Pleasant. Saunders was the town's first merchant, banker, and postmaster, and for 55 years, its foremost citizen. It was he who lobbied successfully to have Mount Pleasant named the Henry County seat. He and his brother Alvin also successfully argued that the state's east and west boundaries should be the two great rivers, the Mississippi and the Missouri.[5]

During the settlement's first year, two Baptist ministers arrived in Mount Pleasant. Methodists and Presbyterians soon followed. Church buildings were central to social as well as religious life, so they were erected before the schools. For other entertainment, early residents watched log-rolling contests, gathered to help build houses and barns, held spelling bees and singing parties, and attended prayer meetings. Doctors were in short supply, so nurses and midwives tended to many of the sick. Epidemics like diphtheria and cholera hit Mount Pleasant as hard as elsewhere, and it seemed like everyone had the ague, a fever akin to malaria that caused recurring spells of chills.[6]

The snow was so deep in winter, and the mud so deep in spring, that roads were often impassable except in summer, when farmers were too busy to come to town. The first plank road was built in 1853, connecting Mount Pleasant to Burlington, Iowa, the nearest river city. A tall tale developed to illustrate why the plank road was needed. Often told during Mount Pleasant's yearly Old Settlers Reunion, the tale went something like this: "I was picking my way into town inside the rail fences along Scott's Lane, when I saw a hat floating southward. I secured a long stick and rescued the hat, uncovering the head of an indignant man who shouted, 'Leave my hat alone. No, I don't need your help; I'm alright. There's a perfectly good horse under me.'"[7]

Mount Pleasant farmwives had little use for fashion, but in town, the Reconstruction-era ladies knew when *Godey's Lady's Book* would arrive, with pictures and descriptions of the latest hats and dresses. In the second half of the 19th century, fashions weren't much more comfortable than the crinolines of the previous generation. Mrs. Lincoln's hoop skirts had been harder to maneuver, but in the 1870s, there was still a half-cage contraption to arrange at the back of the skirt, and yards of material to gather and drape just right. And underneath it all, there was the suffocating corset. A few courageous women in town had tried bloomers, those Turkish trousers worn under short skirts for gardening or swimming. They were thrilled when Amelia Bloomer came to Mount Pleasant to make a speech.[8] Women's circumstances changed as slowly in Iowa as they did elsewhere. Mary Harlan was enrolled at Iowa Wesleyan University from 1862–63, but she never graduated. The first woman graduated from the university in 1869.[9]

Still, the town provided plenty of opportunities for broadening one's perspective. Mount Pleasant became known as the "Athens of Iowa" because many famous lecturers came to town, including Frederick Douglass, Henry Ward Beecher and Susan B. Anthony.[10] An editorial in the *Mount Pleasant Journal* on October 4, 1871, declared that "Mount Pleasant is Booming Along: What with her new City Hall, in process of erection; her new Gas Works (said to be the finest in the State), nearly completed; and her new Daily paper just issued, she has a right to put on city airs and consider herself advancing several pegs on the road to fame."[11]

Mary Harlan Lincoln and her children enjoyed spending summers in Mount Pleasant, and Robert Lincoln got away to join them whenever he could. But he found that small-town obscurity was much harder to come by for him than for the others.

He was constantly approached about running for political office during the 1870s and 1880s.[12] As the martyred President's son, political strategists knew that his name had magical power.[13] In 1876, President Rutherford B. Hayes offered Robert Lincoln the position of assistant secretary of state, but he declined, citing personal and financial reasons (this was the year after his mother's insanity trial). He did run for local office that year and was elected supervisor for the town of South Chicago. Past supervisors had been described as a "gang of robbers" who voted themselves "enormous salaries for doing nothing," but a decade later, after his term was over, the *Chicago Tribune* said Robert Lincoln had "put the affairs of the town in good shape."[14]

Robert served as a state elector during the presidential election of 1880, when James Garfield beat Democratic contender Winfield Hancock by a narrow margin.[15] Garfield was plagued with requests for patronage during his short four months in office. He offered the secretary of war post to Robert Lincoln, who had not asked for it and did not want it, but felt compelled to say yes. When Garfield was shot four months later and subsequently died, Robert Lincoln was the only one of his Cabinet members kept on by succeeding President Chester Arthur.[16]

As wife of the war secretary, Mary Harlan Lincoln's job was to support Secretary Lincoln, to host social functions, and to attend public receptions. When she was feeling well, she was a wonderful hostess, but she was sometimes stretched too thin. While in Washington, the Lincolns became acquainted with Gail Hamilton, a writer living in Secretary of State James Blaine's household. She described Mrs. Lincoln as having "almost everything to make her handsome but health...She seems very sweet, and simple, and attractive."[17]

During her husband's term as war secretary (1881-1885), Mary was busy nursing her ailing mother, taking care of her young children, and distributing her mother-in-law's many possessions. Both her mother and her mother-in-law died during this time; Mary Todd Lincoln died in 1882, and Ann Eliza Harlan in 1884. Mary's own health concerns probably came last.

Robert Lincoln approached his job as war secretary like he did everything else—with careful attention to detail. The *Chicago Tribune's* assessment of Lincoln's tenure as secretary, published after his term, must have pleased both Robert and Mary Lincoln. It said: "Secretary Lincoln undoubtedly received his appointment through his family position, but the appointment has proved to be one of the best that could have been made. Mr. Lincoln stands today solely upon his own merits."[18]

Still, choosing to run for the presidency or the vice presidency was quite different from accepting an appointment. In 1884, rumors circulated that Robert Lincoln would run for President, and *The New York Times* ran editorials supporting his nomination.

Lincoln wasn't interested and tried to discourage the rumors, but they persisted. In a letter to H.H. Warner, a lawyer from Rochester, New York, he wrote, "I am so sincerely not a candidate that in answer to your inquiry I can only say that I have no 'working friend' at Chicago. I have discouraged all use of my name..."[19]

A year after leaving the Cabinet, Robert Lincoln was happy to be out of the public eye. To John Hay, he wrote, "I am let alone in the papers and I don't want my name in them again until I am assured of the regular complementary [sic] notes written by some member of my afflicted family with 'no flowers' attached...God willing I will never again be in the jaws of that damning hyena, the public at large."[20]

God wasn't willing. In the spring of 1886, a southern Negro journal called the *Atlanta Defiance* declared that Lincoln should run for President in 1888. A few days later, when asked by a Chicago reporter for a reaction to the *Defiance's* suggestion, Robert Lincoln replied, "I'm entirely out of public life. I attend strictly to my private business and have no time, nor if I had time, any inclination to discuss public matters." The speculation didn't stop there, however, and by early 1888, Lincoln resumed his former practice of refusing invitations to public occasions, lest he be seen as a candidate.[21]

During these years, Mary and the children spent many months in Mount Pleasant. They entered into the social life there in a way they didn't feel free to in Washington or Chicago. The Lincoln daughters were never formally introduced to high society, but in Mount Pleasant, their mother organized lots of lawn socials, receptions and birthday parties in their grandfather's home. She told cousin Florence that Mount Pleasant was "so very restful and so good for the children growing up."[22]

On September 20, 1883, the *Mount Pleasant Journal* reported that Mrs. Lincoln and the children had accompanied the former senator to Salem, Iowa, a few days before, where he gave a speech. "Little Jackie was on the stand attentively listening to his grandfather's speech. Perhaps few knew that a grandson of Abraham Lincoln was present," the *Journal's* report noted.[23]

In Mount Pleasant, the children had the run of the house, from attic to cellar. Outside, there was a big yard with lots of shade from maples, oaks and elms. At the back of the property were an apple orchard, a garden, and the stables, where Grandfather Harlan kept their ponies. Townspeople were quite familiar with the sight of the children riding around, the "trio of Mary, Jack and Jessie, with the pony."[24]

The Lincoln children carried themselves with "no pretensions of inherited greatness,"[25] and so they were well liked and popular in Mount Pleasant. Olive Cole Smith, who knew them from girlhood, wrote in an article for the *Mount Pleasant News* that, "We knew them and liked them, because they were just one of the crowd of boys and girls their ages."[26] Another writer declared that the Lincoln children "have made themselves very dear in many homes, from the time they were young children. Mary, the eldest, with her rarely lovable nature and sterling qualities of character, has made many devoted friends..."[27]

Senator Harlan called his oldest grandchild "a good armful of lively girlhood."[28] Cousin Florence agreed with this positive assessment. She described Mamie as:

> ...one of the people who never waste time in getting acquainted, having intuition as well as breeding. She was a well-grown, substantial girl of fifteen, medium brunette in complexion, with abundant hair in two braids wound about her shapely head. Her eyes were either brown or violet according to the light. She had a generous mouth, a lovely chin and throat, and a sensitive nose. Her hands apparently were ready for whatever might come, and withal she possessed the appeal of a simply nurtured fortunate child on the brink of a womanhood already surprisingly expressive.[29]

On September 17, 1884, Mamie was initiated into the P.E.O. Sisterhood, an international women's organization founded in Mount Pleasant in 1869. By the time Mamie joined the society, it was 15 years old and spreading far beyond the Iowa Wesleyan University campus. Jessie joined the P.E.O. on New Year's Eve, 1895.[30]

The original seven members banded together to form their own organization because the other women's society on campus did not invite all seven into its membership. Instead of Greek letters, they chose the acronym P.E.O. (Providing Educational Opportunities for Women) as their organization's name. The first constitution specified that their aim was "General Improvement," meaning they vowed to continually improve their minds through education, and to improve their charity and manners toward each other and society as a whole. Loyalty and mutual respect were important P.E.O. virtues.[31]

In the beginning, P.E.O. meetings usually included an educational component. The report of one meeting in the *Mount Pleasant Journal* named members visiting from Kansas, Missouri, India, and London, England—this latter one was Mamie Lincoln. "Like ships on the ocean the P.E.O.'s drift hither and thither, but sometimes they meet, and it needs only the signal light to shine, and love and goodwill will flow," the Mount Pleasant report concluded.[32]

Mamie found other cultural opportunities in Mount Pleasant. Local sculptor Harriet Ketcham chose Mamie and two friends, Clara Cole (Olive's sister), and Frances Wheeler (daughter of the university's president), as models while she designed a Soldier's Monument [PLATE 14] for the Iowa Statehouse in Des Moines.[33] She won first prize, but she died before the work was finished.[34] Mrs. Ketcham provided the girls with an example of a pioneering woman. When she died in October 1890, her obituary remarked on how unusual it was for a woman to pursue sculpting:

> For fifteen years or more she has studied and worked, has breasted opposition, has faced cold apathy, has conquered every obstacle, all for her Art. She discovered in herself a passion for sculpture and despite the fact that this is an unusual branch of art for women to adopt, and more so fifteen years ago, than now, she moved steadily forward undaunted...[35]

Robert Lincoln often came to Mount Pleasant for short periods of time while his family was visiting there. On August 6, 1887, he spoke at Mount Pleasant's Old Settlers Reunion,[36] presided over by its first settler, Presley Saunders. Mr. Lincoln was only one of several dignitaries, including the Governor, who gave an address that day, but he was the only one mentioned in the headlines of the *Mount Pleasant Journal.* Iowa Congressman John Gear, an ex-Governor, was quoted as saying he attended the event only to shake the hand of Robert Lincoln, "whose father's name was a household word in this land, but who was also loved for his own good deeds for he had the good sense to come into Iowa to select his wife."[37]

Robert was scheduled to talk in the afternoon, and the space around the speaker's platform got more and more crowded throughout the lunch hour. When finally introduced by Saunders, he remarked that he was not there to make a speech, but he did deliver the following comments, showing that, despite his aversion to public appearances, he inherited the voice and sensitivities of a politician. Although he professed to be unwilling to make a speech, clearly, he had done his homework:

> I am glad to meet with so many of those who have helped to found so great a state as Iowa. I came to make no speech, that has fallen to abler speakers. I understand the genuine old settler came here before 1850. It is almost impossible to conceive the changes that have occurred since that time. Taking the census of 1880, which now seems out of date, we see that since 1850 the population of your state has multiplied more than ten times and the acreage has increased from one million acres to twenty millions. The character of your people is best shown in the fact that the percentage of population over the age of ten who can read is greater than that of any other state in the union. I am too good a republican not to believe that that same fact has had something to do in the attitude you take on politics. A gathering such as this should be taken up wholly with greeting old friends and with reminiscences of struggles and successes. Time dulls the edge of troubles that are gone but sweetens the pleasures that are past. I hope that may be your pleasure here to-day.[38]

Rumors that Robert Lincoln would run for a national office persisted. By the time of this Old Settlers Reunion appearance, speculation had already begun about the 1888 elections. Over the next year, the *Chicago Tribune*, the *Omaha Bee*, the *Buffalo Courier*, the *Springfield (Massachusetts) Republican*, and other papers published editorials suggesting Lincoln would make a good senator or president. The *Toledo Blade* also noted that Lincoln's was the only name mentioned for vice president. When a *Blade* reporter asked him about all the speculation in August 1887, Robert Lincoln replied:

> I have seen too much of the wear and tear of official life to ever have a desire to reenter it. Though I was but a boy when my father became President, I can well remember the tremendous burden he was called upon to bear. True, the conduct of the war made the cares of office then infinitely more exacting; but I have seen enough of Washington official life to have lost all desire for it. The Presidential office is but a gilded prison. The care and worry out weigh, to my mind, the honor which surrounds the position.[39]

He did, however, admit that, while he did not seek any office, "I will say this: a duty might be imposed upon a man which he could not honorably avoid."[40] So, when he was pressed to accept the position of Minister to the Court of St. James's (in London, England) in 1889, he felt he had to accept.

The mayor of Liverpool, England, met their steamer, the City of Paris, when the Lincolns arrived there on May 22, 1889. A special boat decorated with flags came out to the ship to bring them in, while the mayor waited at the landing. He took them to the train station in his carriage, and they headed immediately for London.[41] Upon arrival there, the "honorable Minister Lincoln" was greeted with the *Pall Mall Gazette's* assurance that he would find "his father's name everywhere a talisman to conjure with in England... We welcome the son for the sake of the father."[42] Even in England, he could not escape allusions and comparisons to his father. He resolved it there as he did at home, by striving to be worthy of his position and above all reproach.

On Saturday, May 25, Robert Lincoln met Queen Victoria at Windsor Castle. The queen's carriage met him at the railway station in Windsor and brought him to the royal palace. The day before, the press had reported what would occur: "Mr. White of the American Legation will accompany Mr. Lincoln to Windsor, but will not be present at the presentation to the Queen. Mr. Lincoln will make no set speech on the occasion, nor will the Queen make a set reply. They will merely exchange compliments..."[43] That same day, Lincoln met the Prince and Princess of Wales at Lady Salisbury's reception. Throughout the next several days, he was introduced to a number of other dignitaries.[44]

On Wednesday, Mrs. Lincoln and one of her daughters (unnamed in the press report) were presented to the Queen in the drawing room of Buckingham Palace. Mrs. Lincoln probably took Mamie, since she was the oldest. The paper said they "both came through the ordeal remarkably well" and in the process satisfied a "good deal of curiosity" about them. The newspaper report said that Queen Victoria wore mourning clothes, but her attire only served "to show up the costumes of those who came to be presented." Creating a proper impression was so important. The first paragraph of the report focuses on the "splendid costumes worn," which are later described in detail:

> Mrs. Lincoln wore a handsome jupe of black silk trimmed with black tulle and embroidered with jet. A long tram of black silk hung from the waist, for, though it is optional to wear it from the shoulders, one feels the weight more when it is so placed. The low cut corsage was of the same material trimmed in the same manner. The court plumes and lappets were black. Mrs. Lincoln wore a collarette of diamond stars fastened on black velvet and small diamond earrings. She carried a bouquet of purple flowers. Miss Lincoln, who was presented by her mother, looked fresh and pretty in a charming debutante's gown of white poule de soie. The front of jupe was covered with tulle hung with tiny silver pendants that shimmered as she walked and were held in place by a chatelaine of daisies and grasses. The train was also of white poule de soie. The corsage was trimmed with tulle, daisies, and grasses. Her court plumes and lappets were white. Pearls were her sole ornaments and her bouquet consisted of pure white exotics, and maidenhair fern.[45]

On Independence Day 1889, Reverend Newman Hall conduct-ed a patriotic service for Americans in his London church, a special dinner was held at the Century Club, and Mary Lincoln made her debut as the diplomat's hostess, with a grand Independence Day cel-ebration held at their residence, 5 Cadogan Square. So many people attended the afternoon reception that the house was taxed beyond its capacity. Those who had attended previous Independence Day parties at the minister's home declared this was the best ever. The press report noted that:

> Minister Lincoln's residence was decorated with great taste. The English and American flags adorned the balcony over the entrance and curtained the halls and doorways. There were flowers in profusion. The reception was informal, yet many elegant dresses were to be seen. 'I have seen more beautiful women here than at any reception for a long time,' a gentleman who has been in London society for years was heard to remark.[46]

The Lincoln daughters had learned that the family name could sometimes be used to their advantage. One news article from London tells a story attributed to Madame Waddington,[47] describ-ing a large crowded party at the Foreign Office in London, attend-ed by the Lincolns. Also present was the Prince of Wales, who would one day be King Edward. Someone approached Mrs. Waddington, asking if she could arrange for an American girl to meet the prince.

"I did not think it would be easy. The prince was not well—he had hurt his knee and walked with a cane and looked tired..." she said. "However I was willing to try, particularly as the young lady was a goddaughter [granddaughter] of President Lincoln" [the arti-cle doesn't say which one, but by manner, it seems like Jessie].

When the prince heard that one of Robert Lincoln's daughters wished to meet him, he got up immediately and went to her. He said he was quite happy to meet Abraham Lincoln's granddaugh-ter, and she was not the least bit shy, according to Madame Waddington. The prince shook hands with her, and they talked for a few minutes. He reminded her to be proud of her famous grandfather. Then he suggested she tour the building and meet the other guests.

"Thank you, very much," Miss Lincoln reportedly replied, looking straight at him with her big blue eyes, "but I don't want to see anything else. I only wanted to see the Prince of Wales, and now that I have seen you and talked to you I don't want anything more."[48]

CHAPTER NINE:
Abraham Lincoln II

London, England, March 5, 1890

The Lincoln family was quite popular in England, partly because of the British people's admiration for Abraham Lincoln, but also because of the respect they felt for Robert Lincoln himself, who "in a very short time has won the confidence of the English Government and people."[1] Mrs. Robert Lincoln fulfilled her role as the American minister's gracious hostess and companion, and the children were intelligent, lively, and well mannered.

Soon after the family's arrival in England, 15-year-old Jack was sent to school in Versailles to learn French. He was preparing to follow in his father's footsteps, first by attending Phillips Exeter, then Harvard, then joining his father's law firm. One reporter later described Jack as "an exceedingly intelligent young gentleman, of a most lovable nature, and those who knew him best had entertained bright hopes for his future..."[2]

Everyone described Jack in similar terms. Olive Cole, a childhood friend from Mount Pleasant, described him as "a handsome, gentlemanly boy, with charming manners...a boy of much promise...a boy worthy of his name and inheritance."[3] Another childhood friend described Jack as "a manly little fellow, and a peacemaker in the ball games," adding that on Jack's last visit, the day before the family sailed to England, the friend's mother remarked on how tall Jack had grown and warned him not to grow as tall as his grandfather. Jack quickly replied, "I would like to be as good, as kind and as wise as he was, but not so tall; he must have bumped his head many times."[4]

Although everyone called him Jack, whenever he penned his name to something he considered official or serious, he signed himself "Abraham Lincoln."[5] He could perfectly imitate his grandfather's signature, and he was known for the prank of selling these copies to his friends as authentic relics.[6] But who could accuse him of forgery? He was only signing his true name.

Although he was officially Abraham Lincoln II, Jack was actually the third of his immediate family to carry the name. In each case, the name skipped a generation. President Abraham Lincoln's paternal grandfather was also named Abraham. This Abraham, whose ancestry could be traced back to Quakers and to prosperous colonial landowners, heard tales of rich and fertile land in Kentucky from a distant relative, Daniel Boone, and he decided to seek his fortune there. He sold his farm in Virginia in the early 1780s and moved his family over the mountains to a largely unsettled area that was then still part of the Virginia Commonwealth. Within a few years, he owned 5,544 acres.[7]

In 1786, he and his three sons, Mordecai, Josiah, and Thomas, were planting a cornfield when Indians attacked. Abraham was killed instantly while his sons watched. Mordecai, the oldest, sent Josiah for help and ran for cover, but eight-year-old Thomas was left behind, still sitting beside his father's lifeless body. Mordecai quickly grabbed a rifle and shot the Indian heading for Thomas before his brother could be harmed. This instinct to protect Thomas apparently did not last. As the eldest, law dictated that Mordecai would inherit all of the family property, and he grew into a wealthy man with a passion for raising racehorses, while the two younger sons were left without an inheritance.[8]

The second Abraham Lincoln, son of Thomas, was not very interested in his namesake or his family genealogy, although he had heard the story of his grandfather's death many times. He did not care to trace his family tree and considered his own early history to be devoid of interest to anyone. When pressed for biographical information about himself during his first campaign for the presidency, he told a Chicago editor in early June of 1860 that, "It is a great piece of folly to attempt to make anything out of my early life. It can be all condensed into a simple sentence, and that sentence you will find in Gray's 'Elegy,' 'The short and simple annals of the poor.' That's my life, and that's all you or any one else can make of it." He avoided adding details about his background.[9]

His grandson, however, took great interest in him. As recipient of the best-loved name in American history, it was appropriate that Jack Lincoln be especially interested in studying President Abraham Lincoln and the Civil War. Robert's law partner, William Beale, recalled seeing Jack on the floor of his father's library with Civil War maps spread all around him. Jack could discuss the various battles in detail.[10]

Jack also had his grandfather's unshakable honesty and sense of responsibility. One day Jack and some friends were playing baseball, when the ball went astray and broke through a neighbor's window. The friends all scattered, so that when the neighbor emerged from his house, angry and demanding to know who had swung the bat, he found only Jack Lincoln.

"Who are you?" the man asked.

"Abraham Lincoln," the boy replied.

The man quickly disappeared, as if he'd seen a ghost.[11]

One example of young Jack's courteous manner is a polite thank you note written to Charles Isham, one of his father's secretaries in England, and eventually his sister's husband. The letter was written soon after Jack went to Versailles. In response to some unspecified offer of help, he wrote, "I am very much obliged to you for your kind offers of assistance, but there is really nothing I need."[12]

Shortly thereafter, Jack contracted blood poisoning when a series of boils under his arm became infected. On November 6, 1889, a French doctor operated on Jack to remove the carbuncle, and the long incision refused to heal. On November 26, Jack's temperature was elevated two degrees; on December 1, he showed signs of improvement; but on December 15, he seemed to be getting pneumonia. While that never developed, the wound was still open and Jack was weaker by Christmas. This seesaw continued for the next three weeks.[13]

Some British-French animosity appeared in a letter written by British physician Dr. H. Webster Jones, later called to the case, who wrote, "Whether Jack gets well or not, I shall always be of the opinion that French surgery was his greatest foe." Jack's life lay in the balance, so Dr. Jones went to Versailles at Robert Lincoln's request and accompanied the boy back to England, "where he is far happier, none the worse for his journey." Dr. Jones added that, "There never was a braver, lovelier character, and Jack deserves to live."[14]

Both the French and the British were accommodating to Jack Lincoln during his difficult journey from Versailles to London. The Nord railroad of France provided a special hospital car. So did the London, Calais & Dover Railroad, which also sent a railroad agent, Alfred Thorne, to meet them at Calais. Jack rested on a swinging bed during the Channel crossing and was fine most of the way, but he felt sick just before reaching the Dover pier.[15]

A week later, the strain of worrying over his son showed in a letter Robert wrote to a friend. The man who was so well known for being careful and precise made several mistakes in the letter, dated January 21, 1890:

My dear Hale:

Many thanks for your letter of the 18th. We have had a very bad time with poor Jack. I left Versailles [he first typed Marsailles, then crossed out "Mar" and handwrote the "Ver"] December 29 with the assurance and in the belief that he had turned the corner but when I saw him again on May 9 [he meant January], I could not fail to discover his very serious condition. A consultation was held but the assembled doctors could suggest no change in the theory or treatment of the case and I learned that they gave him from thirty to sixty days before he would die of exhaustion. His illness causes him little pain and we resolved to utilize his strength remaining, to give him a chance here...Under a radical change of treatment he has seemed to improve and we are considerably encouraged but the doctors will not go further than to say they are really hopeful. The bottom trouble is blood poisoning under the effect of which a great cut under his arm, a foot long, has become inset and does not heal, while it means a very exhausting drain on his system—he is plucky and patient, eats and digests well, reads papers and light books and really to see his face in bed and hear him talk, one would not think him seriously ill. He owes his living to now to [sic] his Mother who has been out of the sound of his voice only once in twelve weeks and more, and for days together in France he could eat nothing that she did not herself cook. She is as healthy and well and as outwardly undisturbed as any mother taking care of a healthy baby...I suppose I am getting along here as well as could be expected and we certainly are treated very well but I dreadfully miss my friends and some amusement once in a while. Every thing goes like clockwork and one's regiment of servants keep a fellow in a ceaseless stupid routine which gets very tiresome...[16]

Jack's father hoped a change in doctors and treatment plans would help his son. The large doses of "Quinia" prescribed by the new doctors had brought down Jack's fever by January 23, and the wound was healing. Notes on the case for February 5 said, "Trouble now all local and, in sense external (open wound). Appetite and digestion never impaired in whole 13 weeks."[17] On February 6, 1890, the *Mount Pleasant Journal*, which closely followed the course of Jack's illness, reported that:

Everybody will be glad to know that the recent newspaper statements as to the hopeless condition of young Abraham Lincoln, son of Robert T. Lincoln, our minister at London, England, and familiarly known here among the boys as 'Jack Lincoln,' were not fully justified by the facts, as the following cablegram[s] will show:

London, Feby. 4th, 1890. To [Senator] Harlan, Mt. Pleasant, Ia. Little change in fortnight, quite hopeful. LINCOLN.

London, Feb. 5th. Two eminent surgeons to-day, expect recovery barring accidents. LINCOLN.[18]

The new doctors, Dr. Jones, Dr. Thos. Smith, and Dr. Maclagen, were pleased with Jack's progress early in February. Dr. Jones wrote a letter to a friend, published February 15, saying, "I believe [he] has yet many chances for recovery."[19] That very day, Jack took a turn for the worse. His pulse rate and breathing became rapid, and he was visibly weaker. The doctor administered a stimulant. On February 21, the doctor noted that Jack passed a "critical day yesterday. Today much relieved as to breathing and restlessness...Wound about the same."[20]

A second operation was performed on February 27. That day, the *Mount Pleasant Journal* reported both good news and bad. First, it stated, "a recent operation gives fresh hope." But an addendum tacked on at the last minute read: "LATER:—Just as we go to press the dispatches announce the death of Master Lincoln, at a late hour last night. His grandfather, Senator Harlan, has the sympathy of his townspeople in this grief."[21]

It was a bizarre and cruel twist to the story; Master Jack was not dead at all. He lived another week. On the morning of March 5, Robert Lincoln was sitting with the secretary of the American legation, Henry White, when Mamie interrupted, telling him to go upstairs quickly to his son's room. Within ten minutes, Jack was dead.[22]

And so, in its next issue, on March 6, 1890, the *Mount Pleasant Journal* had to run a correction, retracting its first death announcement, and then announcing the death again:

> Last week we announced the death of Minister Lincoln's only son, Abraham Lincoln, at London, England, on the authority of a dispatch that was published in all the papers, and which was premature. The brave boy lingered almost another week, Senator Harlan receiving a cablegram at 8 o'clock yesterday morning announcing his death. Jackie's young friends in this city are very sad over his untimely death, and the blow to his parents and sisters and his grandfather, Senator Harlan, is a very severe one. The regret is widespread that the only grandson of the martyr president, Abraham Lincoln, has been taken in his youth.[23]

A number of obituaries eulogized Master Jack, mourning the loss of the boy who had such promise. One writer was particularly eloquent:

> The sympathy of the whole American people will go out to Minister Lincoln in his great bereavement. There is probably no deeper sorrow than that of the death of an only son, and in this instance a special cause of grief exists to emphasize the bitterness of the loss. The young man, Abraham Lincoln, was not only the pride of his parents, but the representative of one of the most illustrious names in American history, which is not likely now to have continuance. Well may the stricken father exclaim as Burke did under like circumstances, 'I am stripped of all my honors; I am torn up by the roots, and lie prostrate upon the earth.' It is not to be doubted that the future of this beloved and promising son was the thing of most interest and importance to him. From all accounts, he had good reason to expect the best in that regard. 'Jack,' as he was familiarly called, had many of the traits of his famous grandfather, and was developing rare qualities of intellect and of character. Had he lived he would surely have chosen a public career. That was his manifest bent and destiny; and all the conditions were in his favor. His early death must, therefore, be considered a calamity of far more than ordinary cruelty and pathos—a loss that in a certain sense gives occasion for national mourning...[24]

The writer of this obituary also pointed out that Robert had been through something like this before. As the eldest son, he had watched all of his brothers die at young ages: Eddie at four, Willie at 11, Tad at 18. He lost close friends and relatives during the war, including the family friend who was the first Union casualty, Colonel Elmer Ellsworth. He also blamed himself for his father's death, thinking if he'd gone with his parents to Ford's Theater, he could somehow have prevented the assassination. He was estranged from his mother after the insanity trial, and then orphaned when she died in 1882. Still, none of these tragedies affected him like the loss of his son, who represented the future to him. Writing to his friend John Hay, Robert called it "the hardest of many hard things." He added:

> Jack was to us all that any father and mother could wish and beyond that, he seemed to realize that he had special duties before him as a man, and the thoroughness with which he was getting ready was a source of the greatest pride to me. I did not realize until he was gone how deeply my thoughts of the future were in him...My wife has surprised us all, in not breaking down...I would not have believed that any human could have stood the strain of the months as she did with apparent cheerfulness, even when she had no hope.[25]

On November 8, 1890, at the Oak Ridge Cemetery in Springfield, Illinois, Abraham Lincoln II was interred in the crypt that once had held his grandfather. Fourteen years before, almost to the day, thieves had tried to steal the body of President Abraham Lincoln from this crypt, and Robert had re-buried his father in another vault there, under four feet of concrete. Jack's body was placed in the original vault.[26]

Although all of Robert Lincoln's brothers, his father, and his mother were buried at the President's gravesite, Robert still needed permission from the Lincoln Monument Association to bury his son there. A committee controlled the President's burial place, and it took several months to get approval for Jack's committal there. In early September, Robert wrote the committee a characteristically proper request:

CROMWELL HOUSE, S.W. LONDON, September 10, 1890.

Hon. O.M. Hatch: MY DEAR SIR—I beg to thank you for your letter communicating to me the resolution of the Lincoln Monument Association, inviting a correspondence with me as to the propriety of depositing the remains of my son in a crypt in the monument erected in memory of his grandfather. In reply, I beg to say to you that when, upon the death of my son, I foresaw the extinction of my descendants bearing his name, the desire came upon me that if it met the view of every member of the Monument Association, arrangements might be made for the burial in the monument of my son, and thereafter of myself and my wife and my two daughters, unless they should marry. This is the arrangement I would make under the peculiar circumstances, if the tomb of my father were, as would usually be the case, in my care, but I trust that it may be understood that I know that the monument was not erected or arranged for such a purpose; and that I would abandon my desire if it does not seem proper to each member of the association...I need not say that any expense caused by such an arrangement would be borne by myself. I will be highly gratified by the kind consideration of my wishes. Believe me, very sincerely, Robert T. Lincoln[27]

On October 18, the association voted to honor his request, and the interment was scheduled for November.

On November 5, Robert Lincoln arrived in New York, having crossed the Atlantic in the steamer City of New York. His wife and daughters had already been in the United States for nearly three months.[28] A special car was sent by the Pennsylvania Railroad to carry him and his son's body to Springfield.[29] Robert's long-time friend, Edgar Welles, who was then vice president of the Wabash Railroad, accompanied Robert on his sad errand. Mrs. Robert Lincoln, who was reported to be "in delicate health," stayed in Mount Pleasant with her daughters.[30]

On the morning of November 8, a small group of men went to Springfield's Oak Ridge Cemetery for the interment. The ceremony was private, with only a dozen or so men present, including several from the monument association, plus Mr. Lincoln, Mr. Welles, Illinois Governor Fifer, Senator Cullom, and former Governor Oglesby. When the deed was accomplished, Robert reportedly turned to the men and said quite simply, "Gentlemen, I thank you for this kindness."[31]

Eventually, after Robert Lincoln's death, Jack would be reburied alongside his father in Arlington National Cemetery, as directed by Mary Harlan Lincoln, Robert's wife. In time, she would be buried there too. But for nearly 40 years, the two Abraham Lincolns lay in the same ground—the elder shot down just after fulfilling his promise, to preserve the Union, the younger one lost on the eve of promise. With Jack gone, there was no one left to carry on the family name. He had been so much at one with his grandfather's legacy that, once again, the nation mourned for Abraham Lincoln.

CHAPTER TEN:

A Storybook Wedding

Brompton Church of the Holy Trinity, London, September 2, 1891

Two months after Jack's burial in Springfield, Robert returned to his duties in London. Mamie, Jessie and their mother sailed back to England a month and a half later, after a six-month stay in Mount Pleasant.[1] Mary Harlan Lincoln had stayed in Mount Pleasant during the burial because of "delicate health."[2] While her son survived, she had managed to wear a cheerful mask, but it had later crumbled, and she retreated to her father's home in Iowa to begin to recover. As long as possible, she stayed away from London, where she had social obligations as a foreign minister's wife, and where places would remind her of her son's illness. Mount Pleasant offered privacy and seclusion for a while, but eventually, she and the girls rejoined her husband.

For Mamie, the return to London must have been especially bittersweet: bitter because London would undoubtedly remind her of Jack's excitement as he expounded on some bit of British history, perhaps the building of Westminster Cathedral, or tales of royalty, or of brave admirals, but sweet because of her upcoming nuptials.

Charles Isham, one of the secretaries of the American ministry in England, had had a meeting with Robert Lincoln on January 7, just before the minister sailed back to England.[3] Could it be that he asked for Mamie's hand in marriage that day? Charles was at the Washington train station to meet Mamie and her sister and mother on February 18, when they came east to prepare for their sea voyage to England. He went home to New York, then traveled to Cambridge, Massachusetts, on February 21 to give a speech (he was a noted historian). On the morning of February 23, he was back in Washington, and he took a walking tour with Mamie. Two days later, he and Mamie had dinner with his family in New York, and then he took her to meet her mother and Jessie; it was time to board their boat to London.[4] The three Lincoln women sailed from New York to Southampton on the steamship Saale on Wednesday, February 25.[5] By July, Charles was in England, too.[6]

While Robert Lincoln was away from England, Henry White, first secretary of the American legation, had acted as chargé d'affaires. Through their duties together, he and Lincoln had formed a friendship that would be long lasting. So it was appropriate that Mr. and Mrs. Henry White hosted the ball on July 21 to announce the engagement of Miss Mamie Lincoln to Mr. Charles Isham.[7]

It was a natural match, one that both families could support. The two were alike in temperament and enjoyed the same cultural entertainments. Charles Isham was a distant cousin of Robert Lincoln's law partner, Edward S. Isham. Charles' father, William, president of the Metropolitan Bank of New York City, was Edward Isham's second cousin.[8]

Charles Isham was listed as secretary to Lincoln in London, but that was mostly a formality, allowing him access to British research materials. First and foremost, he was an historian and a writer, a graduate of Harvard with law degrees from Harvard and the University of Berlin. He was also a librarian for the New York Historical Society, a member of its Committee on Publications, and the author of a five-volume biography of Silas Deane, an American colonial agent in France during the Revolution. Isham's premier area of research continued to be the American revolutionary period.[9]

Mamie Lincoln and Charles Isham had been casual acquaintances until November 1889, when Robert Lincoln asked Charles to accompany his daughters to France so they could visit their ailing brother. During that trip, Mamie and Charles got better acquainted, and over the next year and a half, their friendship warmed and blossomed into romance.[10]

Born July 20, 1853,[11] Charles was 16 years older than Mamie, but Mamie was often praised for her poise, grace, and maturity. A childhood friend of Mamie's remembered his mother remarking that, "Mamie has the poise of a woman ten years older, and yet she enjoys the things of girls of her age." This friend also recalled in a letter to Jessie that with gentle authority Mamie could always get her younger brother and sister to behave when the adult in charge could not. "I remember her motherly care for you when you were a little one of about six and Jackie about ten, and both of you resisting Emma's orders, she in a few pleasant words explained why you should obey. She did not threaten to tell, as most big sister's [sic] would...and Jackie and you gladly obeyed," he wrote.[12]

Charles and Mamie kept in touch while she was in Iowa after Jack's death. His diary for that year before his marriage is full of daytime business appointments and evening social engagements: business and real estate transactions handled for his father, walks with his cousin, dinners with family and friends, nights at the theater or opera, church on Sunday, and meetings of the historical society, plus notations about letters written to "M.L."[13]

When the *P.E.O. Record* announced Mamie Lincoln's marriage, its writer described her as "a pretty petite girl of sweet and winning nature and a great favorite with those who know her. While she is thoroughly well educated she is not a bookish woman."[14] A graduate of Miss Kirkland's School in Chicago, Mary Lincoln was in every description, and in every picture, the epitome of Victorian womanhood. She was the perfect model for the Gibson girl look, with her narrow waist, flowing skirts, and hair coiled softly atop her head. She was graceful, smart, maternal, and feminine, with a style both simple and elegant. One Manchester, Vermont, resident said Mamie Isham was "a lady from her fingertips, oh, she was a marvelous woman."[15]

The Mount Pleasant newspaper's announcement of the engagement of Mamie and Charles reminded readers of the town's proud connection to the Lincolns and praised Mamie like this:

Mary, the eldest, with her rarely lovable nature and sterling qualities of character, has made many devoted friends who will feel that Mr. Charles Isham, Secretary of the Legation, must be pure and brave as Sir Galahad himself, to be worthy of such a maiden's heart and hand. Report says Sept. 9th is to be the wedding day [it actually occurred on Sept. 2]—that they will travel for a year. The good wishes that will go from Mt. Pleasant homes for the young couple will float over like a fleet of fairy ships to wish them joy and bon voyage.[16]

On the morning of September 2, 1891, London's skies were full of rain, but by early afternoon, the rain had stopped, the sky had cleared, and sunlight dappled the quiet courtyard of Brompton Parish Church of the Holy Trinity. Wedding guests walked through an ancient graveyard and along an avenue of arching lime trees to reach the blackened, ivy-covered brick church edifice, its Gothic doorways framed by evergreens.[17]

Inside, the perpetual gloom was brightened by shimmering light coming through the stained glass windows, and by the sweet scent of flowers. The chancel steps were filled with palms, ferns and flowers, and the air was sweetened by the fragrance of Easter lilies, which covered the church's lectern.[18]

The church sanctuary was merely one-quarter full. Mamie and Charles had wanted a quiet wedding, and only sixty invitations had been issued, all verbal. Mamie's mother and sister sat in the front row. Behind them, among the other guests, were Charles' parents and sisters from New York, the Edward Ishams of Chicago, Mr. and Mrs. Marshall Field of Chicago, members of the U.S. diplomatic staff, Mr. and Mrs. Henry White, a few friends, some American officials, and a handful of foreign dignitaries. Mr. White and another member of the legation, Mr. Larz Anderson, served as ushers.[19]

At twenty past one o'clock, the minister and a robed boys' choir filed into the church. A few minutes later, Mamie appeared at the back of the sanctuary with her father. While the choir sang, "Oh God! Our Help of Ages," father and daughter proceeded down the aisle. The bride wore a white satin dress with a long train trimmed with orange blossoms. She also wore a lace veil and a diamond neck-lace given to her by the groom. She carried an ivory prayer book.

Charles met his bride at the altar steps, where they knelt together. Robert Lincoln and the best man, Major James C. Post, military attaché of the U.S. delegation, flanked the couple during the service. There were no bridesmaids.

The couple knelt at the altar while Cannon Farrar began the service. Throughout the ceremony, the bride's and groom's voices could be faintly heard, responding to the minister. The service ended with the congregation singing "The Voice That Breathed O'er Eden," and after that, the happy couple departed together while the organist played the traditional recessional, Mendelssohn's march from "A Midsummer Night's Dream."[20]

Outside the church, London reporters surrounded the newly-weds, bombarding them with questions and asking for details.[21] They were probably not really interested in the couple personally, but were sent to get the story about Abraham Lincoln's grand-daughter getting married. Even the report in the *P.E.O. Record*, a publication of Mamie's sorority, focused first on her famous blood-line, opening its story with the following:

> The marriage of Mary Lincoln is an event of no small inter-est to our sisterhood. She is, herself, an interesting character, as the daughter of the great War President's only surviving child. American people have a great regard for the sensible unobtrusive son of Lincoln, who accepts honor and respon-sibility, given by the people that have found him worthy of his name, but never seeks it. And Miss Mary Lincoln is a daughter of a great race, fit to be its representative.[22]

As usual, the first reason given for Mamie being worthy of notice was her genealogy. And because of this, Mamie Lincoln Isham, like the other descendants, retreated as much as possible from public view. For Robert Lincoln, this was virtually impossible, because he was the President's son, because his business associations were with well-known institutions, and because he accepted sever-al public appointments. But even he did not seek or enjoy publici-ty. No matter what they did, the descendants' best qualities and accomplishments were always somehow attributed not to their own personal integrity or hard work, but to the fact that Lincoln's blood flowed through their veins.

Little else is known about Mary Lincoln Isham. Of all the Lincoln women, she left the fewest records, mostly a few years' worth of appointment books with a handwritten scrawl very hard to decipher. There is nothing unusual in the many years' worth of diaries kept by her husband, where he noted a routine of evenings at the theater, drives in the park, family illnesses, and social gatherings.[23] Charles and Mamie split their time between their home in New York City, where they spent winters, and their village home in Manchester, Vermont,[24] where they spent summers. Charles especially liked to grow roses, and he always recorded the weather in his diary, including the first and last frost dates for both Manchester and New York City.[25]

After their wedding, Charles and Mamie apparently spent some time traveling. They returned to the States later that fall. Mary Harlan Lincoln, her mother, and sister Jessie returned to the U.S. at the end of May or early June 1892. Robert Lincoln was therefore alone in London when he received a letter from Charles, announcing the birth of his first grandchild, who was named Lincoln Isham. It was a bright spot in his lonely foreign existence.

Like his mother a quarter of a century before, he was in Europe when he became a grandparent and had to wait for months to meet the newest family addition. His reply to his son-in-law's news was full of a father's love and a grandfather's pride, but it was also tainted by his lingering bereavement:

11 June 92
2 Cromwell Houses S.W.

My dear Charles

Your telegram of early Monday morning met me on my return from a country visit to Lord Coleridge...it is needless to say that I was very glad to know that the most anxious part of Mary's ordeal had been safely passed. In the absence of any later news I am trusting that she is still going on well.

Give her my best love and congratulations on this achievement which puts us all in another category. It is only by the doctrine of great probability that I am [sure?] that the young man's maternal grandmother and aunt were in time to hear his first exclamation of disgust at this beastly world...With my chief anxiety about Mary allayed...I am about as easy in mind as I ever hope to be. With all good wishes, Affectionately, Your R.T.L."[26]

CHAPTER ELEVEN:
Scandal and Rebellion

Milwaukee, Wisconsin, November 10, 1897

With such well-acclaimed siblings as Mamie and Jack, what role was left for Jessie in the family structure? Mamie was described as a perfect young woman; Jack was idolized as one ready to match his grandfather's legacy if fate had not intervened. And then there was Jessie, the youngest, a female Lincoln coming of age on the cusp of a new century, and at the dawn of a new era for women.

While it is hard for any of us to fully understand what motivates another's attitudes and behavior, especially someone we've never met, current psychological theory stresses that family members are part of a system, with each member having effects on the others. Sibling position often affects personality. According to family system therapists Monica McGoldrick and Randy Gerson, the oldest child in a family tends to be saddled with more responsibilities than younger siblings, and first-born sons are often expected to achieve great things. McGoldrick and Gerson explain some common sibling dynamics in the following ways:

> An oldest child is more likely to be over-responsible, conscientious and parental, while the youngest is more likely to be child-like and carefree. Often, oldest children will feel they are special and particularly responsible for maintaining the family's welfare or carrying on the family tradition... Great things are often expected of a firstborn...The

youngest may feel more carefree and less burdened by family responsibility, and often has less respect for authority, and convention...Parents' attitudes and beliefs about gender roles influence their expectations for their different children in profound ways. For example, families in most cultures have always shown a preference for sons...an older sister who has a younger brother...will often have the responsibilities of an oldest, while her younger brother will get the glory and high expectations.[1]

With these ideas in mind, we can begin to speculate about some of the dynamics within the Robert Lincoln family.

Traumatic events like deaths can also have a profound ripple effect on family systems. Both the Harlan and the Lincoln families had a pattern of premature deaths, including Robert Lincoln's father, all three of Robert's siblings, all three of Mary Harlan Lincoln's siblings, and Robert and Mary Harlan Lincoln's son. The difficulty that a family member has in adjusting to a loss may be seen months or years later in an illness, an accident, or a lifestyle choice.[2]

Fame is also a tough act to follow. Some children may strive extra hard; others may rebel. As Martin Freud, son of Sigmund, once said, "I have never had any ambition to rise to eminence...The son of a genius remains the son of a genius, and his chances of winning human approval of anything he may do hardly exist if he attempts to make any claim to fame detached from that of his father."[3] The fame of Abraham Lincoln no doubt affected Robert Lincoln profoundly, pushing him to succeed, while creating in other family members a lack of ambition, and a great need for privacy.

Rebellion was brewing in society as Jessie Lincoln came of age. In 1890, the year Jack died, two leading suffragist organizations decided to merge and pool their resources in the campaign for the right to vote. Other powerful women's organizations were having an impact on public policy. Young American women had better educational opportunities than ever before, and their voices and actions were increasingly seen as significant. Most colleges now admitted women, and one third of all professional workers were women.[4]

In the fall term of 1890, Jessie was enrolled as a junior in the Iowa Wesleyan University college preparatory department, where her mother had gone to school, and where her grandfather had once been president. During the years after her brother's death, she was constantly with her mother, and after her sister married and moved away, she was her mother's chief project. By then, Jessie was a teenager, and she must have longed for more freedom. Perhaps her parents were feeling particularly protective because so many of their family members had died young, or perhaps they could see in Jessie the seeds of rebellion.

To be admitted as a junior in the prep school, Jessie had to pass entrance exams in spelling (covering a list of at least 100 words, dictation of at least 300 words, phonetics, and the general rules of spelling), reading (including proper pronunciation and expression), English grammar (parts of speech, declensions, and verb conjugations), descriptive geography (names and boundaries of countries, capitals, principal cities, physical features of the earth, and longitude and latitude), and arithmetic (decimals, fractions, and common denominators).[5]

Once admitted, juniors continued to study arithmetic and grammar and had classes in English composition, physiology and U.S. history.[6] What would it be like to sit in U.S. history class while a teacher discusses your grandfather's military strategies and the effects of his political decisions? Did all eyes turn to Jessie for her reaction? Did others students press her for details? How much did she already know about the subject?

Like her mother, Jessie's main interest was studying music, so she also took voice and piano lessons at the college's conservatory department that fall semester in 1890. She missed spring semester because of the family's return to London. In September 1891, her sister got married in London, and for the next year, she and her mother shuttled back and forth between the Harlan home in Mount Pleasant, the Lincoln home in Chicago, and the Isham home in New York City.[7]

By October 1892, Jessie and her mother were back in Mount Pleasant, and Jessie was again enrolled in the Iowa Wesleyan prep school. Because she had missed part of the previous year, she was not advanced to the middle year of prep school, but was listed as "unclassified." So was a young man named Warren Beckwith, a resident of Mount Pleasant.[8] That October, Mamie came to Mount Pleasant with a nurse and her four-month-old son and stayed until late November. The next month, her mother and Jessie went to New York to visit her.[9]

Robert Lincoln finished his term as minister to Great Britain in 1893, then moved back to Chicago with his wife and Jessie. During the next year, they made several trips to Mount Pleasant and visited the East Coast. Jessie lived with her grandfather part of that time, enrolling in the Iowa Wesleyan Conservatory of Music during the 1894-95 school year, and studying voice and piano. She spent the summer of 1895 traveling with her father.[10]

That fall, Mrs. Lincoln arranged for major renovations to the Harlan house, including additions to the existing porches. She also hosted several parties.[11] On Tuesday, October 15, 1895, a party honoring Mamie Isham's 26th birthday caused a minor scandal in town. It made the front page of the *Mount Pleasant Daily News* two days later, in both a news story and an editorial. The news story gave basic information, listed some of the party's guests, then went into great detail about the ladies' dresses:

> Mrs. Lincoln received in a Parish [sic] gown of black satin, low corsage, trimmings of black irridescent [sic], ornaments diamonds. Mrs. Isham wore a Paris gown very artistic, of silver white silk, scattered over with rose buds, trimmings of white lace, black velvet and black flowers, low corsage, no ornaments, but carried in her hand a large bouquet of La France roses. Miss Lincoln was gowned in a lovely blue silk, trimming of cream lace, simple but beautiful in effect, no ornaments, save a bouquet of American Beauties in her hand.[12]

The report also described the house, the ballroom decorated with autumn leaves and palms, the hidden orchestra, the music, and the refreshments that followed, but it made no mention of the scandal caused by one feature of the celebrated party.[13]

The town's other newspaper, the weekly *Mount Pleasant Journal*, also carried a story about the party titled "An Elegant Entertainment." While it hinted about the disagreement, it didn't take a stand:

Three more attractive and accomplished ladies are rarely found in society than the receiving party...Mrs. Lincoln in a lustrous black satin, decollete with garniture of irridescent [sic] jet and diamond ornaments, Mrs. Isham in white silk, brocaded with pink rose buds; and Miss Lincoln in delicate blue satin, both without jewels, formed a picture of fair women not easily forgotten by their guests. Mrs. Lincoln had given her thought unreservedly to the perfection of every feature that could contribute to the enjoyment of the young people. An orchestra was engaged in a programme of dances...For those who entertained conscientious scruples against measured paces and gliding feet, were the quieter pleasures of a tete a tete, or the conversational sparkle of mental interchange.[14]

Both newspapers commented that Senator Harlan warmly greeted his guests, and the *Daily News* said the senator "beamed with happiness to see his old home so full of life and gayety."[15] But the senator's obvious endorsement of an entertainment that included dancing must have raised an eyebrow or two among the Iowa Wesleyan University trustees. The Methodist Church supported this school, which he had so ably led 40 years before, and the Methodist Church didn't allow dancing.

Seven young men and women from the college were among those invited to the party. Iowa Wesleyan President Charles Stafford gave them permission to attend, but they were instructed to leave at eleven o'clock, before the dancing began. Marsa Fee, then of Centerville, Ohio, was one of those students invited. A friend of Jessie's, she had received her lavender dance card for the party, decorated with a purple "L," and she wanted to use it. She didn't think the no-dancing rule was fair, so she wrote to her father, Judge Fee, begging his permission, which he granted.[16]

The party started at nine o'clock with a reception, followed by a supper with a wide variety of delicious offerings, prepared by caterers sent from Chicago for the occasion. The reporter for the local *Journal* remarked that, "The gentleman who served his lady fair to the delicacies as well as more substantial viands felt that his task was an easy one on the principle of selection."[17]

Just before eleven o'clock, the gentleman in charge of the school's military department approached Marsa and asked if she was ready to leave. She said no, and explained that she had her father's written permission to stay. The teacher was supportive, but he said he couldn't protect her from the consequences. Five students said good-bye, but another girl, Helen Hughes, decided to stay with Marsa. Sixty-two years later, when she was interviewed about the experience, Marsa could still remember her red flowing chiffon gown with its accordion-pleated skirt whirling around the dance floor, and she still had her copy of the lavender dance program.[18]

The college president met Marsa in the hall the next morning after class. "I hate to tell you this, I really do, but you are to be expelled from the campus for one week," he told her. Perhaps he had doubts about the rule too, but as president, he was bound to enforce it.

"Dr. Stafford, I expected something like this," she replied, "But I had my father's permission to stay, and I thought it would not be often that I am invited to a dance given by Mrs. Robert Lincoln." Perhaps the president smiled at her courage and plucky spirit despite his serious mission.

Marsa and Helen received the same sentence, but they knew no chagrin. Joy Smith, who later interviewed Marsa about the event, wrote that instead of hiding their heads in shame, the two girls flaunted their freedom and notoriety:

> Behind their gentle bearing lived a fine steeled will. Accordingly, each morning Helen would call for Marsa at her dormitory, with an open top one-seat buggy, and dressed in their best, the young ladies would ride sedately around the campus just as eleven o'clock classes were dismissed. Friends saluted them, impressed no doubt by the sight...All week class mates watched for the girls to wave to them. The Coventry period passed, and Marsa and Helen were re-admitted to school.[19]

The *Daily News* editorial was not so cavalier. The paper supported the president's decision to expel the two students in an editorial titled "Should Enforce Discipline," which appeared alongside its own news story. It said:

> The Lincoln ball has of necessity caused a clash between the college authorities and society. Contrary to the well known rules of the college and after being especially advised, a number of the students attended the ball and participated in the dancing. A number of young men and women have been suspended therefor [sic] by President Stafford. He could not do otherwise. Methodism as a faith and Methodists as an organization have resolved and declared against dancing. The position of the church on this question is too well known to necessitate discussion. The Iowa Wesleyan University is a Methodist school, completely controlled and managed by Methodism. Consequently, one of its rules, and very properly so, forbids students from dancing. This rule was formulated or endorsed by the Board of Trustees which expects Pres. Stafford to enforce it. Senator Harlan is a Methodist and a member of the Board of Trustees. The ball was at the home of Senator Harlan and given by his daughter in honor of his granddaughters. It was a swell affair, the event of the season unquestionably...To enforce the college rules was a question that President Stafford settled with energy. He decided that the rule should apply to the Lincoln ball as at a Carmencita dance at the Grand....This action of President Stafford has brought a storm of abuse about his head from society circles. But society is off, clear off. Without entering into a discussion of the morality or immorality of dancing, the News puts itself on record as endorsing President Stafford's action. If the rule is a proper one enforce it, if improper abolish it. The whole question is a matter of discipline.

Three weeks after the scandalous dancing party, Jessie had her own dramatic birthday party with dancing. This time, the Harlan home was the setting for what was called a "domino" party, marking Jessie's twentieth year. Guests came masked and in pairs, dressed in loose fitting, hooded robes, either matched or color-coordinated with their partners. Again, both local papers reported on the event.[20]

The Harlan home was beautifully decorated with vines, palms, ferns and chrysanthemums. The library, with its long polished floor, was transformed into the ballroom. The dancing included waltzes, round dances and reels, and this time it apparently caused no public controversy. The mix of colors and patterns in the dancers' costumes created a moving kaleidoscope during dances like the Virginia Reel, as a small white-costumed sprite danced down the line to meet a tall Mephistopheles in black and red, or blue and pink met black, or red met cream, and so on.[21] At a signal, masks were removed amid merry shouts of recognition or surprise. Then an elaborate supper was served on Mary Harlan Lincoln's elegant china. After time to rest and talk, the dancing began again.[22]

The next day's *Mount Pleasant Daily News* told the story of the party with the usual hyperbole and attention to fashion detail. The *Journal's* account was similar, but added a compliment for Senator Harlan, much of which could have described Jessie's other grandfather as well:

The young people were glad and proud to greet Senator Harlan, Mrs. Lincoln's honored father. His kindly face and warm grasp instantly disapated [sic] the most unconscious feeling of awe which the dignified and honorable position of the eminent Senator inspired in minds of those who had not yet found out that his is the kindly heart, the helpful hand, and sterling worth of the man that has enthroned Senator Harlan in the hearts of his fellow towns men....[23]

Jessie's domino partner for her birthday party was a girlfriend, but letters written just before the party indicate that she was closely watching at least one young man in attendance. Jessie made a pact with the young man that they would wear the same rooster feathers in their headdresses so they could recognize each other in masquerade. James Burd later recalled that Jessie sent him a note that said, "Have this feather sewn on the front of your cap & I will have done likewise & I think we will have no trouble in finding each other. Come early. Yours very sincerely, Jessie Lincoln."[24]

Although the recipient of the letter was not Warren Beckwith, a later news report said that he and Jessie became secretly engaged around this time.[25] Warren was the youngest son of Captain Warren Beckwith, of Mount Pleasant, a Civil War veteran who was a well-respected member of the Mount Pleasant community. The captain came to Iowa as roadmaster for the Burlington and Missouri River Railroad. When this railroad later consolidated with the Chicago, Burlington and Quincy Railroad, Capt. Beckwith was retained in an administrative position. Seven years later, he left the railroad, and with some other Mount Pleasant citizens, he founded the Western Wheel Scraper Company there. When his company headquarters moved to Aurora, Illinois, the captain stayed in Iowa, where he also managed a 600-acre farm with purebred Hereford cattle and a collection of trotting horses. Capt. Beckwith was a model member of his church and his community.[26]

Capt. and Mrs. Beckwith were among the chaperones for the domino party at the Lincoln home. Robert Lincoln had great respect for the captain, but he didn't want his daughter to marry the captain's son. He didn't exactly say why, but Warren Jr. hadn't shown much ambition for anything besides sports, and Robert Lincoln may have judged Warren as too full of himself and impractical. Apparently, he hid his opinion from Warren, who later told a reporter, "There has been talk that I didn't get along with Robert Lincoln, but that's not true. I was a frequent visitor at his home and he was always nice to me."[27]

Warren was well known in Mount Pleasant for his athletic abilities. He was the star quarterback of the Iowa Wesleyan football team [PLATE 18] and third baseman for the college baseball team.[28] He was described by the *Milwaukee Journal* as "a harum-scarum young fellow devoted to athletics...a good horseman, shot and bicyclist but with a decided aversion to educational matters and to the confining requirements of a business career." Another paper used that quote and noted that young Beckwith was "just such a fellow as would attract the attention of a romantically inclined girl."[29]

Jessie probably fit that description. Her interests and romantic pursuits throughout her life tended toward the arts and adventure. Both Jessie and Warren attended school only sporadically. He was enrolled in Iowa Wesleyan's college prep department from 1891–93, took the next year off, and enrolled again in 1894–95. In the fall of

1895, at the time of the domino party, he was 22 years old. In June 1896, he was away from campus, working for the Gas and Coke Company in Chicago. During the 1897 baseball season, he pitched for a farm team in Dallas, Texas. He was offered a tryout for the Chicago Cubs, but his father opposed his making a living in baseball, so Warren was back in college by the fall of 1897, focused on playing football.[30]

A short news item about Warren's baseball career in the November 18, 1897, *Mount Pleasant Daily News* described him as "well-behaved," but a bit of a dandy: "Beckwith was popular with base ball patrons and cut something of a social figure over the circuit. He was known among his associates as 'The Dude' and the 'Lady Killer.' It was said that he would never go into a game to pitch without first combing and brushing his hair faultlessly."[31]

Early in November of 1897, Jessie and Warren went to the Mount Pleasant town clerk's office and applied for a marriage license. Despite the objections of Jessie's parents, a sympathetic minister was willing to perform the ceremony at a friend's house. They intended to keep the marriage secret for one year, and they asked the town clerk not to tell anyone. Even though they were of age, the clerk refused to keep their secret, and he quickly informed Jessie's parents of her intentions. She was immediately taken to Chicago, where her parents hoped she would forget about Warren Beckwith. But young love is too determined for that. The two communicated through a mutual friend in Chicago and arranged to meet a week later at the train station and elope in Milwaukee.[32]

November 10, 1897, was a mild fall day with a light south wind blowing. Warren arrived in Chicago on the 9 a.m. train, and he and Jessie went on from there, arriving at Milwaukee's St. Paul Depot at 1:45 p.m. The cabbie they hailed remembered later how nervous they appeared. They asked him to take them to Hotel Pfister. They stayed only a few minutes, then got back into the hack and asked for a ride to the home of Rev. O. P. Christian, pastor of the Sherman Street Methodist Episcopal Church. They arrived around 2:30 p.m.[33]

The minister was impressed with their dignified manners and thought they suited each other. They were of age, twenty-four and twenty-two, so he agreed to marry them on short notice. They had no witnesses with them, so he called his wife and his next-door neighbor, Mrs. Henry Baumgartner. He led them all into the parlor and got out the necessary forms. Then he put the young pair under oath and asked their ages and other pertinent facts. He didn't suspect anything unusual, until he asked the bride the name of her father, and she replied, "Robert T. Lincoln." This startled him, but he had already agreed to perform the ceremony, and they seemed to know their own minds, so he went ahead.[34]

It was the first time he had married runaways, but he later said he did not regret it. "I have never married a couple who appeared to be better suited to each other and it gave me a great deal of pleasure to perform the ceremony. She is a cultured, refined and beautiful woman. He is a handsome man. Both carried themselves with a dignified air," the minister later told a reporter. He added that the two young people were far above the sort who usually asked for hasty marriages.[35]

The neighbor, Mrs. Baumgartner, wasn't so sure. She liked the bride well enough, but she told the reporter, "I did not like the groom. There was something about him to which I could not reconcile myself. I cannot tell, though, what inspired my dislike."[36]

A cab driver took the newlyweds to the Plankinton House, where they registered as husband and wife, but used a slightly altered version of Warren's name. He signed in as "Warren Wallace and wife of Chicago." A hotel clerk noticed that they seemed evasive. They paid for dinner and supper in advance, then they went to their room and had their midday meal served there. During the afternoon, a servant noticed that their door was ajar, and upon inspection discovered the room was empty. They never returned. They had taken the four o'clock train back to Chicago.[37]

Jessie returned to her father's house as if nothing had happened. Warren got a room in a hotel, Chicago's Clifton House. Newspaper accounts differ on some of the details, but that night, Jessie's parents somehow learned what had happened and confronted her. Her father was furious. For several days, he refused to let her leave the house, especially to meet her new husband.

For the next week, Jessie Lincoln was in the headlines. The *Chicago Times-Herald* got the tip and broke the story, but other

Chicago papers were quickly on the trail and "lavish" in the space devoted to the story. The *Chicago Chronicle* started its story with, "Miss Lincoln Weds, Sensational Case of Elopement in Chicago, Warren Beckwith the Man, The daughter of Robert T. Lincoln and the Mt. Pleasant youth outwit watchful parents."[38]

The *Mount Pleasant Daily News* ran stories on the elopement, the forced separation, and the final reunion on its front pages, covering the scandal nearly every day for a week. "It has been a long day since anything stirred the social sea of Mt. Pleasant to such depths as the sensational elopement and marriage last week of Warren Beckwith to Miss Jessie Lincoln...The Chicago papers have been lavish of their space in discussing it," the weekly *Mount Pleasant Journal* later reported.[39]

Jessie's timing for such scandalous publicity was particularly bad from her father's point of view. Robert Lincoln was in the middle of negotiations with Pullman Palace Car Company officials, and was about to be named the company's acting president, on the same day the elopement became public.[40] As usual, he was averse to having family matters made public. Still, he faced the reporters and gave them a statement:

> About a year ago my daughter and young Beckwith became sweethearts while she was visiting her mother's old home at Mt. Pleasant, Ia. Both Mrs. Lincoln and I objected to the young man. We broke off the attachment, separated the young people, and thought that settled it. While Miss Jessie was in Mt. Pleasant, on a recent visit, it seems the attachment was renewed, unknown to us. We still disapprove of the young man as much as we did at the outset. He is not satisfactory to us to be the husband of our daughter. He is the son of Capt. Beckwith, a good friend of Mrs. Lincoln's family at Mt. Pleasant—and the father is altogether an estimable old man. It is the son, not the father, we are opposed to...[41]

He told another reporter, "I have not seen Mr. Beckwith. I have no inclination to see him. I refuse to discuss the matter any further. My daughter will remain at home."[42] Robert Lincoln may have been nice to Warren in person, but these statements were decidedly negative, and it's a wonder that Warren later said they got along!

Indeed, for a few days, the new Mrs. Beckwith did remain in her father's house. The papers described her as a prisoner of sorts. One Chicago gossip columnist was so miffed at Robert's response that she conjured up the ghost of President Lincoln. She wrote that:

> It was a pity when Abraham Lincoln freed the colored women of the south that he did not at the same time liberate the white ones of the north. The granddaughter of the great emancipator, sitting in her fortified chamber, in all probability wishes that her grandsire had declared the enthralldom of all women at an end, so that she might choose her life mate without consent of her father...The people in the elegant set of Chicago are showing that they are a bit independent in their ideas for they are asking each other, "Who is Robert T. Lincoln that he should say he is so much better than anyone else?"[43]

The *Chicago Chronicle* reported the following state of affairs:

> Tears and sighs in the loneliness of seclusion from her husband were the sad portion of Mrs. Jessie Lincoln Beckwith all day yesterday...Almost beneath her latticed window the waters of the lake broke on the wall of artificial stone in slow cadences. A lone coal barge interrupted the gray monotony of the watery horizon and the chill November wind whistled past...Mrs. Lincoln and her newly wedded daughter remained on the upper floor all day and admitted none but the most near and intimate friends.[44]

Robert Lincoln had told reporters that both he and his wife opposed the match, but whatever opposition Jessie's mother had felt in the beginning, she began to take her daughter's side. Like any good mother, most of all she would want her daughter to be happy. While her husband met with Pullman officials, sometime on Thursday afternoon, November 11, Mrs. Lincoln took her daughter in a covered carriage to the house of one of the Beckwith relatives, where they met with Warren for several hours and planned what to do next. They all agreed he should return to Mount Pleasant and wait for a reconciliation. Mrs. Lincoln would take her daughter to New York for a few days to let things die down and to secure a trousseau. After that, the Lincolns would hold a public reception for the couple in their home.[45]

On the night of November 11, Warren arrived back in Mount Pleasant, unperturbed by all the commotion he had caused, according to the reporter who telegraphed the following story from Mount Pleasant:

> Warren Wallace Beckwith, who eloped with Miss Jessie Lincoln, returned to this city last night apparently no more concerned over the hubbub he has raised than if he had just scored a touchdown or made a forty-five yard dash. Mr. Beckwith was alone, but not at all disconsolate. That he had returned home was no indication that he had given up his bride or bowed in submission to his imperious father-in-law. He is a true athlete and when he gave his word to the captain...that he would be here Friday to practice for Monday's hard game with Monmouth his captain knew that nothing would detain him.[46]

The weekly *Mount Pleasant Journal* reported on Warren's hero status, stating that, "Everybody he met on the streets wanted to shake hands with him, and congratulations were showered upon him on account of his nerve as well as his good fortune in securing such a lovely bride."[47]

Jessie was a bit more shy about the affair. When she finally left Chicago, a reporter commented that, "Despite her affected unconcern, it was apparent that Mrs. Beckwith was embarrassed over the possibility of her discovery and the consequent attention that would be paid her. Her entrée at the depot was made with great dispatch." She wore a veil to obscure her face, and once the train was ready, she entered her drawing room quickly and shut the curtain. She had hoped to travel on Saturday, but when she learned she could not secure a private room, she postponed the trip for a day.[48]

On Sunday evening, November 14, Warren met his bride in Aurora, Illinois, and brought her triumphantly back to Mount

Pleasant. Apparently, Jessie and her mother did not make the trip to New York after all. A correspondent for the *New York World* wrote that, although it was almost midnight when their train arrived,

> Beckwith's parents, sisters, cousins and half the town were on hand to welcome the homecoming bride. Only at the urgent plea of the bridegroom the Wesleyan college students refrained from tin horns, brass bands and fireworks. Beckwith and his wife were quickly surrounded on the platform by the great throng, and under the lead of the students three hearty cheers were given for the bride...the new Mrs. Beckwith bowed her acknowledgments right and left.[49]

Eastern urban attitudes about the supposed uncivilized rural Midwest were apparent in the New York City reporter's assurance to readers that, by leaving Chicago for Iowa, Jessie Lincoln Beckwith "will not go into a wilderness, by any means. Mt. Pleasant is a pretty little college town, and its society is as pleasant as its name."[50]

A few nights later, the new Mrs. Warren Wallace Beckwith, Jr., watched proudly as her husband battled for glory on the school's football field. She may have watched Monday night's game against Monmouth, and she also was there on Wednesday, watching Warren help Iowa Wesleyan defeat the Keokuk Medics 48-0.[51] On Thursday, November 18, the *Mount Pleasant Journal* reported that:

> The general sentiment in Mt. Pleasant is that the young people are not to be blamed for their runaway marriage. Mrs. Beckwith certainly has lost none of the high esteem in which she has always been held, and her husband plays as good a foot ball game as he ever did in his days of single blessedness. The *Journal* joins with others in extending congratulations, and hopes that their pathway will ever be strewn with roses.[52]

But the marriage wasn't as happy as that.

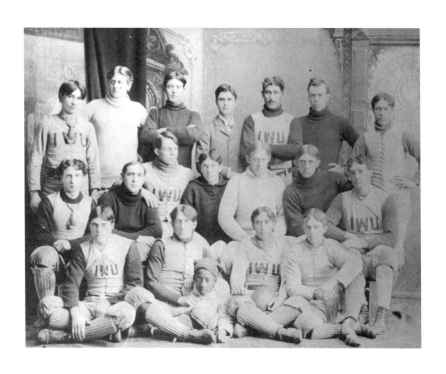

PLATE 18 Iowa Wesleyan College football team 1896-97.
Warren Beckwith is in the back row, far right.

PLATE 19 Robert Todd Lincoln with his baby granddaughter,
Mary Lincoln (Peggy) Beckwith, 1899.

PLATE 20 Formal baby portrait of Peggy Beckwith, circa 1900.

World of Women

A GRANDDAUGHTER OF LINCOLN: A previously unpublished portrait of the late Mrs. Jessie Lincoln Randolph, daughter of Robert Todd Lincoln, with her daughter, Mary Beckwith, who resides in Manchester, Vt. Jessie died in 1948. This photograf is owned by her first husband, Warren Wallace Beckwith of La Jolla, Cal.

PLATE 21 Jessie Lincoln Beckwith and her daughter Peggy, photographed circa 1901.

PLATE 22 Peggy Beckwith with one of her ponies, circa 1905.

PLATES 23 AND 24 Peggy Beckwith and her cousin, Linc Isham, with two
playmates, sailing their toy boats in Hildene's reflecting pool.
Beckwith is second from left in top photo and at far right in bottom photo.
Linc is far right at top and second from left at bottom.

PLATE 25 Peggy Beckwith and her brother Bud with the pony cart
they rode around the Hildene property, circa 1907.

PLATE 26 Peggy Beckwith with one of her many canine friends.

PLATE 27 Jessie Lincoln Beckwith with her children
Peggy and Bud, circa 1912.

PLATE 28 Peggy Beckwith and her two hunting dogs.

PLATE 29 Peggy Beckwith in one of her first cars.

PLATE 30 Bud and Peggy Beckwith as young adults.

PLATE 31   Peggy Beckwith in her fur-lined pilot's jacket.

PLATE 32 Ethan Allen IV and Peggy Beckwith
on dedication day for the Ethan Allen Highway in Vermont,
September 20, 1930.

PLATE 33 Peggy Beckwith's house at Bullhead Pond, built in the 1930s.

PLATE 34 Bud and Peggy Beckwith at the christening of the
U.S.S. Abraham Lincoln submarine, Portsmouth Naval Shipyard, May 14,
1960. By this time, Bud was generally known as Bob.

PLATE 35 "In the name of the United States of America,
I christen thee Abraham Lincoln," Peggy Beckwith said as she
struck the bow with a champagne bottle.

CHAPTER TWELVE:

"Who Has a Better Right?"

Robert Todd Lincoln's Hildene, Manchester, Vermont, circa 1907

Nine months and twelve days after Warren Beckwith and Jessie Lincoln eloped, on August 22, 1898, the fourth Mary Lincoln was born. Although she was officially named Mary Lincoln Beckwith, she was known as "Peg" or "Peggy." The earliest known photographic portrait of her [PLATE 20] was taken in Mount Pleasant, Iowa, probably in 1900 or 1901. It shows a tiny tot all bundled up in winter garb, standing in front of an ornate curlicue wicker chair.[1] Peggy looks to be one or two. She stands chin up, her face expectant, as if she's trying hard to please, despite the constricting mass of fur engulfing her tiny head and neck. Her hands are hidden in a matching muff of long white fur. She does not look comfortable in her miniature princess outfit. Years later, a friend who knew her well would comment that Peggy "should've been a man."[2]

Peggy and her brother, Robert Todd Lincoln Beckwith, were born into an affluent home, but apparently not a happy one. The dynamics of the marriage weren't recorded, except for a few comments published later on, but their parents' celebrated romance did not withstand the test of time or the practicalities of everyday life. Perhaps Robert Lincoln had been right, after all. Warren and Jessie didn't spend much time together, as Warren was often away for periods of time, working for the railroad, or cattle ranching in Oklahoma and western Iowa, or serving in the army during the Spanish-American

War. Jessie gave birth to two more children after Peggy, a stillborn infant in 1901, and Robert Todd Lincoln Beckwith, called "Bud" or "Bob," born July 19, 1904. Jessie and the children stayed with her parents for extended periods of time, in Mount Pleasant, in Chicago, and after 1911 in Washington, D.C.[3] Beginning in 1905, when the construction of Robert Todd Lincoln's summer home, Hildene, was complete, Jessie and the children spent summers in Vermont.

While Jessie's father had voiced the strongest opposition at the outset of the marriage, Jessie's mother was blamed for helping to end it.

"Mrs. Lincoln was always interfering in our marriage," Warren Beckwith later told a *Chicago Tribune* interviewer. "She kept taking Jessie and our children away from me. Mrs. Lincoln said she was lonely since the death of her son..." In 1906, Mary Harlan Lincoln wanted to take Jessie and the children to London. Warren objected, saying he would divorce Jessie if she went. Maybe Jessie didn't believe him; maybe she didn't care. In either case, she went, and he carried through on his threat.[4]

"I said I was going to get a divorce. Mrs. Lincoln said I couldn't get one, but I showed her. I charged Jessie with desertion and got the uncontested divorce in 1907 in Mount Pleasant. I didn't ask for custody of the children because they were with Jessie, and she and her family were much better able to support them than I was."[5] The divorce was final on February 12, the anniversary of Abraham Lincoln's birthday.[6]

Warren never saw his children again, although friends sent him pictures. In 1917, while serving in World War I as a field artillery captain, he was passing through Washington, D.C., and he called Jessie, asking to see their children. By then, Peggy was 19 and Bud was 13. "She said there was no point to it, to let the past be, and that was the end of that," Warren said. He did include his two Lincoln-Beckwith children in his will, along with their two stepbrothers from a subsequent marriage. Later in life, Peggy kept a book of Beckwith family history and made notes in the margin, showing that she was still interested in the father she hadn't seen since she was eight.[7]

A later photograph of Peggy Beckwith, taken around 1905, shows a marked difference from her classic Victorian baby portrait. In this snapshot, she looks comfortable and confident. She is wearing a romper playsuit (back then, some called them "gymnasium suits"[8]), and she squarely faces the camera, proudly presenting her pony. Her bare legs are sturdy, ready to run around the field in which the picture was taken. She smiles at the camera. She seems to know who she is and to not be shy about it. She looks like a little girl who could smile and talk her way out of any mischief—and knows it. This picture was probably taken at Hildene, the summer estate in Manchester, Vermont [PLATE 22].[9]

Robert was at the height of his career when he built Hildene. He was president of the Pullman Palace Car Company, and as one of the nation's leading businessmen, people called him a "captain of industry."[10] He had power, influence and money, but his happiest days were those spent quietly at Hildene. In November 1912, he told a friend in a letter, "We are all very well and happy up here in the mountains and all dread being driven away by the cold winter to come."[11] In 1911, he had resigned as president of Pullman (though he remained as chairman of the board until early 1922). He also sold his Chicago home and moved his official residence to Washington, D.C., in 1911. From then on, until his death in 1926, he, Mrs. Lincoln, Jessie, and the children came up to Hildene every summer, arriving early enough in May to watch spring green creep up the mountains, and staying until after the leaves blazed into color and fell away in the fall.[12]

If the legend is true, then a cow in Chicago helped bring the Lincolns back to Vermont, 40 years after Mary Todd Lincoln's first visit to Manchester and the Equinox House during the Civil War. Legend says that Mrs. Patrick O'Leary's cow knocked over a lantern on the fateful Sunday evening of October 8, 1871, and while this has never been proven true, the Great Chicago Fire did indeed start that night in the cowbarn behind Mr. and Mrs. O'Leary's house.

Ironically, the O'Leary home was spared, but the great conflagration raged until early Tuesday morning, and in the process it took the lives of 600 Chicagoans, left 90,000 homeless, and caused $200 million in property damage.[13] In the process, it destroyed the law offices of Edward Swift Isham and of Robert Todd Lincoln, and as they searched for new offices, they also found each other.[14]

Lincoln's relationship with his previous law partner, Charles T. Scammon, had been troubled almost from the beginning, the result of what Robert called Scammon's "succession of sprees." Scammon was the son of Jonathan Young Scammon, head of the Chicago firm that had taken Robert in to study law in 1865 or 1866. Robert Lincoln quickly wanted to leave this partnership with Charles Scammon, whom he saw as "utterly worthless." He told his fatherly friend Judge David Davis that, "I cannot tell to what extent his debauches damage me personally." Sometime in 1867, he apparently began practicing on his own for a few years. In 1872, the year after the fire, he formed a practice with Isham. The two were almost neighbors, both living on Wabash Avenue in Chicago, so it is not surprising that they would get together. Lincoln looked up to Isham, who was a more experienced lawyer. They got along well together, and they prospered.[15]

Isham was a native of Bennington, Vermont. He had a summer home in Manchester, a place he called "Ormsby Hill,"[16] and from 1872 until the turn of the century, Robert Lincoln was a frequent visitor there, both as Isham's partner and as his friend.[17] But when Robert told his partner he would like to buy some land from him and be his neighbor in Vermont, Isham wouldn't sell. "His partner thought that was too close," explained Mary Porter, one of Peggy Beckwith's friends.[18]

After Isham died in 1903, Lincoln bought several parcels of land, about 500 acres in all, including some of the Isham land and the 400-acre Walker farm, next to the Ormsby Hill property. There, he built his own summer retreat, calling it "Hildene," combining two words meaning hill and valley, because the property had both features. The site Robert chose for the house was on a bluff overlooking the meandering stream of the Battenkill. The house site was on a high meadow where the Walkers used to graze their cows.[19]

Lincoln hired Shepley, Rutan & Coolidge, an architectural firm from Boston, to design the house, and Boston builder Ira Hersey oversaw construction.[20] Perched halfway to heaven, Hildene still commands a spectacular view of both the valley and the surrounding mountains.

Robert Lincoln chose "the ledges," as the house site was called,[21] because of the beautiful view, but the rocky slope prevented bringing in building materials via the nearest road, which ran below the cliff along the Battenkill. The next closest road was a mile in the opposite direction, on the other side of a thick woods. Lincoln wanted to build a road through those woods, and to do so he would need to purchase a piece of land owned by Henry O'Hare, a farmer and veteran whose leg had been wounded in the Civil War. Lincoln's personal secretary, Freddy Towers, approached O'Hare about buying the land, but O'Hare gruffly replied, "I'll be damned if I'll sell my land to anyone."[22]

Robert Lincoln was not so easily dissuaded, according to Manchester resident Helen Pearson, who recounted the story. The next time, Robert Lincoln went to see Mr. O'Hare in person. When he introduced himself to the farmer, O'Hare was so impressed to be shaking the hand of the President's son that he abruptly changed his tune, generously offering, "You can have my whole meadow."[23]

Shepley, Rutan & Coolidge, who had designed the Chicago Public Library and the Art Institute of Chicago, drew up plans for a 24-room estate in the Georgian Revival style. Ground was broken in 1904, and over the next year, artisans and construction experts were imported from New York and Boston to oversee various stages of the project. Local residents provided labor and materials, including the marble used on some exterior details, which was brought to Manchester Village on special railroad flatcars from nearby Dorset quarry. Helen Pearson, who later did work for Hildene, remembered watching Hildene's construction. "It was such a mansion in comparison to so many of the other houses in town that it really was quite a thing to go out and see it," she said.[24]

The people of Manchester were proud to be associated with the Lincolns, and almost universally, there was mutual respect. The Lincolns took a genuine interest in their community, and the historical record includes testaments to the Lincolns' many kind acts and generosities, everything from giving Easter candy and flowers to paying for college educations and cars.

Robert Lincoln was naturally generous to the community's children. He had a regular round of appointments when he was in town, and because of his punctual ways, the children of Manchester Center could mark to the minute when he would arrive at Factory Point Bank to do business each morning. At 9 o'clock sharp, they would gather in front of the bank to watch his black carriage pull up.[25]

Theresa Zullo, one of those children, later recalled that Mr. Lincoln was always dressed in a dark suit and wore a hat. On the rare occasions that Mrs. Lincoln accompanied him, the children remembered her wearing a long black coat and a large black hat. The Lincolns' carriage driver had a very serious look about him. He never said hello to the children, instead concentrating all of his attention on helping Mr. Lincoln out of the carriage. But Mr. Lincoln was always nice to the children, even though they made a regular nuisance of themselves, always showing up and asking for his autograph. Theresa Zullo was nine or ten at the time. She recalled that:

> We must've been a perfect nuisance, because every morning we'd be there, and we'd ask that poor man for his autograph every time, and I think he gave us like ten cents or a nickel, I know he used to give us something...He always stopped. He never seemed to be annoyed at the fact that we were there...I never remember him saying once, 'What are you bothering me for, why are you bothering me every day?'[26]

The children knew he was Abraham Lincoln's son. "He had a reputation in town, he was a very important character!" Zullo said. Did the children save their nickels and dimes forever, as special mementos of this famous historical figure? No. They took them to the nearest candy store and spent them!

The grounds around the Hildene estate were designed by Frederick Todd, an apprentice of Frederick Olmsted, who is credited as the father of American landscape architecture and was designer of New York City's Central Park. The grounds at Hildene included several outbuildings, among them a carriage barn, a pony barn, a workshop, a potting shed and a greenhouse. A grape arbor was attached to the potting shed, and the terraced area under the arbor led to a brick pathway, which led to several small planting beds. The vegetables, herbs, and flowers grown in these kitchen and cutting gardens supplied the household with various edibles and fresh-cut flowers.[27]

In 1907, Jessie Lincoln Beckwith designed the formal gardens behind the house as a present to her mother. Inspired by the elegant stained glass windows in Europe's Gothic cathedrals, she imitated that look by arranging "panes" of colored flowers and using privet hedge for the "leading."[28]

The gardener who tended this profusion of color was especially proud of the peonies and roses, and he treated them protectively. The cutting garden by the potting shed had fresh flowers meant for picking, but one day, little Peggy went into the formal garden and picked some of the gardener's prized roses. When he discovered her transgression, the gardener angrily went to his employer to complain. He told Mr. Lincoln that he "didn't relish the idea of anyone invading his garden."

Robert Lincoln listened thoughtfully to the complaint, good lawyer and diplomat that he was. He hesitated, then he replied. "She's been picking your flowers?" he asked.

"Yes," the gardener nodded.

"Well, I don't know who has a better right."[29]

Growing up wealthy, Peggy was used to having what she wanted. Grandpa Lincoln had been indulged as a child, and he happily passed this habit on to his children and his grandchildren. Each year, the grandchildren were given extravagant birthday parties.[30] At Hildene, they had their own miniature two-room playhouse, complete with a fireplace, a tiny wood cookstove, and a porch covered with rose trellises. Near the playhouse, there was a brick gazebo and a shallow concrete pond where the children could race their toy boats [PLATES 23 AND 24].[31]

In 1907, Grandpa Lincoln bought Peggy a pony from Dr. S. B. Elliot, of Bedford, Massachusetts, as a present for her ninth birthday. Perhaps the pony was not what he expected, because a few weeks later, he wrote a polite note back to the doctor, instructing him to "send Pansy and I will probably return Auricula. [It] is not the color Mrs. Beckwith would like for her little girl." But Peggy apparently wouldn't give the pony up once it arrived, for shortly thereafter, Robert Lincoln wrote to the doctor again, reporting that he would keep Auricula after all.[32]

This was the year Peggy's parents were divorced, in 1907. Because Peggy's father was often absent during her first years, and because she never saw him after the divorce, Grandpa Lincoln served as a father figure for Peggy. She did not record her impressions of him, but one of her closest friends, Mary Porter (great-niece of Robert's law partner), remembered how Mr. Lincoln used to give her fatherly advice. In particular, she remembered him telling her to always carry a little notebook so she could record her thoughts. He said he had one in his pocket at all times. Since she often saw him at the local Ekwanok golf course, he may also have given her advice for her game.[33]

Peggy shared her grandfather's love of golf, and she was pretty good at it. In 1925, Robert Lincoln bought Peggy a lifetime membership at the Equinox Links golf course, owned by the Equinox House and opened in 1927. Peggy played in women's state golf tournaments for several years. In 1930, she scored 101, shooting from the men's tees. "There were no women's tees...it was very tough," according to Virginia Pierce Smith, a charter member of the Vermont Women's Golf Association.[34] But Peggy gave up the tournaments after just a few years because the media wouldn't leave her alone.

Peggy certainly loved and respected her grandfather, but she rejected the conventions of his era, including its expectations for female manners. Jessie still honored many of these conventions, at least in manner and appearance. She sent her daughter to the exclusive Miss Madeira's school in Washington. By the early 1930s, Jessie owned her own home in the Georgetown section of Washington, down the block from her mother, and she helped redecorate some of the homes in the neighborhood. She had a flair for the arts and interior decorating. Peggy's friend "Beanie" Graham said Jessie was "such a true Southern lady who would love entertaining," but she added that, "I'm sure Peg must've been a little trialed at times. She didn't like it at all, wouldn't dress for that sort of thing...Up here in Vermont, she didn't have to."[35]

Growing up at Hildene and in Washington, D.C., Peggy could see that there were two worlds to choose from. Her family connections allowed her access to the elite social life of Manchester's summer residents and to high society in Washington, but Peggy didn't want that lifestyle. A story about the Lincoln descendants, written in 1931, included the following comment:

> Mary Lincoln Beckwith, Lincoln's great-granddaughter, certainly could have from Washington society anything she might ask, if she but lifted her finger. But quite to the contrary, she never has made the slightest move in the direction of the life of a social butterfly. Other wealthy girls have their debuts and are introduced to society. Not Mary Beckwith.[36]

According to Mary Porter, the Lincolns enjoyed a relaxed version of the life of luxury in Vermont. Mary Porter and her parents came to Manchester from Chicago every summer. Early on, they stayed at the Equinox, but around 1920, they built a home in the village, across the street from Mark Skinner Library. Mary Porter and Peggy first became acquainted around 1913, when Peggy was fifteen, and Mary was twelve or so.

During summer afternoons, they played golf together at the Ekwanok Country Club, where Mary's father and Peggy's grandfather were members. The two girls also hiked through the woods at Hildene, studying the animals and flowers. Sometimes they went canoeing and fishing in the Battenkill or at Equinox Pond, bringing home their catches for the servants to clean for supper.[37]

The Lincolns occasionally invited Mary Porter over for lunch or dinner at Hildene. She recalled that the meal was served in courses, first soup, then meat and vegetables, then salad, and finally dessert. Servants waited on them at the table. "I wouldn't call it formal," she said. "We didn't call it formal then. This was ordinary!"[38]

Helen Pearson, who had watched the construction of Hildene, later made linens for Mary Harlan Lincoln, and she sometimes went to Hildene for lunch and to collect instructions. "Their living was never in an extravagant way. Their meals were simple, whole-some, and never any display of anything that made you feel you weren't just in the same social strata they were in. They sat to eat together, with the kids there too...Everything at their table was very gracious, and served family style. If you wanted second portions, you got second portions," she recalled.[39]

Occasionally, the Lincolns hosted formal dinner parties at Hildene, but they did not go to social occasions at the Equinox, though Robert Lincoln would visit there sometimes after his daily round of golf. Life at the Equinox was definitely more formal. "You never went to the Equinox without your white flannels and a blue jacket," recalled Bruce Smart, whose father was the local Congregational minister in those years. Both he and Mary Porter could remember dances at the Equinox, held several times a week with four-piece ensembles playing the music. Other Manchester summer residents went to these affairs, but not the Lincolns.[40]

Peggy Beckwith was in her teens and twenties during this peri-od, and if she had wanted to go to the Equinox to look for a well-connected husband, she certainly could have. But party clothes and formal manners did not suit Peggy. She preferred the informal life she found at Hildene.

Vermonters have a reputation for being stubborn and inde-pendent, and they certainly have their share of strong opinions and prejudices, as anyone who has been to a town meeting will attest. Perhaps the rural nature of the state and the space between people and houses allows for a greater spirit of tolerance. Many people describe Peggy Beckwith as "quite a character," but in Manchester, that's considered a kind of compliment. She enjoyed the same spir-it of tolerance that was extended to Vermonters who were even more obviously eccentric than she.

Peggy didn't seem all that strange in the rural Vermont of the 1940s where, as essayist Van Wyck Brooks once wrote, "One seemed to encounter simpletons, and worse, idiots and homeless lunatics, freely walking about."[41] Many Vermont towns have their local home-town eccentrics, some of whom are carefully watched over by their neighbors. Perhaps this is just the nature of small-town living.

As a girl, Peggy may have seen one of Manchester's most eccentric residents, Icy Palmer, walking the streets. Icy lived in Manchester until 1909, when she was well into her 80s. Palmer was a Tuscarora Indian. No one is sure how she got to Manchester, but some say her parents were transients, that she had been born a few miles from the village in a sugarhouse, and that her parents gave her to a local family when she was a few weeks old. Two local families, the G.S. Purdys and the W.P. Blacks, raised her. Icy was one of Manchester's "darlings." As an adult, she lived in a house built for her by the Ladies Benevolent Society of the Congregational Church. Local benefactors provided a small income, which she supplemented by collecting butternuts in the fall and mixing them with maple sugar to sell. Every day, whatever the weather, Icy was out walking, often without a coat. Toward night, she would return home with a bundle of firewood. When she met someone on the street, she turned her back and bowed her head until they passed.[42]

Joe Sherman, a writer who grew up in Quechee, Vermont, during World War II, remembered his town's tolerance of eccentric characters as well. In his book of Vermont history, *Fast Lane on a Dirt Road,* he remarked on the state's "long tradition of tolerance, at least if you were white or able to pay someone like my sisters to look after you. The rich who were odd seemed to command a special respect...The message seemed to be: be weird, if you could afford it."[43]

Peggy wasn't weird, just strong-minded and independent in an era when that was considered eccentric. But she could certainly have afforded to be. She lived on a trust fund her whole life, set up by her grandparents' wills. This, however, didn't keep her from working hard on her farm. She proudly told a reporter in 1962 that her 20-head dairy farm was "in danger of running out of the red," based on her careful management, "but don't tell the tax collectors about it."[44]

Alice Colonna, an Isham descendant who was a distant cousin of Peggy's and knew her for years, said Peggy was "well-disciplined and totally honest. She was impulsive in ways that never got anybody into difficulties." Examples include trading cars on a whim, taking flying lessons on a moment's notice, and taking in stray raccoons. People sometimes ask why she never married. Some say she preferred the 'company' of women, but no one has offered to prove that. Alice said, "I never had the slightest evidence of her being interested sexually in a man or a woman. Problems in the family (mother and brother both having three marriages) geared her, in my opinion, to plunge into other sublimated interests."[45] Peggy didn't need the kind of financial security many women sought through marriage. And in a traditional marriage, she would have been expected to play second fiddle. Peggy wouldn't have liked that. She liked being in charge of her own life.

In 1888, ten years before Peggy's birth, at the International Council of Women, 72-year-old suffragette Elizabeth Cady Stanton predicted how it would be for the next generation of women. She said, "The younger women are starting with great advantages over us. They have the results of our experience; they have superior opportunities for education; they will find a more enlightened public sentiment for discussion; they will have more courage to take the rights which belong to them...Thus far women have been the mere echoes of men...The true woman is as yet a dream of the future."[46]

In the first two decades of the twentieth century, while Peggy was growing up, women in Europe and America were still fighting for the right to vote. They were also asserting that women should be paid the same as men for equal work, that they should be admitted to medical and law schools, and that they should be allowed to enter a broad range of careers. Young women known as flappers were beginning to assert all kinds of new rights and were acting out of a new sense of independence. Four days after Peggy's 22nd birthday, on August 26, 1920, the Nineteenth Amendment finally won approval from enough states, and women got the right to vote.

Peggy was not active politically, but she dressed and behaved like she wanted to, despite what people might think. She was more at home in a barnyard than in a ballroom, and that attitude won her support in Manchester. "Miss Beckwith...is no 'grande dame,' nor is she interested in 'society.' Genuinely loved and respected by the farm and country folk who are her neighbors and friends, she's more at home, they say, sitting in their kitchens talking about the latest methods in farming," explained local writer Nancy Otis, adding that one acquaintance had said, "She probably loves the lack of artificiality she finds there."[47]

Peggy's friend Beanie Graham said that Manchester gave Peggy a place "to be left alone more or less and be herself...She was far ahead of her time. She found herself, which all the young people are trying so desperately to do...Well, Peg was fortunate. She found herself, and she was happy here."[48]

CHAPTER THIRTEEN:

Tractors and Fast Cars

Hildene's dairy barn, after 1956, daily at 5:20 p.m.

In the mid 1950s, the daily routine for Vermont's dairy farmers hadn't changed that much since Mary Todd Lincoln's first visit to Vermont, nearly a century before. Of course, by 1956, most farms had electricity and plumbing, and most farmers used tractors instead of horsepower, but the types of chores and the turns of the seasons were still just the same. Farmers still got up at dawn to do the milking and milked again before supper. In the spring, there were maple trees to tap; in early summer there were seeds to plant; in midsummer, there was hay to cut; and in the fall, corn and oats to be harvested.

Joe Sherman's Vermont history, *Fast Lane on a Dirt Road,* describes the family farm in the mid 1940s as "a Vermont institution." At the time, there were more than 24,000 of these small farms scattered throughout the mountains and valleys of the state. The typical farm had 15 to 20 cows, 150 rocky acres, a sugarbush for tapping maple trees, a woodlot for firewood and building materials, a two-story farmhouse with dirt floors, some chickens in the kitchen, an outhouse, and a muddy barnyard.[1]

For many young people, the family farm seemed like a trap, poor and dirty, a perpetual hard existence. By 1964, the number of family farms in Vermont was down to about 9,200, and by 1970 the number had dwindled to 6,800.[2] Many of the soldiers who returned from World War II had seen a larger world, and they wanted nothing more than to get out of Vermont as fast as possible. As Sherman wrote:

> They wanted possibilities and newness, not the same old jobs and dirt roads and low standard of living most Vermonters had accepted—it seemed like forever—as their inheritance and destiny...Vermont was a losing hand in cards, the wrong card in Bingo...Life lay out there in Connecticut, Boston, New York, Michigan, Wisconsin, points west. Vermont remained a great place to be from, a scenic backwater...But as far as challenging a young adult who wanted to get ahead, it was nowhere.[3]

Peggy countered that trend. She had come from that larger world, and she was disillusioned by it. She didn't need to get ahead—she had a trust fund to live on. And everything she loved was in Vermont: open spaces, privacy, nature, an unpretentious lifestyle, friends and animals. She could have chosen to live like her mother and grandparents, spending the warmer months in Vermont and the winters in D.C., but she chose Vermont as her year-round residence. For her, farming was a welcome choice, not a dead end.

She especially loved the yearly ritual of making maple syrup. Around town meeting time, in early March, or just before that if the winter was mild, she tapped a dozen or so maple trees and hung up her buckets.[4] Sap collecting was an excuse to get out of the house when the weather was starting to turn bearable again. It was an affirmation of spring, something to do until the weather got warmer.

Early on, her operation was small, and she used an old iron kettle, Indian style, to boil the sap over an open fire. She and Mary Porter had a wonderful time, stirring the boiling sap and talking all the while. With the open fire method, smoke got into the syrup and affected the taste. Ken Hill, her farm supervisor, recalled:

> [The syrup] was black and strong when she got done, but it was something to do and she did some every year...Peg liked to get around in the spring and play around with her sugaring. She and Mary Porter'd get together and go down

and sit in the woods in the sunshine and boil sap and have a good time. She got a pipeline and ran the sap down the farm road to the kettle...[5]

In time, she wanted a bigger operation. First, she had a two- by four-foot evaporator; then she sold it and bought a larger one. She bought more buckets, some plastic tubing, and a bigger storage tank.[6] She scribbled notes on scraps of paper, figuring how much syrup she could make and how much she could spare for each person on her list. During World War II, with sugar being rationed, her syrup was in high demand. At one point she was producing dozens of gallons.[7]

Suddenly one day, in the midst of a sugaring season in the early 1950s, she got tired of the whole thing and dumped out the contents of the storage tank, thirty barrels worth of sap, onto the ground. "That was the end of her big operation; she went back to her old iron kettle," Hill said.[8]

By choosing to be a farmer, Peggy Beckwith brought her family back full circle to her great-grandfather's roots. Abraham Lincoln had been embarrassed by his humble beginnings, but Peggy may have been a bit embarrassed by her unearned wealth. Through farming, she could earn her own way. Her farm was more elaborate and comfortable than Abraham Lincoln's boyhood home, but both farms had fields to plow, livestock to feed, fences to mend, and crops to harvest. She farmed because she liked the tradition and the connection to nature, because it made her proud to fill her table with the fruits of her own labor, and because she wanted to be a good steward of the land her grandfather had provided. It also connected her to a more common human experience and to her neighbors in Vermont.

Like the Lincoln legacy itself, inheriting Hildene had been a mixed blessing for her. She loved Hildene—it was the site of many happy childhood memories—but she already owned another house across town, much more rustic in style, and she would have preferred to live there. Peggy bought her place at Bullhead Pond, on the Manchester-East Dorset town line, in April 1932. The property included about 60 acres and a six-acre pond. She had a South

Dorset barn dismantled and the beams and timbers were used to build her house there [PLATE 33]. She later organized the Bullhead Pond Foundation in order to allow Scouts, 4-H clubs, school groups, science classes and nature groups to use the property. 4-H horse shows were held there, and the Scouts had overnight camping trips. In 1938, Peggy inherited Hildene, and about ten years after that, she sold Bullhead Pond to her friend, Clara May Hemenway. In 1961, she bought it back, and in 1965, she conveyed the property to the Bullhead Pond Foundation, with stipulations that the property be kept as a single unit, in its wild state, and be used as an educational facility. The property was eventually transferred from the foundation to the Vermont Fish and Game Department.[9]

Since Hildene needed someone to manage it, upon inheriting the estate, she moved in. She did this for the sake of the family. She provided a home for her mother there, and she re-developed the farm that first had been established by her grandfather. Robert Lincoln had set the standard. He kept the farm operation going after buying out the Walkers, raising beef cattle, keeping a dairy herd for milk and butter, and chickens for eggs.[10] He hired men to do the physical labor, as Peggy later did, but unlike her grandfather, Peggy was willing to pitch in and get her hands dirty. "She was often in the barns shoveling manure," her friend Clara May Hemenway said. Dorothy Wilcox, whose family had several connections with the Lincolns, agreed. "She was not just a gentle lady farmer. She was very evident on the farm," she said.[11]

Peggy was willing to work hard, but she sometimes lacked the patience to carry through. She got bored easily. In any case, when she did experiment, her risk-taking was less dangerous financially than it would have been for most farmers, because she had money to fall back on. And if she didn't feel like working one day, she could count on the hired hands to do her share. Still, she didn't object to hard labor or to the drudgery of farm chores. This was true even before she owned the farm.

Peggy used her grandfather's farm to make a contribution to the war effort in the final year of World War I. She took a short, intensive agricultural course at Cornell, and then organized a group of young women farmers to help produce food. As was true during other wars, when men went off to fight, women stepped into leadership roles on family farms and other businesses and proved themselves quite capable. A news story published in 1930 describes Peggy in similar terms:

> Miss Beckwith...is known to be a level-headed woman of great ability and plenty of common sense. Vermont knows her as an able farmer. The place at Manchester, a dozen years ago, did its part in helping out the nation's food supply...Miss Beckwith did her bit by taking a short but intensive agricultural course at Cornell...On her return to Manchester, she found only eight men left to cut the hay on the 800-acre farm. She pitched in and did the work of a half a dozen ordinary men herself. Incidentally, the rest of the help lifted their feet, and there was no motion lost. The hay was all saved.[12]

When she inherited Hildene, she began rebuilding the farm. Her grandmother had gotten rid of the livestock, so Peggy started with a few chickens and a couple of cows. At first, most of the produce from the farm went to feed the household and her staff. Around 1941, she bought a herd of Black Angus beef, which she planned to breed and raise for meat.

During World War II, Peggy had her own victory garden. "She raised all her own vegetables and canned a lot," Hill said. "She was very patriotic and war-minded, trying to conserve all she could. In fact, she was that way right up 'til the day she died."[13] Peggy also helped to train first aid workers during World War II.[14]

In 1947, Peggy interviewed Ken Hill for the job of farm manager. Ken had worked on dairy farms before. Peggy met him in her front hall at Hildene, and they talked for fifteen or twenty minutes about his experience, which included agricultural classes. "That all sounded good to her, she didn't want any references," Hill said.[15]

Ken recalled that he and his wife, Lois, went with Peggy to the Eastern States Exhibition in Springfield, Massachusetts. They took four head of cattle to the show. Peggy added sides to a flatbed truck to make it into a trailer, and they pulled it along behind an old Jeep. Ken drove, and he said it was a scary trip, pulling that trailer up and down and over the hills. Going downhill, the trailer's weight pushed them faster. Going up, the Jeep struggled more and more slowly to pull the weight. Halfway up one steep hill, the vehicle lost power. Ken shifted into a lower gear, and they began to move again.[16]

They also went to cattle auctions around Northampton, Massachusetts. "I don't remember her buying, but it was fun to go and see the auctions and the prices," Hill said. Asked if Peggy knew much about raising cattle, Hill laughed and said, "Well, she thought she did. She had studied a certain amount, so she probably knew a lot more than a lot of people did."[17]

Peggy was not patient if a farm experiment turned sour. She didn't want to be in a position to be criticized, and she didn't wait to see if things would improve without intervention. The story of the "throwback" cattle illustrates this trait. Peggy's cattle were polled Herefords, bred specifically to be without horns. Around 1954, she sold eight or ten young cattle to a man in New York. Later, the man wrote to her to say one of the calves had developed horns. "With horns, it was not worth anything," Hill said.[18]

Even though it was a fluke, Peggy was quite upset. "She got worried more would do that...She could get really worked up with something like that. But it's just one of those things. It may go on another thousand before it happens again," Hill said. Peggy couldn't be convinced, and there was no reasoning with her. She felt so bad about the throwback that she offered the man his money back, not just for that one calf, but "for the whole blooming bunch of them. And he kept the cattle," Hill said. Soon after that, she sold the herd, around 65 head. "She got sick of it, she'd had her fun."[19]

For a few years, the workload was a lot lighter for Ken, just a couple of milk cows, some hens, and haying to do. Then in 1956, Peggy came up to him one day and asked, "How'd you like to milk cows for a change?"

What could he say? It meant more work for him, but she was the boss, and if she wanted him to milk cows, well then, he'd milk cows. For Peggy, it was fun, a chance to try something new. She studied up on the latest technology, installed a mechanized pipeline to carry milk through the barn, and bought a dozen cows from a farmer in Brattleboro, some Holsteins and some mixed Jersey-Guernseys.

Hildene began shipping raw milk to the Wilcox dairy down the road, which had its own processing and bottling plant.

For the first year or two, Peggy was very active in the dairy. At haying time, she liked to drive the tractor with the baler behind, and she helped out in other ways too. After a while, her interest tapered off, but she still came around often to supervise. "You never knew when she was going to pop in on you," Hill said.

She expected the milking to be done on a strict schedule—her schedule. Most farmers of that era started milking around 5 p.m., so if they had a big herd, they wouldn't be in the barn all night. Not Peggy. Ken Hill recalled that, "No, we couldn't start at five o'clock. She had always milked at 20 minutes past five in her little dairy up here, so that's when it had to be, 20 minutes past five. And if she happened to pop in the barn...if she caught you starting a little bit early, she didn't hesitate to say something. We'd pass it off by saying our watches must be a little fast!"[20]

The amount of milk produced was not her top priority. She was more concerned that the cows were happy and comfortable. Bruce Smart, the man who grew up as the local Congregational minister's son, sold Peggy some dairy cows from his farm in Peru, Vermont, in the late 1950s or early 1960s. He said, "I tried to sell her cattle with good breeding that would produce milk. She was more interested in their looks and that they'd be nice pets! I asked her once, 'How's their milk production?' She said, 'Oh, I don't worry about that.'"[21]

Peggy liked new gadgets and machines. Lynn Walker, whose father, uncle and grandfather had sold Robert Lincoln their farm in 1902 or 1903, installed the brand-new Pyrex milker in Peggy's dairy barn. He also sold her farm machinery, fishing tackle, guns, and hardware. He knew that whatever Peggy bought, she was more than likely to bring it back. She'd buy a piece of equipment, then decide she didn't like it, and trade it in for something else. "She was a funny gal. She'd change her mind about every day," he said. "The bookkeeper said, 'You never charge Peg for anything.' And I said, 'No, it's easier to carry it in my head because she'll send it back tomorrow!'"[22]

Peggy was definitely a great one for changing her mind, and this affected her employees too. "She could say one thing one minute and a few minutes later, she could be completely different.

I always said she was an Indian giver. She'd give you something one day, and the next day she'd want it back. And if she wanted it back, you gave it back, too. Yea. You got used to it. But she was funny that way," Hill said.[23]

Pete Brooks, who had been fired by Peggy as a teenager for sleeping on the job (he was the gardener's helper at the time), was later invited back to do Peggy's electrical work. Brooks endured her changing moods as she vacillated about how to heat Hildene for the winter. She took the coal-burning furnace out and put an oil burner in when she thought coal prices were too high. Then she got mad at the oil man, and she wanted to switch back. This indecisiveness showed up in other ways as well. Pete said that:

> She was a nice lady, awfully set in her ways, but...you never had any problems if you did what she asked you to do. She didn't ask you, she told you. That was her way...and whether she had to change it the next day was none of your business...I'd try to save her some money on a job that I knew was ridiculous...and she'd say, 'Well, are you going to do it, or is someone else going to do it?' We never knew what she was going to do next, but she kept a lot of us busy for a lot of years, just changing her mind.[24]

Peggy was just as fickle about the automobiles she bought. Ken Hill said that during one single year in the late 1950s, she traded cars seven times. "She had a great love for cars. I think that was one of her biggest fads. She'd have several cars at a time, several different sizes," he said. Oscar Johnson, Peggy's friend and neighbor, remembered seeing her in an open Model T Roundabout. Other cars included a Corvair, a Chevy wagon, a Jeep pickup, a Dodge pickup, a Plymouth, a Saab, a Valiant, a Nash Metropolitan, a Buick wagon, and a Chevy Nova.[25]

She bought a Corvair with an automatic transmission, then immediately regretted her decision and took it back for a standard. She also took back the Chevy wagon after owning it for only a week. She wanted her old car back. This time there was a problem —it had already been sold. But Peggy wouldn't take no for an answer. She insisted the dealer get it back, and Ken said it took "some serious finagling" to get the new owner to accept a trade.[26]

Oscar recalled that the Chevy Nova had a sunroof that slid back. She ordered it from Eddington's in Bennington. Even before she went to pick it up, she had decided she didn't really want it, but she wouldn't call the dealer and cancel the order. Ken told her that the dealership wouldn't care, they'd just sell it to someone else. "She said she couldn't do that, so she took it but never drove it. She just parked it in the car barn." Eventually she sold it to David Wilson, now headmaster of Long Trail School in Dorset. "Peggy knocked about $1,000 off the price," Hill said. Wilson said it was the fastest car he ever owned![27]

Being a Lincoln did have its advantages when dealing with car salesmen. One day she went to a showroom in Troy to buy a new car, dressed as usual in her work shirt, cap, and overalls. She didn't look like she could afford the cars they were offering, so the salesmen tried to ignore her. Finally, she came over and insisted on getting some attention. One of them reluctantly followed her. When she picked out a car and offered him a check, he excused himself and quietly went to call the bank. The Factory Point Bank official who handled his inquiry replied that he better treat his customer well, because the woman standing before him could buy the whole dealership if she wanted to. The salesman hung up and quickly changed his manner.[28]

Peggy usually got what she wanted, but not always. She bought a black 1958 model Corvette at Eddington's. Soon afterward, she decided she wanted a newer model, so she traded in the black one, and an architect from Arlington bought it.

"It wasn't too much after that, Peggy decided she didn't want that new one, she wanted the old one back," Ken said. "She tried her darnedest to get that car back." Ken didn't know how much money she offered, but he thought she probably offered the architect enough to buy another new car. "He wouldn't budge. 'I like that car,' he said, 'I don't want to sell it. I wouldn't have bought it if I hadn't wanted it.' She didn't get it back. That was one time."[29]

CHAPTER FOURTEEN:

Manchester's Amelia Earhart

Curtiss Airport, Baltimore, Maryland, February 1930

Peggy Beckwith startled officials at the Curtiss Airport in Baltimore one day in late 1929 or early 1930 when she arrived dressed in knickers, heavy laced boots, a man's shirt and sweater, and an old hat, asking for a ride in one of the airplanes. She said she wanted to see what this flying business was all about.

Perhaps it was the women's air derby of August 1929 that inspired her. This eight-day race from Santa Monica, California, to Toledo, Ohio, was the first such event open exclusively to women, and it attracted a lot of attention. Twenty women started the race, and sixteen crossed the finish line; Amelia Earhart, already famous as the first woman to cross the Atlantic in an airplane, finished third. Many women came to see what these "sweethearts of the air" looked like. Earhart said the race was "the event which started concerted activity among women fliers...It captured the public interest and proved invaluable in interesting other women in aviation."[1]

Peggy Beckwith liked her first airplane ride so well that she convinced the pilot to stay in the air for three hours, and upon landing, she announced that she was ready to learn to fly by herself.

Reporters assigned to write the Lincoln's birthday stories of 1930 were fascinated to find this new angle on the descendants of Abraham Lincoln, and several articles featured Peggy's flying lessons that year. In one, she was photographed standing beside a

Gipsy Moth, with her first instructor, W. H. Hampson, in the cockpit.[2] A photograph in *The New York Times* showed Peggy in the driver's seat, with the following caption: "A great-granddaughter of Lincoln trains for a pilot's license: Miss Mary Lincoln Beckwith in the plane which she flies daily at the Washington airport in preparation for her test permit."[3] Another article had the headline, "Descendant of Lincoln Prefers Plane to Teas."[4] Yet another of these stories declared that,

> The spirit of Abraham Lincoln lives, and in his great granddaughter, Miss Mary Lincoln Beckwith, many of his outstanding characteristics continue...she now is taking up aviation, owns her own plane and is qualifying for her pilot's license...[She] is known to be a level-headed woman of great ability and plenty of common sense. Vermont knows her as an able farmer...[T]hose who have been honored with her acquaintance unite in declaring her to be one upstanding United States woman in whom the spirit of pioneering is dominant.

That paper told about her daily flying lessons and said Peggy understood the machine from propeller to rudder, could design and build a plane, and could make her own repairs.[5]

In the September 1930 issue of *Popular Aviation*, Peggy's name appeared in an article listing the recent accomplishments of early female fliers, including Amelia Earhart:

> Miss Amy Johnson has just completed a flight from London to Australia in nineteen and a half days, finishing her remarkable feat last week...She has been made commander of the British Empire for her wonderful performance, the highest award ever given to a woman in aviation. On May the 15th Miss Amelia Earhart reached Washington, Bolling Field, escorting the Women's Advertising Club from Philadelphia in her Lockheed Vega. On June the 2nd Miss Bobby Trout of Los Angeles claimed an American woman's height altitude for light airplanes. She climbed to a height of 15,200 ft...Miss Laura Ingalls, 25, of New York

City recently beat her record of 344 loops by accomplishing 966 loops in a Moth Machine in St. Louis...Miss Mary Lincoln Beckwith, granddaughter [sic] of Abraham Lincoln owns a Waco plane as well as a Moth, in which she is approaching her commercial pilot's license time in Baltimore.[6]

The report had several inaccuracies. Peggy Beckwith was Lincoln's great-granddaughter, not his granddaughter. She never flew commercially, although another report said she was planning an aviation career. She never had a pilot's license as far as the Federal Aviation Administration can tell. Their only record is an application for a student permit dated April 3, 1931, and by that time, Peggy had been flying for over a year.[7]

Peggy also took lessons from Lee Bowman at the airport in Springfield, Vermont. While flying lessons weren't regulated in 1930, every pilot needed to learn certain basics. After taking lessons and building up enough flight time, a student pilot who wanted a license had to take both written and flying tests with an examiner from the U.S. Department of Commerce. The test would ask about the plane's instruments and parts, navigation, meteorology, maneuvers, takeoffs and landings. In her flying memoir, *The Fun of It*, Amelia Earhart wrote that she believed it was a good idea for beginning pilots to also learn a few stunts, like slips, stalls and spins, so they could learn to control a plane in any situation that might arise.[8]

The *Newark Star-Eagle* reported in February 1930 that Peggy's lessons also included some of these stunts:

Abraham Lincoln, whose birthday is celebrated today, never rode in an auto, yet his great-granddaughter, Miss Mary L. Beckwith, is learning how to fly at Washington airport...From the historic city over which her illustrious forebear presided during the Civil War, Miss Beckwith drives daily to Washington airport for instruction in flying. Howard French, her instructor, reports that she is rapidly becoming proficient in takeoffs, spiral climbs and three-point landings.[9]

In the early years of aviation, any mistake on the part of a pilot could prove disastrous. Courageous air pioneers pushed the technology forward even as they pushed back the psychological barriers. These brave pioneers included women. On March 6, 1931, Ruth Nichols ascended to 27,740 feet (over five miles high), breaking an altitude record held by Elinor Smith, who promptly went up to get her record back. During this flight, Elinor's oxygen tube broke at 25,000 feet, and she fainted. The plane dropped four miles while she was unconscious. At just over 2,000 feet, Elinor regained consciousness and managed to save herself. And just to show she hadn't lost her nerve, she went up again the following week.[10]

One woman flight instructor, Phoebe Omlie, ended her teaching career abruptly after her plane crashed with a student at the controls. The student had panicked. Other instructors, faced with this situation, had resorted to knocking their students unconscious so they could take over the controls, but either Phoebe was too short to reach the student in the front seat, or the student's grip was too tight. She waited helplessly while the plane crashed. She survived, but she never took a student up again.[11]

Harriett Quimby, the first American woman licensed to fly, was also the first woman to fly across the English Channel. This flight was on April 12, 1912, just nine years after the first flight at Kitty Hawk. Quimby wrote for a newspaper in Boston and was the dramatics editor for *Leslie's Weekly*. She was known for her stylish flying costumes. For the Channel crossing, she wore a purple satin outfit, with bloomers and high laced shoes, and a scarf wrapped around her head like a monk's cowl. During the crossing, the fog was so thick that she could not see the water below and had to use a compass to find her way. Amelia Earhart wrote that Quimby's crossing was "probably the most perilous heavier than air flight up to that time attempted by a feminine pilot...In appraising this fine feminine feat, it must be remembered that the pilot had no parachute and none of the instruments known today."[12]

Quimby was killed at a Boston air show just two and a half months later. She was flying a Bleriot monoplane, which performed well as long as strict balance was maintained. When the airplane carried only the pilot, a bag of sand had to be placed in the passenger's seat. If a passenger rode along, that person had to sit still as a statue. The organizer of the air show went up with Quimby, and at one point he moved. The plane took a sharp dip and Quimby lost control. Both passenger and pilot were thrown out.[13]

In this era when land rovers are traveling to Mars and Saturn, and trips to the moon are "old hat," it's hard to imagine just how revolutionary airplane travel was in 1930, when Peggy Beckwith started flying. Just three years before, Charles Lindbergh had landed his Spirit of St. Louis at the Bourget Field in Paris, on May 21, 1927, having completed the first solo trans-Atlantic flight. The crowds who waited to greet him were so ecstatic that they broke through police barriers, dragged him from his plane, and carried him around on their shoulders. Some even ripped pieces off his plane for souvenirs. "In the days that followed, Lindbergh's stature as a hero grew until it almost blotted out the sun," one account reported.[14]

There had been other firsts—the first flight at Kitty Hawk in 1903, the Navy's first trans-Atlantic flight in 1919, the first non-stop flight across the United States in 1923, the first trip across the North Pole in 1926—but Lindbergh's feat caught people's imagination like no other. Lindbergh proved that flying was a real alternative to automobiles, boats, and trains. As one writer put it, "The impact of Lindbergh's achievement on American aviation was explosive. From May 21, 1927, onward, men knew that the airplane was actually capable of all that the dreamers and pioneers had claimed...Like the first four-minute mile in foot racing, the flight broke through an invisible psychological barrier..."[15]

In the year following Lindbergh's achievement, applications for pilot's licenses jumped dramatically in the United States, from 1,800 to 5,500.[16] Most of these applicants were men; as late as January 1929, only a dozen American women had pilot's licenses.[17] Licenses weren't required, so the statistics don't accurately represent the total number of fliers, women or men.[18] Still, the gap between the statistics tells a familiar story. Men were encouraged to be adventurous, but women were not. It took someone like Amelia Earhart to break through that psychological barrier.

Amelia Earhart started flying long before Lindbergh's trans-Atlantic crossing. Her first flight as a passenger was on December 28, 1920. Like Peggy, she was immediately hooked. "As soon as we left the ground, I knew I myself had to fly," she said. "I told my family casually that evening, knowing full well I'd die if I didn't."[19] She added that, "Unfortunately I lived at a time when girls were still girls. Though reading was considered proper, many of my outdoor exercises were not...In 1920 it was very odd indeed for a woman to fly," she wrote in her memoir, *The Fun of It*.[20]

Her parents were more progressive than some. Her father encouraged both of his daughters to participate in the dramatic games he invented, and her mother bought each of them a pair of bloomers. "We wore them Saturdays to play in," Amelia wrote, "and though we felt terribly 'free and athletic,' we also felt somewhat as outcasts among the little girls who fluttered about us in their skirts. No one who wasn't style conscious twenty-five years ago can realize how doubtfully daring we were."[21]

Amelia wanted other women to believe, as she did, that they were equal to men when it came to flying. She criticized the socialization of women, who she said were "bred to timidity." She blamed both public education and tradition for limiting women's visions. She wrote:

> Too often little attention is paid to individual talent. Instead, education goes on dividing people according to their sex, and putting them in little feminine or masculine pigeonholes. Outside of school, similar differences are noticeable, too. In the home, boys and girls usually follow the pursuits which tradition has decreed...Girls are shielded and sometimes helped so much that they lose initiative...Probably the most profound deterrent of all is tradition which keeps women from trying new things and from putting forth their whole effort when once they do venture forth...[22]

Amelia was so determined to learn to fly that when her father refused to pay for lessons, she got a job at the telephone company, working all week so she could afford lessons on Saturdays and Sundays. Flying required "unladylike" attire. "The fields were dusty and the planes hard to climb into," she wrote. Despite the necessity, she felt self-conscious wearing what she called "breeks" [Scottish for breeches] and a leather coat. She didn't bob her hair like some female fliers; instead she secretly snipped it off little by little, "lest people think me eccentric...I had tried to remain as normal as possible in looks, in order to offset the usual criticism of my behavior," she wrote.[23]

When Peggy Beckwith first brought her airplane to Manchester in 1930, the town already had an airport. The construction of this airport had been organized and supervised by a woman, Mrs. George (Anna Louise) Orvis, proprietor of the Equinox House (she inherited the business from her husband). She got the idea to create Manchester's first public airstrip in 1928, hoping it would help bring in more summer visitors.[24]

On a large, flat piece of land east of the Equinox, workers leveled land, cut brush, picked out stones, filled holes, constructed a hangar, and laid out runways, while Mrs. Orvis had the words "MANCHESTER, VERMONT" painted on the roof of her hotel in ten-foot-high letters. The field was officially opened on July 4, 1928. It was Vermont's eleventh public airport. A report in the *Manchester Journal*, quoting a St. Albans writer, said that, "While other communities in Vermont are talking, haggling, and arguing over airports, their cost, their advantages, their drawbacks, the town of Manchester-in-the-Mountains is up and doing."[25]

According to the Federal Aviation Administration, Peggy's first registered airplane was a De Havilland Gipsy Moth, registration #NC-970H. This biplane, built in July 1929 by the Moth Aircraft Corporation, of Lowell, Massachusetts, was originally sold to the Curtiss Flying Service of the South, but it crashed en route from the factory and was sent back to Lowell for repairs. The landing gear, rudder, lower wings, and other parts were replaced, and it was re-inspected the day before Christmas, 1929. On February 4, 1930, Curtiss sold the plane to "Mary L. Beckwith, Washington, D.C."

The FAA granted Peggy a license for the plane the same day. The agent who typed the FAA form had trouble with the Lincoln part of Peggy's name, because in two different places, the middle initial was listed as "K," then scratched out, and an "L" was written in.[26]

Peggy kept this plane for only eight months. A letter to her from the FAA, dated October 25, 1930, acknowledged transfer of the plane to Perley L. Goodwin, of Franconia, New Hampshire.[27]

After the Moth, Peggy bought a brand-new Fleet Model 1, registration #NC-772V, built in Buffalo, New York. She drove to the Consolidated Airport in Tonawanda, New York, to pick it up on August 29, 1930, just after her 32nd birthday. This is the plane she flew over the dedication parade for the Ethan Allen Highway, from the Massachusetts border to Manchester, on Sept. 20, 1930.

On May 18, 1931, Peggy sold the Fleet to her Springfield, Vermont, flying instructor, Lee Bowman, who had worked on it while she owned it, repairing the fuselage and fitting it with new wings. Peggy signed the plane over to him, minus her copy of the plane's records—she told the FAA the records had been destroyed in a hangar fire. The FAA record does not say, but the fire may have been what necessitated repairs to the plane.[28]

Lee Bowman wrote a very apologetic letter on Bowman School of Aviation stationery to "Miss Beckwith" on June 19, 1931, saying that he was sending an installment on what he owed for the plane, and he was sorry he couldn't send the whole balance. Apparently, she'd had this kind of thing happen before. He wrote:

> I will tell you frankly that business has been very poor this spring and with all the expenses the fire has put on my shoulders I am broke...I know that you have had such a lot of bad luck with airplanes and collecting for them that I would rather pay it all...but it is impossible...I would be glad to work off part of the bill if you would care to take some time either solo or duel [sic] in the Fleet or the Command-Aire...If this is not satisfactory please advise and I will do anything I can to pay the debt.[29]

Letters showing how this was resolved have not been found, but knowing Peggy, her response was probably generous and sympathetic.

An article in the *Atlantic Flyer* said Peggy owned another plane, a Waco, but the FAA does not have any record of this, nor of a Boeing Travel Air (#NC-399M) some say she owned.[30] At any rate, she kept flying for two more years after she sold the Fleet.

Pete Brooks, the electrician that Peggy fired as a teenager for sleeping on the job, remembered that back then, when he was working in the gardens, Peggy went flying every couple of days. The workers paid close attention to this because, as Pete said, "That's the only time we knew she wasn't around to be watching us." Peggy had a habit of standing in the upstairs parlor window and shouting directions at them through a megaphone, or blowing a bugle when she wanted their attention. "It seemed like every other day she'd go up, if the weather was decent," he recalled. "She seemed to keep busy all the time on something, trying something new."[31]

A February 1931 article about the Lincoln family described Peggy's competence as an aviator and gave further details:

Of the three great-grandchildren of Lincoln now living, Mary Lincoln Beckwith stands out as most colorful. She startled officials at the Curtiss Airport in Baltimore one day about a year ago by appearing on the field and asking for a ride in the air so that she could see what it was like. So much did she enjoy it that she had the flight continued for three hours, and after landing, she announced without any further formalities that she would like to learn to fly by herself. She bought a Waco plane for $3000 and had her instructor, W. Morris Hampson, keep it in the Baltimore airport for her. He would fly to the Washington airport and give her lessons there. Mary appeared on the field dressed in knickers, heavy laced boots, woolen socks, a man's shirt and sweater, and an old hat. This has continued to be her costume, as the months have progressed, and she has become a pilot who solos and has no need of instructors. Mary is tall and heavy and doesn't care if she is. Friends are enthusiastic about her. They say she is so sweet and genuine, such a thoroughly nice person—a girl you'd be sure to like if you ever met her. They admit she doesn't give a rap about clothes or how she looks, but they say they believe Abraham Lincoln would have liked this great-granddaughter of his immensely just because of her courage and her indifference to public opinion...She is too shrewd to be bothered with fortune hunters. They couldn't fool her and they seem to know it. She seems to have the thoroughgoing admiration of every man who has met her. 'It's just this way,' they explain, 'she knows what she wants and goes after it wholeheartedly'... Mary's flying teachers say that she learned to handle her plane rather easily, but was very deliberate about it, preferring to be sure of herself, rather than take chances. As soon as she had soloed, she sold the Waco plane and bought a little Curtiss Gipsy Moth with slotted wings, for around $4000; also a larger Travelair, with a 300-horsepower motor. The latter machine set Mary Beckwith's bank account back some $6000. Her Gipsy Moth is the same type of plane in which Amy Johnson flew from England to Australia, and the Prince of Wales has one of this type for little air jaunts too...Though she now has her private pilot's license [this has not been verified by the FAA] and is working for a commercial pilot's paper, she has never taken any of her friends up for a ride, nor any member of the family...Bob aspires to be a flier like his sister. His wife, his mother and his grandmother, however, are very much against any such career, and so far they have succeeded in keeping him on the ground.[32]

In the summer of 1930, when Peggy went into Hemenway's store in Manchester Village to ask the father of her friend Clara May Hemenway to order her an airplane hangar, he looked at her with surprise and replied that he didn't have the foggiest idea where to get one. As usual, Peggy was insistent. He did finally manage to locate one, but the price seemed outrageous. Horrified, he passed the news on to Peggy, who asked, "What's the matter? Don't you trust me?" When the hangar arrived, she had it set up on Hildene's meadowlands, down along the Battenkill.[33]

Peggy's grandmother owned Hildene at this point, and she didn't relish the idea of her granddaughter flying. Amelia Earhart acknowledged that flying could be dangerous. Early on, she said, "Motors had bad habits of stopping at inopportune moments. Pilots just naturally expected to have to sit down once every so often because of engine failure," she wrote.[34] By 1930, the engines were much better. But other problems came when a pilot overestimated her plane's ability, underestimated the distance between two points, misjudged wind speed, or ran into unexpected weather.

"Trouble in the air is very rare. It is hitting the ground that causes it."[35] This statement by Amelia Earhart seems absurdly obvious! That principle proved itself painfully true for Captain Charles Stickney of Bellows Falls, Vermont, whose plane won the dubious distinction of being the first airplane to remain in Manchester for any length of time. He was giving passenger rides one day in 1920 at the Manchester fairgrounds, presumably hoping to sell people on the idea of flying with his firm, either as passengers or pilots. The last flight of the day probably left them unconvinced. Capt. Stickney had to land unexpectedly, and his plane hit a swampy area. The nose ran aground so badly that all future flights for the day had to be cancelled.[36]

These kinds of accidents were in Mary Harlan Lincoln's mind whenever her granddaughter took to the air. "Her grandmother was so worried she'd get killed in that thing," Peggy's friend Isabel Parris said.[37] Peggy's farm supervisor, Ken Hill, said she was a good pilot and she knew what she was doing. Peggy understood the challenges and dangers of flying in the mountains, especially the way a downdraft could catch a pilot unaware. She flew in the mountains often, so she had plenty of experience, and whenever a plane went down in the area, she would shake her head and say, "People just don't smarten up."[38] Still, Peggy's grandmother was not convinced that Peggy was safe when she was flying.

Howard "Dutch" Wilcox, Sr., who ran a local dairy and milk processing plant and was a friend of Peggy's, recalled that Peggy and her instructor tried to calm her grandmother's fears by landing the plane right on the front lawn of Hildene. They thought if her grandmother could see the plane up close, she wouldn't be so afraid.

But it didn't work. Peggy continued to fly, and her grandmother continued to fret.[39]

Amelia Earhart had her mother's support when she flew. After her first solo flight, her mother helped her buy a small second-hand plane. "If Mother was worried during this period, she did not show it. Possibly, except for backing me financially, she could have done nothing more helpful...the cooperation of one's family and close friends is one of the greatest safety factors a fledgling flier can have," Amelia wrote.[40]

Peggy did not get that kind of support from her family. She gave up flying suddenly, probably in 1933. "Her nervous grandmother wanted her to stop, and since she was her grandmother's favorite, she apparently quit to please the woman," Ruth Owen Jones wrote in an article for the *Atlantic Flyer*.[41] Some say that Mary Harlan Lincoln gave her granddaughter a $10,000 bribe to stop, but that hardly seems credible. She already had a trust fund to live on, so she didn't need the money.

More likely, she gave in to her grandmother's pressure for other reasons. Her grandmother always had a strong influence on her. Dutch Wilcox said Peggy found her grandmother in tears whenever she came back from flying. This, apparently, was persuasion enough. Clara May Hemenway told a *Manchester Journal* writer that Peggy promised her grandmother she would never fly again since it upset her so.[42] Peggy's friend Beanie Graham somehow got the impression that Peggy gave up flying for her mother. "Her mother insisted on it, she was so frightened...she couldn't have her mother so upset so she gave up flying," Beanie said.[43] Whether it was her grandmother or her mother who bribed or begged her, everyone agrees Peggy stopped to keep peace in the family. Ken Hill said, "It's funny in a way that she did because she was a pretty headstrong person."[44]

Even after Grandmother Lincoln died in 1937, Peggy wouldn't fly again. Clara May asked Peggy about this, and Peggy replied, "No, I won't. A promise is a promise. It doesn't matter whether the person you promised is dead or alive."[45]

CHAPTER FIFTEEN:

Peggy's One-Woman Humane Society

Hildene observatory, Manchester, Vermont, circa 1915–25

It's a common saying that a good test of a person's character is how he or she treats children and animals. Robert Lincoln was generous to children, especially in his adopted home of Manchester. Astronomy was one of his favorite pastimes. He had his own observatory built at Hildene, with a powerful eight-foot Warner and Swasey telescope in a little silo-shaped building perched on the edge of the bluff. He enjoyed sharing this treasure with children.

One day when Robert was at the post office, he told the postmaster that, "You've been so nice to me, I'd like to do something for you." Rhoda Orvis Wriston, the postmaster's daughter, was about twelve years old. She remembered her father saying, "Well, there is something you can do for me. You can let us look through your telescope, me and my daughter and my wife." Rhoda remembered the occasion well. "He explained things and he was pleased to do it." She remembered seeing the rings of Saturn, a double star, and close-ups of the moon. She was impressed with how much Robert Lincoln knew about the stars. Later, she was also given permission to ride her horse on Hildene property with a friend.[1]

On that occasion or another, Robert Lincoln also invited his doctor's children to see the observatory. Young James Campbell, who was eight or nine at the time, remembered looking at the moon. Mr. Lincoln also gave him a map of the stars to take home. "It was quite a thrill...It was impressive how much he knew of astronomy," Campbell recalled, adding, "He was a very impressive person, and my dad [Dr. Claude M. Campbell] admired him immensely.[2]

Helen Coburn, whose father owned a jewelry store in town, said that Mr. Lincoln made the shop one of his regular visits. "He was fascinated with watches," she said, and he liked to observe while her father worked on them. "There was very little conversation that went on, but he'd lean over the counter and watch him fix watches," she said, adding that, "He was very nice to us children. He'd pat our heads on the way out, stop and visit with us...He was a very distinguished gentleman."

Helen also remembered going on the rounds with her father, which included a stop in the front hall at Hildene to wind the grandfather clock. Then she waited while her father went through the house, winding all of the clocks. "In those days, wealthy folks had their clocks wound once a week...Imagine having someone wind your clocks!" she said.[3]

Things were run differently at Hildene in Peggy's grandfather's era. In addition to the house staff and a chauffeur, Robert Lincoln had fifteen men each summer just to keep up the grounds, including mowing the lawns, taking care of the gardens, and doing the farm chores. The lawns of the estate were so extensive that the mowers rarely stopped during daylight hours. Some of the grounds crew lived at Hildene, in the two farmhouses down by the river, or in a separate building next to the main house.

Daily house chores were taken care of by maids, the butler and the kitchen staff. Bessie Bushee was first a cook's helper, and then later on was Bud Beckwith's nanny. Her job was to keep her charge happy and occupied from early in the morning until he went to sleep at night. Bessie took care of Peggy's brother for about a year, when he was four and five years old. "He was an awfully good little boy," she said. "He loved to be read to, he played on the lawn, we took walks and picked flowers, anything to amuse him. At the sight of his mother, he ran to be with her. She didn't mind. But she always informed the gardener to keep him away from the flowers."[4]

Because Robert Lincoln was president of the Pullman Company, he and his family traveled in style when they came to Vermont each spring. Bessie said that Mr. Lincoln had his own private train, with a sleeping car, dining car, and kitchen, and that when it arrived in Manchester, it pulled off onto its own special siding.[5] Howard Wilcox recalled that Mr. Lincoln had three automobiles brought up to Vermont on railroad flat cars.[6] In a letter to one of his golfing cronies, written October 20, 1918, Robert Lincoln referred to "two freight cars" that were on the way to Manchester so the family could finish their "final packing" for the season. He also brought his private secretary with him each summer so that he could spend regular hours each day taking care of his business.[7]

When he wasn't working, Robert Lincoln was an active member of the Manchester community. He was a founding member of the Ekwanok Country Club and its president for many years. He and three close friends, the "Lincoln foursome," played golf there nearly every day. He was a trustee of the local Mark Skinner Library, he helped found the local chamber of commerce, and he was active in local charities. When he died at Hildene on July 26, 1926, just shy of his 83rd birthday, one member of his foursome, Horace Young, said that, "Few men...have exerted upon a community an influence at once so strong, so gentle, and so kindly. In this village, he was more than a friend and benefactor; he was a strong and unusual character who enjoyed the universal respect and affection of all who knew him."[8]

The rest of the family followed his lead in terms of generosity. The family files in various historical depositories are full of thank you notes that prove this. Soldier friends got care packages during the war, as did friends in war-torn England. A wide circle of friends got Peggy's homemade maple syrup when sugar was being rationed. The Lincolns gave money to churches, to schools, to the Community Chest, to the Red Cross, to family members, to employees, and to friends in need. They bought toys and clothes for children. They sent flowers and candy. They bought cars and put people through college.

Through the Save the Children Fund, Jessie sponsored several British youngsters whose lives were being disrupted by World War II. In a thank you letter from the organization, Jessie received a picture of one smiling child, wearing a Sunday dress and broad-brimmed hat. The accompanying information said that eight-year-old Gladys was one of six children. Her father was a soldier, and their mother, who was caring for them on her own, was prone to "sudden fits of hysteria." Their home had been bombed and most of their possessions had been lost. Among other things, Jessie's contribution helped buy the children warm winter clothes. Jessie also "adopted" three children of the Kendall family; one of their brothers was a soldier in Asia and another was a prisoner of war in Japan. In her thank you letter, Violet Kendall thanked Jessie for money to buy clothes and said that her mother, her sister and her father had all been ill.[9]

Peggy Beckwith also loved the company of children, and she liked to play with Ken and Lois Hill's children, who she got to watch growing up. She called them her "Little Army," and every summer, she went fishing and swimming with them in the nearby Battenkill. "There was a nice hole down there. She and the kids and all went for years and years...She liked the kids, they were just like family," Hill said. Peggy dubbed Ken's son Errol "the little frog," because he never tested the water before swimming; he just dove in head first, "kerplunk."[10]

Peggy had a generous heart toward all the children of her community. She paid for school groups to see plays and attend concerts. She presented travelogues. One young student, Christopher Madkour (now executive director of the Southern Vermont Arts Center), remembered that when his teacher told his Manchester Elementary School class that the great-granddaughter of Abraham Lincoln was coming to visit them, he imagined an elegant, well-dressed woman. Then Peggy showed up, dressed as usual in her overalls, shirt and jacket, and wearing an engineer's cap.[11]

First at Bullhead Pond, and later when that became too small, at the Hildene meadowlands, Peggy provided space for the local 4-H horse shows. She had a wooden ring built at the Hildene meadowlands to accommodate the shows. But she did more than provide a space for the group to meet. She helped organize the shows, doing everything from figuring out the various classes in which the children could compete, to hiring judges, choosing prizes, getting donations, and selling sandwiches during the event. Mabel Knapp, the Bald Mountain 4-H Club's leader, said a group of adults, including Peggy, would spend six months organizing each show, much of it done around the Knapps' kitchen table. Peggy enjoyed being a part of all that—this woman that outsiders called reclusive. She was always dressed in old work clothes. "Clothes didn't seem to make much of a difference to her," Mabel recalled.[12]

During the shows, while the Knapps worked in the judge's stand and tallied records, Peggy worked in the concession stand handing out sandwiches. "She would buy all the food and soda and then turn the proceeds over to the club when the show was over," Oscar Johnson said.[13] "Peggy seemed glad to do it...She did things, but she didn't like to take credit," Mabel said.[14]

When Peggy first took over Hildene, she had a full crew of servants like her grandfather. At one point, there was a gardener and crew, a cook and housekeeper, and upstairs and downstairs chambermaids. Mrs. Isabel Parris helped out in the house, and her husband Morton ran the farm crew from 1938–1941.[15]

"Things were set up strict in the beginning," said Ken Hill, who was caretaker after Morton Parris. "They always brought Peggy's meals to her on a tray, or tea in the afternoon if it was nice and she was out on the porch. Someone always had to stay until five o'clock; someone had to answer the phone. She'd usually not answer it. They'd see if she wanted to talk or not. That went on for many years," he said.[16]

In later years, though, she cut back on staff. She also sent the staff home on Saturday mornings and told them not to come back until Monday. "She'd say, 'Okay, everybody out, I'm going to have the house to myself the rest of the weekend,' and she would 'til Monday morning. She'd get her own meals and do just as she pleased," Ken said.[17]

For Peggy, the servants were really part of the family. She continued her grandmother's tradition of having tea parties for her staff. As mistress of Hildene, Mary Harlan Lincoln had invited her servants and their families to tea every Thursday afternoon. According to local historian and writer Nancy Otis, "Mary Harlan Lincoln always 'received' while sitting on an Empire sofa in Robert Todd Lincoln's study overlooking the garden...[She] made each visitor sit for a minute beside her for a chat, and she knew nearly every detail about their lives. Mrs. Lincoln was very sweet and very democratic." Otis' story in the *Bennington Banner* recounted these details as provided to her by Margaret Hard, wife of local poet Walter Hard.[18]

By the late 1960s, Peggy was cutting back on staff by attrition. If employees left, she didn't replace them. Two died of cancer, and she didn't replace them either. If they'd been there a long time and they died, she figured she didn't need the position anymore. She also allowed things to be more informal than her grandparents had.

When Ken Hill first came to work for her, he asked Peggy, "How should I address you? Do you want to be called Miss Beckwith?" Peggy replied, "By all means, call me Peggy." But she was definitely in charge. Marie Pearson, who worked at Hildene for 29 years, recalled that, "If she wanted to do anything, if it was right or wrong, it had to go her way. She was the boss." Cutler Severance, who managed the farm along with Ken, once asked to whom he should report. Peggy answered, "I am the boss. You ask me."[19]

"She had a marvelous quality of common folk, but she also... could have a certain arrogance and authority when she wanted to... Generally, she was a very gentle and easy-going, friendly person, and I think it was only rarely that you saw the other side of her, but she could manipulate when she needed to," her friend Beanie Graham said.[20]

Peggy liked to have the latest farm equipment, even if it meant trading in a lot. But she didn't mind sharing these tools with her neighbors. She always told Oscar Johnson, who had a farm down on the meadowland, to come over and borrow whatever he needed. "I never met a more generous person in my life, and I'm 80," he said in 1991. "But she didn't want any credit."[21]

"Peggy was one of the great women...She did so much that she'd never let anybody know. She was doing and doing and doing and doing. Of course it never could be known that she did it," Isabel Parris said, adding that Peggy was "such a dear, and everybody imposed on her."[22]

The French novelist George Eliot once wrote that animals are "such agreeable friends—they ask no questions, they pass no criticisms."[23] Peggy cherished her pets and seemed more at ease with her animals than with most people. The animals weren't impressed because she was a Lincoln. Animal behavior was always honest, direct and unpretentious, and she liked that. With animals, you could always tell where you stood.

Peggy and her brother Bud always had pets growing up at Hildene, just as her mother and Aunt Mamie had had ponies in Iowa. Peggy had a Shetland pony with a wicker cart to pull, and she could take passengers [PLATE 25]. Bud and his nanny Bessie Bushee rode with her in that cart all over the estate, as well as down along River Road, beside the meadowlands. Sometimes they took the cart to visit Bessie's family. Bessie remembered that the children also had a full-size horse and a colt. "She was a great horsewoman," Bessie said of Peggy.[24]

Peggy met her friend Clara May Hemenway because she had just bought two horses and was looking for someone to help her exercise them. She promised riding lessons to whomever would help. Clara May heard about the offer from her father, who ran the hardware store in the village. "I jumped at the chance," she said, and thus began a long and close friendship between the two.[25]

In studying animal behavior, she had come to her own conclusions about human nature as well. Peggy rarely allowed herself to be interviewed, but for Lincoln's birthday in 1963, she did make some public comments about desegregation. Apparently it was one issue that provoked a strong enough reaction in her that she wanted her views to be heard. Stories about this interview ran on both the United Press International (UPI) and the Associated Press (AP) wires. She announced that she opposed the federal government's policy of forced integration.

"Bobby Kennedy is just too impetuous on this whole integration question," she told the Associated Press. She said she agreed with the principle of integration, "but you can't force it down people's throats." She said she thought James Meredith, the first black to attend a previously all-white college, would have had an easier time entering the University of Mississippi if the federal government "hadn't used officers to shove him in there." She said she believed in "gentle persuasion" rather than the use of force.

"It's not the color of skin that causes all the trouble. It's whether you like the individual. And you can't be forced to like an individual. Just remember the old saying: 'A woman convinced against her will is a woman unconvinced still.'" She said she believed that education, rather than forced desegregation, would be the key to solving racial problems.[26]

To the UPI reporter, she said:

> People and animals just don't like strangers. And when strangers are suddenly thrown together, people and animals alike bristle. It's a curious sort of provincialism, yet it is absolutely universal. The question is not confined to the southern Negroes. We have it here in Vermont with the migrant workers in the summer. They have had it in Massachusetts, as I recall, especially with the Portuguese. And it's the same question in Africa and other parts of the world...I realize that the process of integration must seem to be taking a very long time to some people. But I think it may take even more time than it has. It's like nature, which takes an awfully long time in its evolution...I am not a pacifist, but I am concerned by all this aggressiveness and I would probably punch someone in the nose who is aggressive. I think more is accomplished by reasoning, brotherly love and simple human kindness...[27]

Peggy's opinions sometimes changed over time. When Peggy was a young adult, she liked to hunt. Hildene's photo archives include at least one picture of her in hunting gear with two dogs [PLATE 28], and Howard Wilcox recalled that she liked to go deer hunting with her brother.[28] Later, she posted the property against hunting and Hildene became a refuge for deer during hunting season. Some say she paid patrollers to keep hunters off her land. Isabel Parris remembered that on the morning of the first day of deer-hunting season, a group of bucks and does would show up on

Hildene's lawn. "They stayed there until deer hunting was over, and the next day after deer hunting was over, they weren't there," she said.[29]

As Peggy grew older, she became more and more indulgent toward all of the animals at Hildene. "Wild animals or domestic, it made no difference, they came first," Isabel said. Cows, horses, deer, dogs, mice, raccoons—they all were allowed to wander freely about, including in the flower and vegetable gardens. "She would consider the garden second," Beanie Graham said.[30]

Isabel added that Peggy got her kindness toward animals from her mother. In the early 1940s, when she first owned Hildene, Peggy tried raising quail and turkeys, but eventually, she set them all loose. She also set free any mice that were caught in the kitchen. When the maids found evidence of the little critters, Peggy and Jessie refused to have them killed. Instead, they bought catch-and-release mousetraps. In the morning, they would check the traps, and if there were captives, they would take the cage outside and let them out.

"You know they'll just come back into the house," one of the cooks told them. So Peggy tried an experiment. On the tails of several of the mice, she painted Mercurochrome, to mark them. Then she let them go as usual. Just as the cook had predicted, the mice were back in the kitchen the next morning![31] Peggy was "a great one for pets of all kinds," Bessie Bushee said. Peggy had several domestic white mice, which Bessie remembered seeing in one of the bathtubs.[32]

When Peggy inherited Hildene in 1938, she sold Bullhead Pond to her friend Clara May, who wanted to raise Angora rabbits. Clara May named her operation the Wailiilii Angora Rabbit Farm. She started with fifteen rabbits, and twelve years later, when she shut down the business, she had 400 breeding stock and was shipping to most states and to foreign countries. Peggy sometimes helped her.[33]

Peggy also had her own little bunny hip-hopping around her house. Isabel remembered that it was "a regular brown rabbit. She had him for years, and she had a little house for him by the couch." Peggy always made sure her animals were well fed, and the rabbit was so well cared for that he was pleased to share. One day, Isabel suggested they try an experiment, just for fun. She told Peggy to put a mirror on the floor, so that the rabbit could see down into it. Peggy did. The rabbit picked up a piece of its food and dropped it on the mirror. Then he sat there waiting for the rabbit in the mirror to pick up the food. "He thought there was another rabbit," Isabel said.[34]

"She didn't like to abuse any animal, and yet I heard stories told about her when she was young. If her pony didn't do just as she wanted, why, she'd take the crop to him and slap him," Ken Hill said. "That's nothing, though. I'm tender-hearted compared to what I used to be. I guess that just grows on you with age."

Ken once thought he'd be reprimanded for smacking the pigs with a stick. When he went into the pens to feed them, they would grunt and clamor around him so much that it was difficult to walk to the food trough. In order to keep them from jumping up on him, he had taken to carrying a stick with him, and he smacked them on their snouts to knock them down.

One day, Peggy came to feed the pigs. Ken's six-year-old son Brian was watching her. When they jumped up on her, Brian said that he had watched his daddy feed the pigs and he knew just what to do. "My daddy can fix 'em. He'll get a stick and he'll get them down." Ken arrived in time to hear this remark and wished he had a hole to disappear into. But Peggy just laughed.[35]

"All the animals she had, somebody would give them to her, want[ing] to get rid of them. She'd take them...She loved animals and everybody imposed on her," Isabel said.[36]

"Any animal that came to her, she'd take them in," Pete Brooks said. "I think she catered to animals more than she did the place... I think she wanted to turn the place over to the animals." He ought to know. He was the one she called in to fix the damage done by the raccoons.[37]

Driving back into her estate one night, Peggy spotted a couple of baby raccoons with no sign of their mother. She took them inside, fed them, put them in a second-story bedroom, and opened the window. Just outside the window was a tree, and Peggy figured they would be within reach of their mother that way. But their mother never came back, so Peggy just kept them. She kept up the practice of opening the window so they could go in and out whenever they wanted.

The raccoons lived in the house at Hildene for two or three years. She had the door to their room cut in half to make a Dutch door, with the top half screened so she could see them as she walked by and they could hear her around the house. Their room gave off quite an odor, so she installed blue deodorizer lights outside their door, a dozen of them going at a time. When the raccoons were hungry, they climbed the screen and squawked, and she came to feed them.

Pete said, "Those coons were wonderful. They gave her more enjoyment I think than the dogs did. They'd tear the switches out of the wall, short out the circuit, open the bathtub faucets, or the sink faucets." Isabel remembered that, "Those coons went in the bathtub and turned the water on and let it run. Of course, there was water coming down through the ceiling, strong." Pete said, "She finally had to have all that stuff disconnected."[38]

Beanie sometimes came to tea while Peggy had the raccoons. She saw how they had scratched up the walls and the fireplace and destroyed the carpet in the room where she kept them. "I will admit I was taken aback, to say the least, when I saw the animals in those beautiful rooms and on the lovely mantle," Beanie said. "This was Peg. The rug on the floor, the beautiful rug on the floor...it meant nothing to her compared to the two little raccoons she had in here...This was typical of Peg. She was so unworldly."[39]

Among the animals, the dogs were the most privileged. Nearly every day, she could be seen somewhere in the village—at the post office, at Hemenway's hardware store, or somewhere else—making her rounds. Her dogs went everywhere with her, waiting in the car while she did her errands. Sometimes they chewed the seats, but she didn't mind. They got whatever they wanted. When she traded in her convertible Corvair automatic for one with a standard transmission, she wanted them to like it. The old Corvair had a top that opened so they could stick their heads out in the breeze. So before she brought the new one home, she had Ellington's cut a hole in the top. Then she went to an upholstery place and had a special snap-down vinyl cover made. That way, she could get the car she wanted without sacrificing the open top that the dogs loved.

"She had three dogs and they always rode in the car wherever she went," Ken said. Once she brought her collie Jamie with her when she and Mary Porter went to New York City. When they arrived at their hotel and learned the hotel didn't allow pets, they got right back into the car and drove straight home to Hildene.[40]

Hildene, on a summer day, late in the 1960s

In 1927, Peggy Beckwith's brother, Robert Todd Lincoln Beckwith, married a widow named Hazel Holland Wilson. Hazel already had two children, and Bob helped her raise them. Hazel's niece Beverly came up from Virginia with her family to Hildene one day in the late 1960s. Beverly was then in her mid-teens. She later recounted how impressed she had been, driving a mile through the woods on the dirt entrance road to the main house. Suddenly, the forest opened up, and they could see Hildene's impressive face in the clearing: two stories with a gray stucco finish, grand entrance, five graceful chimneys, and green shutters at every window. This house spoke quietly of comfort and wealth.[41]

As they drove in under the pillared portico, two chubby horses ambled over to the fence on their left to greet them. On the massive front lawn where her grandfather once had practiced golf, Peggy now pastured these horses. These two may have been the ones given to her by Manchester veterinarian Dr. Edwin Treat. "Poor animals, she fed them so much they could hardly walk. Like every animal she ever had, she overfed them. They didn't mind," Pete Brooks recalled.[42]

Marie Pearson answered the door when the visitors knocked. Marie was Peggy's cook and housekeeper, but she had been on staff for twenty years or more, and her job title didn't really explain her role at Hildene. She was one of Peggy's closest friends and companions. She had tea with Peggy in the mornings and evenings, and in between, she did the cooking and cleaning and made out the grocery lists. Marie led the family inside.[43]

The entryway where they paused to wait for Peggy was furnished with an antique grandfather clock, ticking away like a sentry on the wide-cut polished oak floor. Straight ahead of them, sunlight streamed in through the floor-to-ceiling windows at the back of the house. Next to the windows was the Aeolian pipe organ that Robert Lincoln had bought for his wife in 1908. It was equipped with an automatic player attachment, but Peggy never played it, and mice had built nests in its pipes.

As Marie led them through the central hall, they could see the formal dining room on their left and the casual sitting room on their right. Beverly began to notice some contrasts. The molding on the walls, the wallpaper, the furniture, the specially-milled floor boards and the beautiful main stairs all gave the place a sense of elegance, but that elegance showed signs of wear. Peggy hadn't kept up with needed repairs. Curtains and light sconces were askew. Unfinished projects lay across some chairs.[44]

In the formal dining room, a large imposing portrait of Robert Lincoln hung over the fireplace. This room looked as it had in Peggy's grandparents' day. So did her grandfather's study down the hall. But in the sitting room to the right, mixed in with her grandmother's mahogany Steinway grand piano and her grandfather's bookcases, Peggy had brought in comfortable chairs and couches, a radio and a television, making a place where she felt at home.

Marie led the family out to the back veranda and seated them in dark green wicker chairs, where they had an excellent view of the gardens and the mountains beyond. The gardens had weeds that needed to be pulled and bushes that needed pruning, but the flowers there still bloomed cheerily. They waited a few minutes, and then Peggy arrived, dressed as usual in what Beverly called "her flying Dutchman denims," loose and full to accommodate her ample figure.[45]

As a young woman, Peggy lived with her mother in Washington, D.C., and as a member of the Lincoln family, she had been invited to fancy parties and receptions. She hated these events, but she sometimes went for the sake of her mother. She may have rejected her mother's clothing and lifestyle, but she did learn some of her mother's gracious manners. After greeting her guests, Peggy asked Marie to bring in the tea set. The family heirloom china and silver were delivered on a large serving tray, and Peggy poured the tea. Dressed as she was, she may have looked like a farmer's daughter, but she could pour tea as gracefully as the finest dressed lady.

Beverly recalled that, "She was very elegant the way she poured. It was very much a dichotomy. The house was quite run down... Hildene was kind of faded elegance at that point. But she knew how to do it right, and she had all the right things to do it with."[46]

Later in the visit, after dinner, they all went into the sitting room to talk some more. When Beverly's father sat in one of the chairs, Bugie the beagle came up beside him and began to whine.[47]

The beagle had his own silver food bowl in the dining room, placed on an Oriental rug beside the fireplace. In Peggy's car, he had a special box on the console to sit in. One day, Peggy had called Pete Brooks out to Hildene and had asked him to hook up electricity to the house's rope-pulled elevator. She said it was for the beagle, who had gotten too old and fat to climb the steps.[48] "The dog owned the house," Beverly joked.[49]

"What's wrong?" Beverly's father asked Peggy when the dog began to whine.

"That's his chair," she replied.

So he moved, and the beagle climbed up on the chair he had vacated. Then the dog began to whine again.

"What's wrong now?" he asked.

"The light's in his eyes," Peggy said, and she got up and fetched the poor creature a parasol![50]

CHAPTER SIXTEEN:

For the Sake of the Family

When interviewed about desegregation in 1963, Peggy was asked by an Associated Press reporter if she thought her great-grandfather would agree with her that forced desegregation wasn't the answer. She replied, "I can't say. I'm as far away from him as anyone."[1] While she was proud to be a member of such a distinguished family, she didn't have much else to say publicly about her great-grandfather.

A year earlier, she had told a reporter that, "It always provokes me when people stare and say, 'There's Lincoln's great-granddaughter.' It's just my luck he was related to me."[2]

It may, in fact, have been her bad luck. Presidential historian Michael Beschloss, who researched the Lincoln descendants for an article in *The New Yorker*,[3] told a *Chicago Tribune* reporter that, "Researching the Lincolns confirmed two things for me...One, that it is very difficult to be the descendant of a great leader—there is just too much extra pressure placed upon them than there is upon the descendants of mere mortals. And two, that America's yearnings for a political dynasty within a family is romantic but not rational."[4]

Beschloss himself was not very kind in his portrait of the Lincolns. He didn't seem familiar with the many warm stories told by those who lived near them and worked for them. Instead, he wrote that:

...history played a practical joke on the Lincolns: the President was followed by a procession of heirs better described by Flaubert than by Tolstoy. Thanks to John Wilkes Booth, the chief influence on later generations of the House of Lincoln proved to be not the great man of New Salem and Springfield but his tormented eldest son, Robert Todd Lincoln. Abraham Lincoln loved the common people, but Robert, from his days at Phillips Exeter Academy and Harvard, had little use for them...[5]

The Lincoln descendants were expected to live up to the legendary Abraham. But in his book *With Malice Toward None*, Lincoln biographer Stephen Oates cautions us against confusing the mythic Lincoln—the one who embodies our most sacred beliefs and values—with "the Lincoln who actually lived. The real Lincoln was certainly honest and compassionate, with a deep commitment to the right of all people to elevate themselves in a free society. But he was hardly the flawless immortal that legend claims."[6]

It is important to remember that the Lincoln descendants were seen differently by those they trusted than by those who watched them from a distance. In Mount Pleasant, Iowa, and in Manchester, Vermont, Robert Lincoln and the other descendants were respected and even loved by the "common people." The descendants didn't think of Abraham Lincoln every time they looked in a mirror. They had lives apart from his. They didn't talk much about him among themselves, and they did not publicize their ancestry.

The last three Lincoln descendants were not interested in studying the details of Lincoln's life and career. Peggy's brother, Robert Todd Lincoln Beckwith, once said that he was occasionally embarrassed by the public's fascination with Abraham Lincoln. He told a reporter that he didn't ask his grandfather Robert Lincoln about the White House years because, "I was not especially interested."[7]

He described himself as a "gentleman farmer of independent means," and once admitted, "I'm a spoiled brat." He said he was a wealthy man whose passions were boats, fast cars, and beautiful women.[8] He explained that he considered it "neither a hindrance nor an asset to be a descendant of a man whose memory is cherished here and abroad" (reporter's words). In his own words, he added: "I just want to live my own life."⁹

Lincoln Isham, Peggy and Bud's only cousin, also found it easy to put his famous ancestor out of mind. He called the Manchester probate judge one day in early February 1959 and said he would like to come down from nearby Dorset on Wednesday or Thursday of that week and review some papers. When the judge said he should come Wednesday because Thursday they would be "closed for the holiday," he asked her, "What holiday?"

"Lincoln's birthday, of course; you should know," the judge told him.

"Oh, I forgot; I'm as bad as Grandpa," he replied.¹⁰

Robert Lincoln also forgot the holiday at least once. He and his wife were in Chicago one day, and he asked her why all the stores were closed. She had to remind him that it was his father's birthday.¹¹ While everyone else regarded the Great Emancipator with awe, the Lincolns were proud to be associated with him, but went on with their lives and pretty much took him for granted.

The portrait of America's best-loved President hangs on the walls of many American school classrooms. Manchester resident Phebe Ann Lewis remembers seeing the famous Healy portrait of Lincoln in Mamie Isham's home in Manchester Village. Seeing it there impressed upon her that the Lincolns had a different perspective on the President. Phebe Ann was a teenager when she went with her mother to visit Mrs. Isham, across the street from the Equinox hotel. Over the Isham's fireplace was the familiar portrait. When she saw it in school, she thought of it as a presidential portrait. But here, in Mary Isham's home, she realized it was a family portrait. "To see it in a house, and think, 'This is where it belongs because it's a relative,' that was impressive to me," Phebe Ann said.¹²

The Lincolns owned this American legend in a way that other citizens did not, but it was an inheritance with a price. Robert Lincoln's obsessive custody of his father's papers was one example of the psychological burden that came to him as the President's son. His father's letters, manuscripts and other public and private records were contained in seven or eight trunks that he inherited in 1865. As early as 1882, he was pressed to dispose of the papers, but he avoided the issue for as long as possible. He had intended to leave the papers to his son, but when his son died, he was unsure about the next best course of action.[13]

He first left them in charge of Lincoln biographers John Hay and John Nicholay. After their deaths, he kept the papers with him in his home, carting them up to Vermont each spring, and carting them back to Washington each winter. Finally, in 1919, he agreed to donate them to the Library of Congress, but they were to be considered his private property until his death, and until then he retained final say as to who could review them. In 1923, he added another restriction—the papers were not to be opened to the public until 21 years after his death. As he had during his whole adult life, he was trying to protect his family from any public injury.[14]

It's quite possible that he destroyed some of the more private family papers for the same reason. At one time, he had hoped to round up the many pleading letters written by his mother that he believed gave too much evidence of her irrationality. He had spent many years during her lifetime trying to put out fires of embarrassment that came from dealing with her behavior. He once wrote that:

> I could not hold her back from doing many things that distressed me beyond any power of description; advertising her old clothes for sale and writing begging letters by the hundreds were only part of what I had to grieve and be mortified about; there was any quantity of newspaper publicity about her actions and writings and much of my time was spent in sadly answering inquiries about her. It all nearly wore my life out.[15]

Historians recount rumors of family papers that Robert Lincoln may have destroyed, including perhaps some love letters between Abraham and Mary. Robert would not have considered this an infringement on history; instead, he considered it as a proper action to protect his parents' privacy. But of course, questions arise inevitably about what details have thus been lost.[16]

✦

The very human Abraham Lincoln fathered an equally flawed and many-sided family. Whatever their mistakes and inadequacies, though, none of them ever broke the family's cardinal rule: never exploit the Lincoln name. Robert Lincoln was praised for this trait, and he passed this habit on to his children and grandchildren. The *Boston Herald* said this in Robert Lincoln's obituary:

> To be known always and everywhere as the son of Abraham Lincoln in itself was a heavy responsibility. Easily Robert Lincoln might have hindered the development of his father's fame. Had he seized upon every opportunity to 'tell stories' of his father; had he leaped into print at the slightest provocation...had he striven to capitalize [on] his father's name in his own interest, he might well have made himself a bore and a nuisance...Robert Lincoln chose to play a far better part. He did not strive for public notice. He went about his business quietly, with dignity, keeping in the shadows...He considered reticence the wise course and he was right...He could not possibly elude the fact that he was his father's son, although he did with decided success avoid the proclamation of it and refrain from its use for selfish purposes...His silence clothed him with an elusive quality, almost of mystery to the general public, however genial and intimate he may have been with a chosen circle...What a responsibility to live a worthy life as the son of such a man. That responsibility Robert Lincoln creditably fulfilled and the American people think of him today with respect.[17]

Robert Lincoln did not need to rest on his father's laurels. He was successful in his own right, as a lawyer, a statesman, and a businessman. Helped in part by a substantial inheritance from his father (about $37,000 initially, then the remainder of his brother's and his mother's portions when they died), he kept meticulous records, invested wisely, and his investments prospered even during the Depression. His reputation for careful and practical thinking earned him government posts as well as the titles of President and Chairman of the Board in one of the nation's most powerful businesses, the Pullman Palace Car Company. During his tenure there,

Pullman underwent its greatest period of growth. From 1898 to 1910, the after-tax earnings for rental of their railroad cars went from $384,000 to more than $10 million.[18]

As the company prospered, so did its leader. When Robert Lincoln died in 1926, his estate included Hildene with 1,000-plus acres, his townhouse in the Georgetown neighborhood of Washington, D.C., and about $3 million (equal to about $30 million in today's currency). In keeping with tradition, Robert gave Hildene and much of the Lincoln fortune to his wife Mary. In addition, he had already given his wife some $1,250,000 worth of securities and had established a sizeable trust fund for his two daughters.[19]

Mary Harlan Lincoln loved Hildene as much as her husband had. She had helped to design the house, and after her husband's death, she continued to spend summers there until her death in 1937. Predictably, in her will, she gave Hildene to her eldest daughter, Mamie Isham.[20]

Mamie, by then 68, had a house in the center of Manchester Village, a couple of miles from Hildene. She also had a home in New York City. She and Charles had spent summers in Manchester throughout much of their married lives, from 1905 until he died in 1919. By the time she inherited Hildene, Mamie had been a widow for nearly twenty years. Apparently, she decided that she would move into Hildene, for she spent the next year redecorating the place to her own taste and adding her own furnishings. But before she could move in, she died.[21]

Jessie was not in line to inherit Hildene. Mary Harlan Lincoln had made it clear that she wanted Hildene to go to Peggy after her eldest daughter's death, and she provided for that in her will. Peggy's grandparents had discussed giving Hildene to Peggy much earlier, but Robert Lincoln thought Peggy was too young. In a letter to her daughter Jessie, written three years before she died, Mary Harlan Lincoln explained that, "Nothing you have done, ever, has had any influence with me in the making of my Will, and I think Hildene is dealt with, as Papa could have liked."[22]

Jessie knew that she had displeased her father by running off to be married, then divorcing, and marrying two more times. Eight years after she and Warren Beckwith were divorced, Jessie married

National Geographic explorer and photographer Frank Edward Johnson. An undated society note remarked that:

> No prettier idyll has flourished with the Spring than that of the Adonis-like archaeologist, protégé of Mrs. Marshall Field, F.E. Johnson, and the charming and rather reserved daughter of the Robert Todd Lincolns. Mrs. Beckwith has been so conservative, so wary of the masculine sex, owing to her disastrous venture with young Beckwith, that it seems absurd to link her name with a matrimonial rumor. But her friends say that Mr. Johnson's attentions can mean but the old, old story, and his constant attendance is evidence that Mr. and Mrs. Lincoln, at first strongly opposed, have become reconciled to the match...[23]

Sound familiar? So is the rest of the story. Frank and Jessie married in 1915, but after ten years, in 1925, they divorced. In 1921, Frank Johnson had written a bizarre request to Robert Lincoln in a letter from Havana, Cuba. He reported that two years before, he had arrived at Jessie's house in Washington to find another man living with her. "They left me at 3038 N Street [the address of Jessie's house] and went off on a cruise on Mr. Randolph's yacht without a chaperone," he wrote.[24]

He said that the only solution seemed to be a divorce, and he asked whether Robert Lincoln would draw up the papers himself, using either "Desertion from bed and board" or "Incompatibility of temperament" as the grounds. "If you will have the papers prepared and forwarded to me to be acknowledged and sworn to before the proper officials in Habana [sic], it will keep things quiet," he concluded.[25]

How that request was received is explained in a letter Mary Harlan Lincoln wrote to her daughter Jessie in June. She sent a copy of Frank's letter and quoted her husband's response to it as, "What a damned fool that man is, to expect me to do this business for him!"[26] Eventually Jessie married Robert Randolph, a wealthy Virginian who raised racehorses.

It may have been a practical decision to leave Jessie out of line for Hildene. With her record for failed marriages, Jessie's parents may have feared she would lose the family home in a divorce. Perhaps Peggy's grandparents saw her as the one family member most interested and capable of taking care of Hildene. They had watched her grow up there, and they knew it was a place where she was happy. Owning Hildene would give Peggy roots, a connection to the family tradition that could help keep her steady.[27]

Did Peggy feel any guilt about inheriting Hildene instead of her mother? To show her loyalty to her mother, she asked Jessie to come and live with her, which she did for much of her last ten years. When Jessie died in 1948, she was buried in Manchester's Dellwood Cemetery, with the back of her headstone just a few feet from the entrance to Hildene. She is the only Lincoln buried there.

Navy Shipyard, Portsmouth, New Hampshire, May 14, 1960

All three of Abraham Lincoln's great-grandchildren found ways in their final years to honor their Lincoln legacy. When the U.S. Navy asked Peggy Beckwith to help christen the nuclear submarine U.S.S. Abraham Lincoln, she accepted the invitation enthusiastically. She later wrote the submarine's captain, thanking him for the privilege and telling him, "I must confess I'm thrilled to be associated with her."[28]

This was a special occasion indeed, in more ways than one — instead of wearing her usual dungarees, she wore a pretty blue and white polka-dotted dress, white gloves, a string of pearls, and a white hat [PLATE 34]. When her friend Beanie Graham commented on how nice she looked, Peggy replied that she hated dressing up, but "there comes a time once in a while...I just have to do this for the sake of the family."[29]

The christening took place on May 14, 1960. Fifth in a fleet of new ballistic-missile nuclear-powered submarines, the Abraham Lincoln was designed to carry and launch the Polaris missile, and it could hold 80 of the deadly weapons at a time. It also had torpedoes. With its nuclear-powered engine, it could reach any part of the ocean. It was 380 feet long, weighed 5,400 tons, and could hold ten officers and a crew of 90. It had two crews, so that while one was training, the other could keep the submarine at sea.[30]

Thousands of people were on hand for the ceremony. After the national anthem was played, Chaplain Cecil Marley gave the invocation and Captain H.P. Rumble, commander of the shipyard, said a few words of welcome. The shipyard employees gave Peggy a gift as the submarine's sponsor, presented to her by a man named John F. Lincoln. After that, a few other officers spoke, as did Republican Senator Styles Bridges, the senior senator from New Hampshire.[31]

Senator Bridges took the opportunity to comment on some upcoming summit talks with the Soviet Union. First, he explained that the new submarine had more destructive capacity than all the bombs dropped during World War II. He warned that while a peace accord might result from the summit, "We cannot forget that the Russians have violated every international agreement to which they have been a party over a period of thirty years." He said the submarine "was built by a nation that loves peace enough to build the strength to prevent war."[32]

Then the three-minute warning was sounded with two blasts on the klaxon horn. Someone shouted the traditional warning, "All clear on ground except at dog shores and trigger." The production officer reported to the commander that, "The Abraham Lincoln is ready in all respects for launching." The ship was blessed by Lt. Commander John P. Fay. Then the one-bell signal was given, telling Peggy to be ready.[33]

A trigger was released and the ship was launched. As it slid into the waters of the Piscataqua River, Peggy struck hard with the champagne bottle on the submarine's bow and declared, "In the name of the United States of America, I christen thee Abraham Lincoln." The Navy band played "Anchors Away," and thousands of spectators cheered [PLATE 35].[34]

Peggy's brother was also called on to make several public appearances as a descendant of Lincoln. In 1965, he was the only Lincoln on hand for ceremonies in Illinois marking the centennial of Lincoln's death and the end of the Civil War. He first attended ceremonies in Chicago, then visited his great-grandparents' home-town of Springfield and participated in several events there. It was his first trip to Springfield, and he toured his great-grandparents' home and visited President Lincoln's grave, with James Hickey, curator of the Lincoln Collection for the Illinois State Historical Library of Springfield, serving as his guide. At one Civil War party there, Robert Beckwith asked the jazz band to play "Dixie," just as President Lincoln had done after the South's surrender at Appomattox.[35]

The year before, in 1964, Robert Todd Lincoln Beckwith went to the New York World's Fair on Illinois Day and posed for pho-tographers with a huge bust of Lincoln.[36] In June 1965, he received an honorary LL.D. degree at the Iowa Wesleyan College com-mencement in Mount Pleasant.[37] In 1976, he received another LL.D degree from the Lincoln College in Lincoln, Illinois, for his "service to mankind."[38]

Lincoln Isham also did his duty to history before his death in 1971. Like cousin Bob, "Linc" gave some of his Lincoln memora-bilia to friends, but the more valuable ones, including some pieces of the White House china and his great-grandmother's watches, he gave to the Smithsonian.[39]

He was also generous within his community. He helped found Manchester's Southern Vermont Arts Center, where his cousin Peggy later helped organize art shows and sometimes displayed her own paintings. He financed a new science laboratory at Burr and Burton Seminary, the local high school, in memory of his wife, Leahalma Correa. His grandmother, Mary Harlan Lincoln, had earlier given Robert Lincoln's telescope to the same school and had paid for an exact replica of Robert's observatory to house it there. That telescope has since been returned to Hildene.[40]

Like his cousin Bob, Lincoln Isham had married a widow who already had a child and he never fathered a child of his own. When he died, he left $440,000 of his $1 million estate to his stepdaugh-ter. The rest went to the American Red Cross, the American Cancer Society, and the Salvation Army.[41]

❦

When Peggy died in 1975, she left all of her Lincoln family possessions to her brother. Lincoln Isham had died in 1971. As the last Lincoln alive, Bob Beckwith inherited the family's final historical responsibilities. He survived his cousin by 14 years and his sister by ten years. During that decade, it was Bob Beckwith's turn to be guardian of the family treasures. Like his grandmother Mary Harlan Lincoln had done with Mary Todd Lincoln's possessions nearly a century before, he worked painstakingly to disburse the various items to the appropriate historical institutions.

With the help of James Hickey, Bob spent weeks going through the contents of "sixty some trunks plus the many rooms of Hildene and his own homes and apartment to make sure that all family relics and artifacts were distributed before his death [in 1985]," according to Hickey.[42]

To Hildene, he returned a number of things, including Robert Todd Lincoln's grandfather clock that stands in the main hall, some family silver, a lamp and some paintings, some of his sister's photography equipment, toys from their childhood, and a trunk full of items that had belonged to his mother Jessie.[43]

To the Smithsonian he gave an unused rifle that had belonged to Abraham Lincoln. The Chicago Historical Society got all of the family's clothing collection and many family papers and pictures. To the state of Illinois he gave $100,000 worth of Lincoln memorabilia, including paintings, china, busts, cutlery, the correspondence of Robert Todd Lincoln (46 letterbooks containing copies of approximately 20,000 letters he wrote), and a portrait that Mary Todd Lincoln had made of herself to surprise her husband (he died before she could present it).[44]

Despite suffering from a fairly advanced case of Parkinson's, which made it difficult for him to write, he slowly and painstakingly handwrote many affidavits attesting to the authenticity of various items, signing his full name, Robert Todd Lincoln Beckwith, which he hadn't used in years. "He would never make an affidavit...unless he personally knew the fact or they could be documented satisfactorily," Hickey said, who added:

Many institutions and Lincoln scholars will always be indebted to him for taking on this burden late in life. I personally know that at times it saddened him and brought on the famous Lincoln melancholy but after a brief rest he would return to the task. I know that he worked hard at this...In fact, Bob Beckwith worked hard all his life to please; he was generous to a fault...He felt responsible for every individual who ever worked for his family and set up trusts for them so they would be paid after they no longer could work ...[He] did not look at all like his illustrious great grandfather, but he had the heart of this great man, that feeling for his fellow man.[45]

Many requests came to him from a variety of people who wanted Lincoln relics. "Bob was very patient. It was very difficult for him to turn anyone down or offend anyone...He was very serious about his heritage...being the last one he had to make the [final] decisions" about things very important to history, James Hickey said.[46]

Elsewhere in the house, in a secret compartment in a closet between Robert Lincoln's bedroom and the entry, James Hickey found the mother lode—a bundle of papers tied with a ribbon and labeled by Robert Lincoln as the "MTL Insanity File." One hundred years after his great-grandmother's insanity trial, new evidence came to light. Bob Beckwith decided to release the file to the public. Although it was a chapter his grandfather preferred not to discuss, Bob Beckwith knew the papers were important historical documents and had been saved for a purpose. In the preface to Mark E. Neely, Jr. and R. Gerald McMurtry's *The Insanity File* book about the trial, Robert Todd Lincoln Beckwith said he believed that the file would help historians "treat my great-grandmother Mary Todd Lincoln more kindly" and would show that "my grandfather acted in the best possible way towards his mother."[47]

The man who inherited all of this family responsibility was the youngest of all the Lincolns. By the time his sister died, making him the last Lincoln, Bob Beckwith was a balding man, hard of hearing, with an occasionally bad stutter. In his youth, he had considered himself a playboy and he had freely admitted, "I'm a spoiled brat."[48]

He had made one of the first cross-country automobile trips in 1925, an adventure that included a female companion and a ticket for speeding in Omaha. Although Bob Beckwith had once proclaimed that his greatest passions were sailing, fast cars, and beautiful women, his first marriage to Hazel Holland Wilson had lasted 37 years, until her death in 1964.[49]

What happened to Hildene after Peggy died?

Originally, Mary Harlan Lincoln's will had established a trust fund to support her three grandchildren. The provision stated that if the Lincoln bloodline should die out after that generation, the residuary of the fund was to be divided equally between the First Church of Christ, Scientist in Boston, the American Red Cross, and Iowa Wesleyan College.

The Christian Science Church was also named in Peggy Beckwith's will. Peggy had never been a member of the church, although she subscribed to several of its publications throughout her life. Peggy's mother was not officially a member, but she wrote letters to one of the church "practitioners," a woman in the church's healing ministry named Ruth Burton. She also corresponded for years with a gentleman friend, Keith Schwinley, who followed Mary Baker Eddy's teachings. These letters are in the archives of the Illinois State Historical Library in Springfield.

Mary Harlan Lincoln and Mary Lincoln Isham were both members of the Mother Church. Mamie joined first, in 1897, and her mother followed suit in 1898,[50] eight years after traditional medicine had failed to save her son's life. Several references suggest that she may have begun to study Christian Science as early as the late 1880s.[51]

In his book about how Hildene became a public museum, *Robert Todd Lincoln's Hildene and How It Was Saved*, author Donald Keelan says that, "One of [Mary Harlan Lincoln's] earliest and closest friends was Mary Morse Baker Eddy." He said the friendship lasted for 30 years, until Mary Baker Eddy's death in 1910.[52] If a letter to the Lincoln Fellowship of Southern California is correct,

Mary Harlan Lincoln was a "devout student" and a member of the Mother Church, but never a member of any branch church.[53] But Yvonne von Fettweis, former historian for the First Church of Christ, Scientist said that Mary Harlan Lincoln was active in the Chicago congregation and may have been first introduced to the church when Mary Baker Eddy taught in Chicago, either in 1884 or in 1888.[54]

Jessie, Peggy and her brother were reportedly students of Christian Science, but not members of either the Mother Church or any branch church, although Peggy's brother apparently attended the First Church in Washington sometimes.[55] However, the Mary Baker Eddy Library collection contains no correspondence between Mrs. Eddy and the Lincoln women other than one letter from Jessie to Mrs. Eddy, apparently requesting a visit in 1893.[56] Jessie Lincoln did come to Mrs. Eddy's home on August 17, 1893, but when asked whether she would see Jessie, Mrs. Eddy said, "No, not today."[57]

As a way of honoring her grandmother, Peggy decided early on that when she died, Hildene would become the church's property. But in the early 1970s, she got other ideas. At one point she considered giving the property to the state of Vermont to be used as a game preserve, farm and museum to her family. Her lawyer Jim Campbell wrote notes about her intentions, making it clear that she "objects to its commercial development," but Peggy never followed through on this idea to make it official.[58]

She called her friend Oscar Johnson one day and asked if he would pay her a visit at Hildene. When he got there, she told him that she was thinking of giving Hildene to her friends in Manchester, along with her million-dollar trust fund to support it, so Hildene could be open to the public as a living memorial to her mother, grandparents and great-grandparents.[59]

Already, a group of her friends had helped Peggy organize and run the Bullhead Foundation, which was preserving Peggy's home in East Dorset as a nature center for the community's children. Peggy asked Oscar if he thought her friends would also agree to organize the preservation of Hildene. He said he thought they would. The two of them met several more times to discuss the idea, and Peggy told Oscar she would change her will to that effect. Typically, though, she never got around to it.[60]

On July 10, 1975, Mary Lincoln "Peggy" Beckwith died of colon cancer in the hospital in Rutland, Vermont, a month and a half before her 77th birthday. Her farm's caretaker, Ken Hill, said she hadn't been feeling well for a year or two, but she had put off going to the doctor. By the time the cancer was discovered, it was too far advanced to respond to treatment.[61]

When she died, her will still stated that the First Church of Christ, Scientist was to inherit Hildene, but it also included the following: "...it being my direction that said Hildene estate shall be a memorial to my mother and grandparents." She did allow that if the "...Board of Directors [of the Church] shall determine that it is impractical to keep and maintain said Hildene estate as a memorial, I authorize and empower them to sell any part and all of said real estate..."[62]

The Christian Science Church did not have the same loyalty to Peggy's ideas for Hildene that her friends did. The church leaders were in the business of advancing religion, not managing real estate or museums, so they thought it was impractical for them to carry out Peggy's wishes. On July 23, 1976, church representative Carl Rechner came to Manchester to address its citizens and to announce that Hildene would be put on the market. He said the church wanted to know if there was a group in Manchester willing to buy the property for the purpose of preserving it. If so, they had 90 days to develop a purchase plan. The church was willing to entertain an offer of $500,000, well below the $625,000 appraisal.[63]

Oscar Johnson attended the meeting that day. He remembered that on another occasion, he was asked to show a developer around the property. He said his idea was to build a housing development and maybe call the place something like Lincoln Acres. Oscar thought to himself, "Over my dead body."[64]

"He had no feeling for the home or for history," Oscar said, "so we got the Friends of Hildene into high gear."[65]

A dozen people at the first meeting met again the same night. One of them was Robert Thum of Dorset, who the *Manchester*

Journal quoted as saying, "We have a valuable historical site and a great tourist attraction along the lines of Schuylerville and Ticonderoga in New York and the Calvin Coolidge Home in Plymouth [Vermont]." That became the essence of their philosophy as they moved forward.[66]

They met again on August 12. "The people who gathered around a table in the [Manchester] Town Office that night in August, 1976, agreed that preserving this piece of Americana for future generations would be a fitting way to mark the [nation's] Bicentennial," John Goff wrote in the preface to his biography of Robert Todd Lincoln. "They were filled with enthusiasm, but they had few resources." Still, they were determined.

Within the month, they had incorporated, written a set of bylaws, and elected a board of nine trustees: Ken Hill, Susan Hill (secretary), Oscar Johnson Jr. (vice president), Romi Perkins, Carl Saladino, Robert Schmid (president and chairman of the board), Robert Thum (treasurer), John West, and William Whitman. But their task was still nearly impossible. The church wanted to sell the property within the next two months, by the end of October, and the asking price was $500,000. Friends of Hildene had only $140 in the bank.[67]

"At that point, the first of three 'miracles' occurred," Goff wrote. The church agreed to extend the deadline while they negotiated with the newly formed group. The negotiations went on for two and a half years. Meanwhile, the Friends of Hildene met with fundraisers and studied the operation of other historic homes, but the challenges of their venture, not the least of which was the church's purchase price, all seemed insurmountable.[68]

Eventually, the church decided to take the question of whether Peggy's idea was feasible to court. The church was arguing that it was not practical, but the Friends of Hildene asserted that they could do it. Before the court could reach a decision, the second "miracle" occurred. The church had already lowered its asking price several times. Now they told the Friends of Hildene that they could have Hildene for $200,000. On faith, Oscar told the group's attorney to say yes.[69] The third "miracle" occurred when an anonymous donor agreed to provide the $200,000.

On July 27, 1978, Hildene was transferred back to Peggy's friends and the Manchester community. The papers were signed at the dining room table of Hildene, with a portrait of Robert Todd Lincoln looking down from the wall.[70]

The Friends of Hildene's heroic effort to preserve Hildene, told with details of its nail-biting suspense by Donald Keelan, and the many dedicated hours given by hundreds of local volunteers over the past quarter of a century, is a great tribute to the Lincoln descendants. All of the Lincolns, and especially Peggy, had been loyal and generous to the community, and in this way, the community returned the favor. Oscar Johnson, who was always characteristically humble about his leading role in saving Hildene, said in August of 1991 that, "Hildene has done much more for me than I ever did for it."[71]

Before Peggy died, she directed that she was to be cremated and her ashes scattered over the lands of Hildene. That was done within a month of her death. With the help of her close friends in Manchester, her ashes were spread from the lookout near the formal gardens.[72]

If it is true that departed spirits can roam, then surely her spirit still strolls through the house and around the grounds of Hildene, grateful for the loyalty of friends, and equally grateful that she is finally, irrevocably, out of the limelight.

Notes

Letters and Manuscript Collections and Common Abbreviations

Book citations refer to the following materials, but each institution's collection contains other materials as well. Abbreviations used in the endnotes are in SMALL CAPS after each institution's name.

Abraham Lincoln Presidential Library (formerly the Illinois State Historical Library), 112 N. Sixth St., Springfield, Illinois. ISHL
- Artwork
- Calling cards
- Correspondence (including Minnie Chandler letters)
- Family and other photos
- Financial receipts, investment records, and cancelled checks
- Hildene maple syrup production notes
- News clippings
- Property records and house plans
- Recipes and diet plans
- Robert Todd Lincoln letterpress books

Chicago Historical Society, Clark St. at North Ave., Chicago, Illinois. CHS
- Isham Family Collection
- Robert Todd Lincoln Collection
- Robert Todd Lincoln—Isham Family Collection

Harlan-Lincoln House Collection, Iowa Wesleyan College, Mount Pleasant, Iowa. HLH
- Correspondence
- Dance party invitation
- Family photos
- News clippings
- Panel from closet door showing heights of Lincoln children
- Rock collection of Abraham Lincoln (Jack)
- Wills and inheritance records

Hildene, Route 7A, Manchester, Vermont.
- Correspondence
- Family photos
- News clippings
- Oral history tapes
- Summer home open for tours

Iowa Wesleyan College Archives, Mount Pleasant, Iowa. IWC
- College catalogs
- Student rosters

Lincoln Museum Research Library at the Lincoln National Corporation, 200 E. Berry St., Fort Wayne, Indiana. LML
- Artifacts
- Artwork
- Family photographs
- News clippings
- Rare books

Manchester Journal archives (microfilm and some bound volumes), Mark Skinner Library, Route 7A, Manchester, Vermont.

Mount Pleasant newspaper archives (microfilm), Iowa Wesleyan College library and Mount Pleasant Public Library, Mount Pleasant, Iowa.

P.E.O. archives, P.E.O Library, W. Monroe St., Mount Pleasant, Iowa. Membership records (microfilm).

INTRODUCTION

1 Roy P. Basler, editor-in-chief, *The Collected Works of Abraham Lincoln,* 8 vols. (New Brunswick, N.J.: Rutgers University Press, 1953-55), 3: 484, 511. Lincoln spoke of the nation's "fathers" at Beloit, Wisconsin, on October 1, 1859, referring repeatedly to "our fathers" a few months later at Cooper Union in New York. He wrote about his parents in an autobiographical sketch around the same time, December 20, 1859.

2 Mark E. Neely, Jr., and Harold Holzer, *The Lincoln Family Album* (New York: Doubleday, 1990), 62.

3 Mary wrote, "I consider myself fortunate, if at eleven o'clock, I once more find myself, in my pleasant room & very especially, if my tired

& weary Husband is there, resting in the lounge to receive me — to chat over the occurrences of the day." Robert would echo: "I scarcely even had ten minutes quiet talk with him during his Presidency." See Justin G. Turner and Linda Levitt Turner, *Mary Todd Lincoln: Her Life and Letters* (New York: Alfred A. Knopf, 1972), 200; Rufus Rockwell Wilson, ed., *Intimate Memories of Lincoln* (Elmira, N.Y.: Primavera Press, 1945), 499.

4 Mary wrote to her mother-in-law a full two years after the President's death to inform Sarah Bush Johnston Lincoln that their youngest son, Thomas "Tad" Lincoln, was named for Sarah's late husband. See Turner and Turner, *Mary Todd Lincoln,* 464-65. For "best friend" reference see David Herbert Donald, *Lincoln* (New York: Simon & Schuster, 1995), 28.

5 Mary Todd Lincoln enjoyed only limited rights, in fact, to defend herself at her insanity trial— although by national standards, Illinois was advanced in this area.

6 Associated Press, "Bobby Kennedy Goes Too Fast, Says Lincoln Kin," story with Manchester dateline, February, 1963, LML. (A United Press International wire story from the *Cincinnati Post and Times-Star,* dated Feb. 12, 1963, contains similar comments.)

CHAPTER ONE:

"I Didn't Ask to be Born a Lincoln."

1 Johnson, *Nature of Vermont,* 14-28.

2 "Road Opening Plans Complete," *Bennington (Vt.) Evening Banner,* Sept. 20, 1930.

3 "Colorful Parade and Pageant Dedicate First Long Link of

Concrete on Allen Highway,"
Bennington (Vt.) Evening Banner,
Sept. 22, 1930.

4 "Pageant Was Used When Road
Opened," *Manchester (Vt.) Journal,*
Oct. 2, 1930.

5 "Road Opening Plans Complete,"
Bennington (Vt.) Evening Banner,
Sept. 20, 1930.

6 "Scout Rumor of Suicide Flight,"
Bennington (Vt.) Evening Banner,
Sept. 20, 1930.

7 "Lincoln Relative an Aviatrix,"
National Tribune, Feb. 20, 1930
(handwritten date), LML.

8 "Great Granddaughter of Lincoln
Takes to Air," Washington, Feb. 12
(1930), LML.

9 Bernice "Beanie" Graham interview, Hildene.

10 Associated Press, "Bobby Kennedy
Goes Too Fast, Says Lincoln Kin,"
unlabeled story with Manchester
dateline, February 1963, LML.

11 *Chicago Tribune* obituary, July 27,
1926; Associated Press on R.T.
Lincoln's burial at Arlington
National Cemetery, Oct. 21, 1926,
Folder #2, Robert Todd Lincoln
Collection, CHS.

12 "Colorful Parade and Pageant
Dedicate First Long Link of
Concrete on Allen Highway,"
Bennington (Vt.) Evening Banner,
Sept. 22, 1930.

13 "Big Celebration Opens New
Road," *Manchester (Vt.) Journal,*
Sept. 25, 1930.

14 "Colorful Parade and Pageant
Dedicate First Long Link of
Concrete on Allen Highway,"
Bennington (Vt.) Evening Banner,
Sept. 22, 1930.

15 See Robert Todd Lincoln Beckwith
foreword to Neely and McMurtry,
Insanity File, ix.

16 Neely and McMurtry, *Insanity File,*
36; Baker, *Mary Todd Lincoln,* 307.

17 Goldsmith, *Other Powers,* 19-22.

18 Ibid, 8-13.

19 Ibid, 28-33.

20 Neely and McMurtry, *Insanity File,*
6-26.

21 Neely and McMurtry, *Insanity File,*
37-73.

22 Turner and Turner, *MTL Life and
Letters,* 616-17, 692-93.

23 Turner and Turner, *MTL Life and
Letters,* 705-06; Baker, *Mary Todd
Lincoln,* 365-69.

24 Turner and Turner, *MTL Life and
Letters,* 716-17; Baker, *Mary Todd
Lincoln,* 368-69.

25 Turner and Turner, *MTL Life and
Letters,* 706; Neely and McMurtry,
Insanity File, 123.

26 Neely and McMurtry, *Insanity File,*
36.

27 Turner and Turner, *MTL Life and
Letters,* 705-06; Neely and
McMurtry, *Insanity File,* 122-23;
Baker, *Mary Todd Lincoln,* 364-69.

CHAPTER 2

The Courtship of Mary Todd

1 Neely and McMurtry, *Insanity File,*
131-33.

2 Neely and McMurtry, *Insanity File,*
xi.

3 Neely and McMurtry, *Insanity File,*
97-99; Turner and Turner, *MTL
Life and Letters,* 615-16; Randall,
Lincoln's Sons, 292-93.

4 Baker, *Mary Todd Lincoln,* 4.

5 Turner and Turner, *MTL Life and
Letters,* 3.

6 Baker, *Mary Todd Lincoln,* 33.

7 Baker, *Mary Todd Lincoln,* 11-12, 17.

8 Baker, *Mary Todd Lincoln,* 20;
Woloch, *Women and the American
Experience,* 8.

9 Baker, *Mary Todd Lincoln,* 22-23.

10 Baker, *Mary Todd Lincoln,* 28.

11 Ibid.; Turner and Turner, *MTL Life and Letters*, 588.
12 Baker, *Mary Todd Lincoln*, 28.
13 Ibid.
14 Baker, *Mary Todd Lincoln*, 29.
15 Wise, *Young Lady's Counselor*, 91.
16 Woloch, *Women and the American Experience*, 41.
17 Gregory, *A Father's Legacy*, 9-10.
18 Welter, "The Cult of True Womanhood," 200.
19 Woloch, *Women and the American Experience*, 59.
20 Bennett, *Strictures on Female Education*, 88.
21 Arthur, *Advice to Young Ladies*, 129-30.
22 Welter, "The Cult of True Womanhood," 205-06.
23 Woloch, *Women and the American Experience*, 60.
24 Kerber, *Women of the Republic*, 191-93; Evans, *Born for Liberty*, 72.
25 Woloch, *Women and the American Experience*, 79.
26 Woloch, *Women and the American Experience*, 80-81.
27 Baker, *Mary Todd Lincoln*, 37-40; Turner and Turner, *MTL Life and Letters*, 5-6; Helm, *True Story of Mary*, 20-21.
28 Baker, *Mary Todd Lincoln*, 35-37.
29 Baker, *Mary Todd Lincoln*, 37-40; Turner and Turner, *MTL Life and Letters*, 5-6; Helm, *True Story of Mary*, 20-21.
30 Ibid.
31 Baker, *Mary Todd Lincoln*, 38-39.
32 Turner and Turner, *MTL Life and Letters*, 5.
33 Baker, *Mary Todd Lincoln*, 40; Helm, *True Story of Mary*, 21.
34 Baker, *Mary Todd Lincoln*, 59-61.
35 Turner and Turner, *MTL Life and Letters*, 7.
36 Baker, *Mary Todd Lincoln*, 41-46.
37 Ibid.
38 Ibid.
39 Ibid.
40 Randall, *Biography of a Marriage*, 4-5.
41 Baker, *Mary Todd Lincoln*, 97.
42 Baker, *Mary Todd Lincoln*, 75.
43 Turner and Turner, *MTL Life and Letters*, 9.
44 Baker, *Mary Todd Lincoln*, 76.
45 Ibid.
46 Baker, *Mary Todd Lincoln*, 77.
47 Turner and Turner, *MTL Life and Letters*, 29-30.
48 Baker, *Mary Todd Lincoln*, 78.
49 Baker, *Mary Todd Lincoln*, 78-79.
50 Baker, *Mary Todd Lincoln*, 83.
51 Baker, *Mary Todd Lincoln*, 85-86.
52 Turner and Turner, *MTL Life and Letters*, 21.
53 Baker, *Mary Todd Lincoln*, 86; Randall, *Biography of a Marriage*, 17-18.
54 Turner and Turner, *MTL Life and Letters*, 16, 20-21, 23, 27; Baker, *Mary Todd Lincoln*, 84-85; Randall, *Biography of a Marriage*, 4-5.
55 Turner and Turner, *MTL Life and Letters*, 11.
56 Turner and Turner, *MTL Life and Letters*, 51-52.
57 Turner and Turner, *MTL Life and Letters*, 18.
58 Baker, *Mary Todd Lincoln*, 85.
59 Turner and Turner, *MTL Life and Letters*, 26.
60 Baker, *Mary Todd Lincoln*, 86-87.
61 Ibid.
62 Baker, *Mary Todd Lincoln*, 89.
63 Ibid.
64 Randall, *Biography of a Marriage*, 182.
65 Baker, *Mary Todd Lincoln*, 85.
66 Turner and Turner, *MTL Life and Letters*, 23.
67 Baker, *Mary Todd Lincoln*, 89-90.
68 Turner and Turner, *MTL Life and Letters*, 24-25.
69 Turner and Turner, *MTL Life and Letters*, 25.

70 Turner and Turner, *MTL Life and Letters*, 27.
71 Turner and Turner, *MTL Life and Letters*, 29.
72 Ibid.
73 Baker, *Mary Todd Lincoln*, 95-97.
74 Drake, "Duel!", 96-97.
75 Turner and Turner, *MTL Life and Letters*, 29-30; Baker, *Mary Todd Lincoln*, 96.
76 Turner and Turner, *MTL Life and Letters*, 30; Baker, *Mary Todd Lincoln*, 97-98.
77 Baker, *Mary Todd Lincoln*, 97.
78 Baker, *Mary Todd Lincoln*, 98; Randall, *Biography of a Marriage*, 69-73.
79 Turner and Turner, *MTL Life and Letters*, 30.
80 Turner and Turner, *MTL Life and Letters*, 21.

CHAPTER THREE:
"Ease, Grace and Fashionability"

1   Randall, *Biography of a Marriage*, 214-15.
2   Baker, *Mary Todd Lincoln*, 165-66; Turner and Turner, *MTL Life and Letters*, 77-78, 85; Randall, *Biography of a Marriage*, 214-16.
3   Oates, *With Malice Toward None*, 100-05.
4   Baker, *Mary Todd Lincoln*, 178.
5   Randall, *Biography of a Marriage*, 206-07.
6   Randall, *Biography of a Marriage*, 89-90.
7   Ibid.
8   Helm, *True Story of Mary*, 1-5.
9   Baker, *Mary Todd Lincoln*, 166.
10 Randall, *Biography of a Marriage*, 214-19.
11 Baker, *Mary Todd Lincoln*, 166.
12 Baker, *Mary Todd Lincoln*, 160.
13 Baker, *Mary Todd Lincoln*, 197.
14 Randall, *Biography of a Marriage*, 217.
15 Baker, *Mary Todd Lincoln*, 164.
16 Baker, *Mary Todd Lincoln*, 166-67; Turner and Turner, *MTL Life and Letters*, 78; Randall, *Biography of a Marriage*, 207.
17 Oates, *With Malice Towards None*, 201.
18 Oates, *With Malice Toward None*, 218-19.
19 Baker, *Mary Todd Lincoln*, 198.
20 Randall, *Biography of a Marriage*, 214-16.
21 Laver, *Concise History of Costume and Fashion*, 151-53, 173-88.
22 Ibid.
23 Ibid.; Randall, *Biography of a Marriage*, 215-16.
24 Turner and Turner, *MTL Life and Letters*, 5-6; Baker, *Mary Todd Lincoln*, 29-30.
25 Baker, *Mary Todd Lincoln*, 29-30.
26 Randall, *Biography of a Marriage*, 215.
27 Randall, *Biography of a Marriage*, 218.
28 Randall, *Biography of a Marriage*, 215.

CHAPTER FOUR:
Public and Private Grief

1   Turner and Turner, *MTL Life and Letters*, 179.
2   Turner and Turner, *MTL Life and Letters*, 88.
3   Baker, *Mary Todd Lincoln*, 183.
4   Turner and Turner, *MTL Life and Letters*, 84-85; Baker, *Mary Todd Lincoln*, 184.
5   Baker, *Mary Todd Lincoln*, 182-84; Turner and Turner, *MTL Life and Letters*, 84-85, 87-89.
6   Turner and Turner, *MTL Life and Letters*, 87-89; Baker, *Mary Todd Lincoln*, 185-89.
7   Ibid.
8   Turner and Turner, *MTL Life and Letters*, 88.
9   Baker, *Mary Todd Lincoln*, 188-90; Turner and Turner, *MTL Life and Letters*, 89.

10 Ibid.

11 Ibid.

12 "The Secession Rebellion," *The New York Times*, May 24, 1861; "Highly Important News: The War for the Union Commenced in Earnest," *The New York Times*, May 25, 1861.

13 Loatman, "Elmer E. Ellsworth: Citizen Soldier," speech.

14 "Highly Important News: The War for the Union Commenced in Earnest," *The New York Times*, May 25, 1861.

15 Ibid.

16 Ibid.

17 Turner and Turner, *MTL Life and Letters*, 92; Randall, *Biography of a Marriage*, 204, 232; Randall, *Lincoln's Sons*, 110-14; Oates, *With Malice Toward None*, 208, 234-35.

18 Ibid.

19 Loatman, "Elmer E. Ellsworth: Citizen Soldier," speech.

20 Ibid.

21 Baker, *Mary Todd Lincoln*, 185; Turner and Turner, *MTL Life and Letters*, 92.

22 Randall, *Lincoln's Sons*, 100-01; Randall, *Biography of a Marriage*, 232-33; Oates, *With Malice Toward None*, 240.

23 Baker, *Mary Todd Lincoln*, 185-86.

24 Randall, *Biography of a Marriage*, 297-98; Baker, *Mary Todd Lincoln*, 185-86.

25 Woloch, *Women and the American Experience*, 138-40; Wood, "War Within a War," 125.

26 Ibid.

27 Wood, "War Within a War," 130.

28 Wood, "War Within a War," 129-30.

29 Baker, *Mary Todd Lincoln*, 205-07.

30 Ibid.

31 Ibid.

32 Ibid.

33 Ibid.

34 Randall, *Lincoln's Sons*, 127-32; Baker, *Mary Todd Lincoln*, 207-09.

35 Randall, *Lincoln's Sons*, 127-32; Baker, *Mary Todd Lincoln*, 208-14.

36 Ibid.

37 Helm, *True Story of Mary*, 180, 197-98.

38 Turner and Turner, *MTL Life and Letters*, 120.

39 Baker, *Mary Todd Lincoln*, 211.

40 Turner and Turner, *MTL Life and Letters*, 147.

41 Baker, *Mary Todd Lincoln*, 212.

42 Ibid; Turner and Turner, *MTL Life and Letters*, 122.

43 Baker, *Mary Todd Lincoln*, 213.

44 Baker, *Mary Todd Lincoln*, 223; Helm, *True Story of Mary*, 203.

45 Baker, *Mary Todd Lincoln*, 223.

46 Evans, *Born for Liberty*, 114; Fullbrook, "Relief Work in Iowa," 212.

47 Aldrich, "Mrs. Ann E. Harlan, Late Wife," 489-94.

48 Ibid.

49 Ibid.

50 Ibid.

51 Ibid.

52 Ibid.

53 Ibid., 500-01.

54 Ibid.

55 "She Pulled Rank on Civil War General," *Des Moines (Iowa) Register*, Sept. 12, 1971.

56 Ibid.

57 "Mrs. Ann Eliza Harlan: A Memorial to Her Life," *Mount Pleasant (Iowa) Journal*, Sept. 18, 1884.

58 Randall, *Biography of a Marriage*, 297-98; Baker, *Mary Todd Lincoln*, 186.

59 Baker, *Mary Todd Lincoln*, 186.

60 Randall, *Biography of a Marriage*, 298.

61 Ibid.

CHAPTER FIVE:
"A Pleasant Land Among the Mountains"

1   Randall, *Biography of a Marriage*, 244-47, 326.
2   Bigelow and Otis, *Manchester, Vermont*, 90-91.
3   Bigelow and Otis, *Manchester, Vermont*, 286.
4   Bigelow and Otis, *Manchester, Vermont*, 204; Lewis, *The Equinox*, 7.
5   Bigelow and Otis, *Manchester, Vermont*, 206; Lewis, *The Equinox*, 6.
6   Lewis, *The Equinox*, 5-6.
7   Bigelow and Otis, *Manchester, Vermont*, 198.
8   Lewis, *The Equinox*, 7.
9   "Local Intelligence," *Manchester (Vt.) Journal*, Aug. 25, 1863.
10 Bigelow and Otis, *Manchester, Vermont*, 91.
11 Lewis, *The Equinox*, 6.
12 Randall, *Biography of a Marriage*, 326; Turner and Turner, *MTL Life and Letters*, 153-54.
13 Randall, *Biography of a Marriage*, 244.
14 Randall, *Biography of a Marriage*, 324-25; Turner and Turner, *MTL Life and Letters*, 153-54.
15 Ibid
16 Ibid.
17 Turner and Turner, *MTL Life and Letters*, 104.
18 Lewis, *The Equinox*, 12.
19 Ibid.
20 Bigelow and Otis, *Manchester, Vermont*, 206.
21 Bigelow and Otis, *Manchester, Vermont*, 198.
22 Lewis, *The Equinox*, 7-8.
23 Lewis, *The Equinox*, 11-12.
24 "State Intelligence" and "Local Intelligence," *Manchester (Vt.) Journal*, Aug. 25, 1863.
25 "State Intelligence" and "News Items," *Manchester (Vt.) Journal*, Aug. 25, 1863.
26 "Sanitary Commission," *Manchester (Vt.) Journal*, Aug. 25, 1863.
27 Lewis, *The Equinox*, 9.
28 Lewis, *The Equinox*, 10-11.
29 Turner and Turner, *MTL Life and Letters*, 123-24; Baker, *Mary Todd Lincoln*, 218-22; Helm, *True Story of Mary*, 226-27.
30 Baker, *Mary Todd Lincoln*, 221.
31 Baker, *Mary Todd Lincoln*, 216.
32 Goff, *Robert Todd Lincoln*, 55; Randall, *Biography of a Marriage*, 326.
33 Goff, *Robert Todd Lincoln*, 235.

CHAPTER SIX:
Who is the Lucky Fellow?

1   Goff, *Robert Todd Lincoln*, 60-61; Helm, *True Story of Mary*, 229-30; Turner and Turner, *MTL Life and Letters*, 197.
2   Ibid.
3   Donald, *Lincoln*, 544.
4   E.J.M., "The Inauguration Ball," *The New York Times*, March 8, 1865.
5   Ibid.
6   Ibid.
7   Goff, *Robert Todd Lincoln*, 67.
8   "Senator Harlan Dead," *Mount Pleasant (Iowa) News*, Oct. 6, 1898; Sandy Williams, "Lincoln's Death is Turning Point in Career of Senator from Iowa," *Mount Pleasant (Iowa) News*, July 7, 1973; Haselmayer, *Harlan-Lincoln Tradition*, 1977 ed., 9-10; Goff, *Robert Todd Lincoln*, 67.
9   Randall, *Lincoln's Sons*, 173-74.
10 Ibid.
11 E.J.M., "The Inauguration Ball," *The New York Times*, March 8, 1865.
12 Minnie Chandler letters are from the Illinois State Historical Library.
13 Goff, *Robert Todd Lincoln*, 67.

14 Turner and Turner, *MTL Life and Letters*, 206-08; Baker, *Mary Todd Lincoln*, 239-40.
15 Ibid.
16 "Grant—Richmond and Victory!," *The New York Times*, April 4, 1865.
17 "From Richmond," *The New York Times*, April 8, 1865.
18 "The Abandonment of Richmond," *The New York Times*, April 4, 1865.
19 Baker, *Mary Todd Lincoln*, 241; Goff, *Robert Todd Lincoln*, 68; Turner and Turner, *MTL Life and Letters*, 208.
20 Goff, *Robert Todd Lincoln*, 68.
21 Goff, *Robert Todd Lincoln*, 71-74; McMurtry, *Harlan-Lincoln Tradition, 1946 ed.*, 5.
22 Goff, *Robert Todd Lincoln*, 74-75.
23 Ibid.
24 Goff, *Robert Todd Lincoln*, 67.
25 W.W. Kimball, "Robert T. Lincoln Inherited His Father's Clear View, Humor," letter to editor, *Washington Star*, April 15, 1928, LML; Kathleen M. Norton, "Lincoln's Son Tried to be Own Man, Letters Reveal," Associated Press, story in *Sunday Rutland (Vt.) Herald*, Feb. 12, 1984; Warren, "Hon. Robert Todd Lincoln," 1-8.
26 Alpheus H. Harlan, *History of the Harlan Family*, 2-11.
27 "History of Old Kennett Meeting," flyer for Harlan Family in America 2002 national reunion (see www.harlanfamily.org); "Straight-Ahead Driving Tour of the Brandywine Battlefield Region," www.ushistory.org/brandywine/drivingtour/car1.htm (accessed Feb. 27, 2005).
28 Louis R. Harlan, *Harlan Family in America: A Brief History*, 2-3; Baker, *Mary Todd Lincoln*, 31.
29 Brigham, *James Harlan*, 1-15; Haselmayer, *Harlan-Lincoln Tradition, 1977 ed.*, 5.
30 Brigham, "Wedding of James Harlan," 101-05.
31 "Mrs. Ann Eliza Harlan. A Memorial of Her Life," *Mount Pleasant Journal*, Sept. 9, 1884.
32 Brigham, "Wedding of James Harlan," 102-03.
33 Haselmayer, *Harlan-Lincoln Tradition, 1977 ed.*, 5-7, 16.
34 Ibid.
35 Ibid.
36 Ibid.
37 Haselmayer, "Memorandum," 5-6.
38 See note #12.
39 Turner and Turner, *MTL Life and Letters*, 478, 482; Goff, *Robert Todd Lincoln*, 88-89; Brigham, *James Harlan*, 237-38; Randall, *Lincoln's Sons*, 255-57.
40 "Bob Lincoln's Marriage: Further Particulars," *Chicago Times* reprint of *Washington Star*, Oct. 2, 1868, HLH.
41 "Bob Lincoln: His Marriage," *Chicago Times* reprint of *Washington Express*, Sept. 30, 1868, HLH.
42 "Bob Lincoln's Marriage: Further Particulars," *Chicago Times* reprint of *Washington Star*, Oct. 2, 1868, HLH.
43 "Bob Lincoln: His Marriage," *Chicago Times* reprint of *Washington Express*, Sept. 30, 1868, HLH.
44 *Illinois State Journal*, Oct. 3, 1868, quoting *Washington Star*, Sept. 27, 1868 (typed notes, HLH).
45 Haselmayer, "Memorandum," 1-2.
46 Yvonne von Fettweis (Manager, Church History, First Church of Christ, Scientist), letter to author, July 13, 1993.

CHAPTER SEVEN:

A Question of Sanity

1 "Mrs. Ann Eliza Harlan. A Memorial of Her Life," *Mount Pleasant Journal*, Sept. 18, 1884.

2 Turner and Turner, *MTL Life and Letters*, 705.

3 McMurtry, "Some Intimate Glimpses," 4.

4 Ibid.

5 Ibid., 1-3.

6 Ibid., 4.

7 Ibid., 3.

8 Ibid., 4.

9 Ibid.

10 Neely and McMurtry, *Insanity File*, 154-81.

11 Neely and McMurtry, *Insanity File*, 154.

12 Neely and McMurtry, *Insanity File*, 174.

13 McMurtry, "Some Intimate Glimpses," 4.

14 Turner and Turner, *MTL Life and Letters*, 481-82, 536; Neely and McMurtry, *Insanity File*, 154; Randall, *Biography of a Marriage*, 368, 420-22; Helm, *True Story of Mary*, 279.

15 Turner and Turner, *MTL Life and Letters*, 481-82; Neely and McMurtry, *Insanity File*, 5, 87; Baker, *Mary Todd Lincoln*, 277-80.

16 Neely and McMurtry, *Insanity File*, 5; Baker, *Mary Todd Lincoln*, 271-80.

17 Baker, *Mary Todd Lincoln*, 275-78.

18 Ibid.

19 Sandburg and Angle, *Mary Lincoln*, 133.

20 Baker, *Mary Todd Lincoln*, 279.

21 Baker, *Mary Todd Lincoln*, 212-13, 280.

22 Brigham, *James Harlan*, 237-38.

23 Neely and McMurtry, *Insanity File*, 153-55.

24 Turner and Turner, *MTL Life and Letters*, 520.

25 Turner and Turner, *MTL Life and Letters*, 522.

26 Randall, *Biography of a Marriage*, 420.

27 Turner and Turner, *MTL Life and Letters*, 533-34.

28 Turner and Turner, *MTL Life and Letters*, 519, 522, 524, 528-29, 537.

29 Turner and Turner, *MTL Life and Letters*, 520.

30 Turner and Turner, *MTL Life and Letters*, 534-37.

31 Turner and Turner, *MTL Life and Letters*, 539-41.

32 Turner and Turner, *MTL Life and Letters*, 546.

33 Turner and Turner, *MTL Life and Letters*, 552-53.

34 Randall, *Biography of a Marriage*, 418.

35 Baker, *Mary Todd Lincoln*, 296.

36 Baker, *Mary Todd Lincoln*, 296-97.

37 Turner and Turner, *MTL Life and Letters*, 555-57, 572; Randall, *Biography of a Marriage*, 419; Baker, *Mary Todd Lincoln*, 299; Neely and McMurtry, *Insanity File*, 5.

38 Turner and Turner, *MTL Life and Letters*, 555-56; Baker, *Mary Todd Lincoln*, 294.

39 Baker, *Mary Todd Lincoln*, 295.

40 Ibid.; Randall, *Biography of a Marriage*, 417-18.

41 Baker, *Mary Todd Lincoln*, 298; Turner and Turner, *MTL Life and Letters*, 555.

42 Baker, *Mary Todd Lincoln*, 299-301; Randall, *Biography of a Marriage*, 419; Turner and Turner, *MTL Life and Letters*, 571-72.

43 Ibid.

44 Turner and Turner, *MTL Life and Letters*, 572.

45 Neely and McMurtry, *Insanity File*, 173.

46 Baker, *Mary Todd Lincoln*, 305; Randall, *Lincoln's Sons*, 267-68; Neely and McMurtry, *Insanity File*, 153-54.

47 Baker, *Mary Todd Lincoln*, 306-08; Randall, *Biography of a Marriage*, 424-25; Randall, *Lincoln's Sons*, 269-71.

48 Baker, *Mary Todd Lincoln*, 308; Randall, *Lincoln's Sons*, 275.

49 Turner and Turner, *MTL Life and Letters*, 595, 608.

50 Baker, *Mary Todd Lincoln*, 309-10; Haselmayer, *Harlan-Lincoln Tradition, 1977 ed.*, 19; Neely and McMurtry, *Insanity File*, 36.

51 Baker, *Mary Todd Lincoln*, 309-10; Randall, *Biography of a Marriage*, 425; Neely and McMurtry, *Insanity File*, 6.

52 Goff, *Robert Todd Lincoln*, 96; Baker, *Mary Todd Lincoln*, 310; Randall, *Lincoln's Sons*, 275-76.

53 Haselmayer, *Harlan-Lincoln Tradition, 1977 ed.*, 19.

54 Baker, *Mary Todd Lincoln*, 310.

55 Neely and McMurtry, *Insanity File*, 36; Randall, *Biography of a Marriage*, 425; Turner and Turner, *MTL Life and Letters*, 608.

56 Haselmayer, *Harlan-Lincoln Tradition, 1977 ed.*, 19.

57 Randall, *Biography of a Marriage*, 425-29; Randall, *Lincoln's Sons*, 276-80; Baker, *Mary Todd Lincoln*, 313; Turner and Turner, *MTL Life and Letters*, 601-02.

58 Neely and McMurtry, *Insanity File*, 6-7; Baker, *Mary Todd Lincoln*, 314.

59 Neely and McMurtry, *Insanity File*, 6-7.

60 Ibid.

61 Ibid.

62 Neely and McMurtry, *Insanity File*, 7-8, 16; Baker, *Mary Todd Lincoln*, 320-21; Turner and Turner, *MTL Life and Letters*, 608-09; Sandburg and Angle, *Mary Lincoln*, 141-43, 305-09; Goff, *Robert Todd Lincoln*, 100-01; Randall, *Biography of a Marriage*, 430-31.

63 Sandburg and Angle, *Mary Lincoln*, 309; Goff, *Robert Todd Lincoln*, 101; Baker, *Mary Todd Lincoln*, 317-18; Neely and McMurtry, *Insanity File*, 13-14; Turner and Turner, *MTL Life and Letters*, 609-10; Randall, *Biography of a Marriage*, 430.

64 Neely and McMurtry, *Insanity File*, 14-17; Baker, *Mary Todd Lincoln*, 318-22.

65 Goff, *Robert Todd Lincoln*, 102, 231-32.

66 Goff, *Robert Todd Lincoln*, 247; Neely and McMurtry, *Insanity File*, 11.

67 Neely and McMurtry, *Insanity File*, 11-12; Baker, *Mary Todd Lincoln*, 319-20; Randall, *Biography of a Marriage*, 431; Turner and Turner, *MTL Life and Letters*, 609.

68 Neely and McMurtry, *Insanity File*, 15-16; Baker, *Mary Todd Lincoln*, 315, 320; McMurtry, "Some Intimate Glimpses," 4; Turner and Turner, *MTL Life and Letters*, 609; Randall, *Biography of a Marriage*, 430; Sandburg and Angle, *Mary Lincoln*, 143.

69 Neely and McMurtry, *Insanity File*, 8-13.

70 Ibid.

71 Ibid.

72 Goff, *Robert Todd Lincoln*, 101-02.

73 Turner and Turner, *MTL Life and Letters*, 610.

74 Baker, *Mary Todd Lincoln*, 316-18; Randall, *Lincoln's Sons*, 284-86; Schreiner, *Trials of Mrs. Lincoln*, 13-17.

75 Baker, *Mary Todd Lincoln*, 318-19.

76 Ibid.

77 Neely and McMurtry, *Insanity File*, 17.

78 Neely and McMurtry, *Insanity File*, 15.

79 Neely and McMurtry, *Insanity File*, 17-26.

80 Ibid.

81 Ibid.

82 Baker, *Mary Todd Lincoln*, 321-25; Neely and McMurtry, *Insanity File*, 19-21.

83 Baker, *Mary Todd Lincoln*, 318-25; Neely and McMurtry, *Insanity File*,

15-17, 60; Turner and Turner, *MTL Life and Letters*, 610-11.
84 Ibid.
85 Neely and McMurtry, *Insanity File*, 34-35; Randall, *Biography of a Marriage*, 430-31; Randall, *Lincoln's Sons*, 288-88.
86 Ibid.
87 Ibid.
88 Neely and McMurtry, *Insanity File*, 27-30, 37-40.
89 Ibid.
90 Ibid.
91 Goff, *Robert Todd Lincoln*, 97-98.
92 Goff, *Robert Todd Lincoln*, 149-50.
93 Randall, *Lincoln's Sons*, 36-37.
94 Randall, *Biography of a Marriage*, 149.
95 Baker, *Mary Todd Lincoln*, 120-21.
96 Goff, *Robert Todd Lincoln*, 98-99.
97 Baker, *Mary Todd Lincoln*, 350.
98 Neely and McMurtry, *Insanity File*, 57-73; Turner and Turner, *MTL Life and Letters*, 612; Baker, *Mary Todd Lincoln*, 339-41.
99 Neely and McMurtry, *Insanity File*, 63-68.
100 Neely and McMurtry, *Insanity File*, 68-73.
101 Neely and McMurtry, *Insanity File*, 62, 75.
102 Goff, *Robert Todd Lincoln*, 149.
103 Haselmayer, "Memorandum," 7.
104 Neely and McMurtry, *Insanity File*, 91-92, 94-98.
105 Ibid.
106 Neely and McMurtry, *Insanity File*, 100-04; Turner and Turner, *MTL Life and Letters*, 612-13.
107 Neely and McMurtry, *Insanity File*, 121-22.
108 For examples, see Neely and McMurtry, *Insanity File*, 152-82.
109 Turner and Turner, *MTL Life and Letters*, 615-16.
110 Turner and Turner, *MTL Life and Letters*, 617.
111 Turner and Turner, *MTL Life and Letters*, 617-18; Baker, *Mary Todd Lincoln*, 355-57.
112 Baker, *Mary Todd Lincoln*, 358-60; Turner and Turner, *MTL Life and Letters*, 619-20.
113 Turner and Turner, *MTL Life and Letters*, 630-32.
114 Baker, *Mary Todd Lincoln*, 363-65; Turner and Turner, *MTL Life and Letters*, 692-93, 705-06.
115 Turner and Turner, *MTL Life and Letters*, 705-06.
116 Turner and Turner, *MTL Life and Letters*, 706; Baker, *Mary Todd Lincoln*, 366, 368; Neely and McMurtry, *Insanity File*, 123.
117 Randall, *Biography of a Marriage*, 384.
118 Neely and McMurtry, *Insanity File*, 123.
119 McMurtry, "Some Intimate Glimpses," 4.
120 Ibid.

CHAPTER EIGHT:
"So Restful for the Children"

1 McMurtry, "Some Intimate Glimpses," 3.
2 Ibid., 2-3.
3 McMurtry, *Harlan-Lincoln Tradition, 1946 ed.*, 4, 7; "Lincoln Grandchildren Write Names on Old Door Discovered in Mt. Pleasant," *Ottumwa (Iowa) Courier*, April 4, 1931.
4 McMurtry, *Harlan-Lincoln Tradition, 1959 ed.*, 14; Haselmayer, *Harlan-Lincoln Tradition, 1977 ed.*, 12.
5 Harper, *History of Henry County*, 22-23.
6 Ibid., 23-24.
7 Ibid., 24-25.
8 Ibid., 23.
9 Ibid., 25.
10 Ibid., 29.
11 "Mount Pleasant is Booming Along," *Mount Pleasant (Iowa) Journal*, Oct. 4, 1871.

12 Goff, *Robert Todd Lincoln*, 106-124, 154-55, 159-166.
13 Goff, *Robert Todd Lincoln*, 143.
14 Goff, *Robert Todd Lincoln*, 108, 110.
15 Goff, *Robert Todd Lincoln*, 112.
16 Goff, *Robert Todd Lincoln*, 112-117, 122.
17 Goff, *Robert Todd Lincoln*, 118.
18 Goff, *Robert Todd Lincoln*, 118, 130-31, 148.
19 Goff, *Robert Todd Lincoln*, 142-146.
20 Goff, *Robert Todd Lincoln*, 148.
21 Goff, *Robert Todd Lincoln*, 159-160.
22 McMurtry, "Some Intimate Glimpses," 3.
23 Untitled news note, *Mount Pleasant (Iowa) Journal*, Sept. 20, 1883.
24 McMurtry, *Harlan-Lincoln Tradition, 1946 ed.*, 7; Will Fenton interview, HLH; Hallie Ott interview, HLH; "Lincoln—Isham," unidentified news clipping announcing the engagement of Mary Lincoln to Charles Isham, "Charles Isham 1880-1919 folder," Robert Todd Lincoln—Isham Family Collection, CHS.
25 McMurtry, *Harlan-Lincoln Tradition, 1946 ed.*, 7.
26 Olive Cole Smith, unidentified newspaper clipping, IWC; Randall, *Lincoln's Sons*, 305.
27 "Lincoln—Isham," unidentified news clipping announcing the engagement of Mary Lincoln to Charles Isham, "Charles Isham 1880-1919 folder," Robert Todd Lincoln—Isham Family Collection, CHS.
28 McMurtry, "Some Intimate Glimpses," 2.
29 Ibid., 3.
30 P.E.O. archives: Mary "Mamie" Lincoln record is on Roll #225, Jessie Lincoln record is on Roll #361.
31 See *www.peointernational.org/about* and *www.peointernational.org/record/2003-11-12/past-prologue.php*.
32 "P.E.O.," *Mount Pleasant (Iowa) Journal*, Sept. 25, 1890.
33 Haselmayer, *Harlan-Lincoln Tradition, 1977 ed.*, 19.
34 "Iowa's Loss: Mrs. Harriet Ketcham," *The Free Press (Mount Pleasant, Iowa)*, Oct. 28, 1890.
35 Ibid.
36 Haselmayer, *Harlan-Lincoln Tradition, 1977 ed.*, 19.
37 "Henry County Old Settlers," *Mount Pleasant (Iowa) Journal*, Aug. 11, 1887.
38 Ibid.
39 Goff, *Robert Todd Lincoln*, 159-164.
40 Goff, *Robert Todd Lincoln*, 166.
41 Goff, *Robert Todd Lincoln*, 193; "Minister Lincoln Reaches Port," unidentified news clipping with the dateline "Liverpool, May 22," from a series of clippings about the Lincolns in London, photocopied together and containing the handwritten title "The News," from "Papers 1861-1905," Robert Todd Lincoln Collection, CHS.
42 "Welcome to Lincoln," unidentified news clipping from "The News," see #41.
43 "Minister Lincoln to Be Taken to Windsor in the Court Carriage," unidentified news clipping with the dateline "London, May 24," from "The News," see #41.
44 "Mr. Lincoln Meets the Prince," unidentified news clipping with the dateline "London, May 26," from "The News," see #41.
45 "Mrs. Lincoln, Miss Lincoln, and Mrs. Robert McCormick at the Drawing Room," unidentified news clipping with the dateline "London, May 29," from "The News," see #41.
46 "Americans Abroad Celebrate," unidentified news clipping from "Papers 1861-1905," Robert Todd Lincoln Collection, CHS.

47 Probably Mary King Waddington, wife of the French ambassador— see Goff, *Robert Todd Lincoln*, 209, footnote #1.

48 "King Edward and Lincoln's Goddaughter," unidentified news clipping, LML.

CHAPTER NINE:
Abraham Lincoln II

1 Untitled, unidentified news clipping announcing the death of Abraham Lincoln II, and beginning with the words "The greatest sympathy...," Folder #3, Robert Todd Lincoln Collection, CHS.

2 "Death of Mr. A. Lincoln," unidentified news clipping with the handwritten date March 6, 1890, Folder #3, Robert Todd Lincoln Collection, CHS.

3 Olive Cole Smith, news clipping with byline but no other identifying information, IWC.

4 J. Allen Boteler[?], handwritten letter to Jessie Lincoln Randolph, April 2, 1934, ISHL.

5 Olive Cole Smith, news clipping with byline but no other identifying information, IWC.

6 From author's tours of Hildene, Manchester, Vermont.

7 Donald, *Lincoln*, 20-22.

8 Ibid.

9 Oates, *With Malice Toward None*, 3-4.

10 Goff, *Robert Todd Lincoln*, 194.

11 Ibid.

12 Abraham Lincoln II to Charles Isham, undated letter labeled "Versailles, Sunday," Box #1 Folder #3, Isham Family Genealogy Collection, CHS.

13 "History of Fatal Illness of Abraham Lincoln II, (aged 16), as gleaned from letters written to Robert S. McCormick, secretary to United States legation in London," typed

notes dated Nov. 6 to March 5, Folder #3, Robert Todd Lincoln Collection, CHS.

14 "Illness of Master Jack Lincoln," news clipping with handwritten label *"Elite News of Chicago,"* Feb. 15, 1890, Folder #3, Robert Todd Lincoln Collection, CHS.

15 "Young Abraham Lincoln," *Mount Pleasant (Iowa) Journal*, Jan. 23, 1890.

16 Robert Todd Lincoln letter to "My dear Hale" [Eugene Hale], from "2 Cromwell Houses, S.W., London," Jan. 21, 1890, Folder 3, Robert Todd Lincoln Collection, CHS.

17 "History of Fatal Illness of Abraham Lincoln II," see #13.

18 "Minister Lincoln's Young Son," *Mount Pleasant (Iowa) Journal*, Feb. 6, 1890.

19 "Illness of Master Jack Lincoln," news clipping with handwritten label *"Elite News of Chicago,"* Feb. 15, 1890, Folder #3, Robert Todd Lincoln Collection, CHS.

20 "History of Fatal Illness of Abraham Lincoln II," see #13.

21 Untitled news brief, *Mount Pleasant (Iowa) Journal*, Feb. 27, 1890.

22 Goff, *Robert Todd Lincoln*, 195.

23 Untitled news brief, *Mount Pleasant (Iowa) Journal*, March 6, 1890.

24 "The Lincoln Bereavement," with handwritten notation "3-7-90 GD," probably *Globe-Democrat* (Springfield, Ill.), LML.

25 Goff, *Robert Todd Lincoln*, 196.

26 Lewis, *Myths After Lincoln*, 266-287; Carson, "The Other Tragic Lincoln," 248, 250-51; "Young Lincoln's Remains," unlabeled news clipping with dateline "Special Dispatch to the *Globe-Democrat*, Springfield, Ill., November 8," LML.

27 "Young Abraham Lincoln's Remains," unlabeled news clipping with the dateline "Special Dispatch

to the *Globe-Democrat*, Springfield, Ill., October 18," LML.

28 Haselmayer, "Memorandum," 9.

29 Goff, *Robert Todd Lincoln*, 196.

30 "Young Lincoln's Remains," unlabeled news clipping with dateline "Special Dispatch to the *Globe-Democrat*, Springfield, Ill., November 8," LML.

31 Goff, *Robert Todd Lincoln*, 196; "Young Lincoln's Remains," unlabeled news clipping with dateline "Special Dispatch to the *Globe-Democrat*, Springfield, Ill., November 8," LML.

CHAPTER TEN:
A Storybook Wedding

1 Goff, *Robert Todd Lincoln*, 196-97; Haselmayer, "Memorandum," 9.

2 "Young Lincoln's Remains," unlabeled news clipping with dateline "Special Dispatch to the *Globe-Democrat*, Springfield, Ill., November 8," LML.

3 Charles Isham diaries, Isham Family Collection, CHS.

4 Ibid.

5 "Cabin Passenger List of the Imperial German & U.S. Mail Steamship Saale," Feb. 25, 1891, ISHL.

6 Goff, *Robert Todd Lincoln*, 197.

7 Ibid.

8 *American Ancestry*, Vol. III, Part I, 1888 ed., 28-29, from Isham Family Genealogy, Box 1, Folder 5, CHS.

9 Osmond, "A P.E.O.'s Wedding in London," 10-11; "Charles Isham," typewritten draft of a biography, with correcting notes, Box 2, Lincoln Isham 1898-1959 Folder, Robert Todd Lincoln —Isham Family Collection, CHS.

10 Osmond, "A P.E.O.'s Wedding in London," 11.

11 "Charles Isham," typewritten draft of a biography, with correcting notes, Box 2, Lincoln Isham 1898-

1959 Folder, Robert Todd Lincoln —Isham Family Collection, CHS.

12 J. Allen Boteler[?], handwritten letter to Jessie Lincoln Randolph, April 2, 1934, ISHL.

13 Charles Isham diaries, Isham Family Collection, CHS.

14 Osmond, "A P.E.O.'s Wedding in London," 11.

15 Helen Pearson interview, Hildene.

16 "Lincoln—Isham," unlabeled news clipping, Box 2, Charles Isham 1880-1919 Folder, Robert Todd Lincoln—Isham Family Collection, CHS.

17 Osmond, "A P.E.O.'s Wedding in London," 10; "Miss Lincoln's Wedding," *The New York Times*, Sept. 3, 1891.

18 Ibid.

19 Ibid.

20 Ibid.

21 Goff, *Robert Todd Lincoln*, 198.

22 Osmond, "A P.E.O.'s Wedding in London," 10.

23 Mary Lincoln Isham and Charles Isham diaries, Isham Family Collection, CHS.

24 Built in the 1770s, the former home of Mary and Charles Isham, in Manchester Village, Vermont, is now an inn, the 1811 House. In fact, it has been an inn continuously since 1811, except for the period when it was the Isham residence, see *www.1811house.com*.

25 Charles Isham diaries, Isham Family Collection, CHS.

26 Robert Todd Lincoln letter to Charles Isham, 11 June 1892, Folder #11, Robert Todd Lincoln Collection, CHS.

CHAPTER ELEVEN:
Scandal and Rebellion

1 McGoldrick and Gerson, *Genograms*, 46-49, 63.

2 Ibid., 88-94.

3 Ibid., 92.
4 Lunardini, *What Every American Should Know*, 126-27.
5 *Annual Register 1890-91*, 28-29.
6 Ibid., 30.
7 Haselmayer, "Jessie Harlan Lincoln," 417-18.
8 *Annual Register 1892-93*, 52-53.
9 Haselmayer, *Harlan-Lincoln Tradition, 1977 ed.*, 20.
10 *Annual Register 1894-95*, 62; Haselmayer, "Jessie Harlan Lincoln," 418-19.
11 Ibid.
12 "Mrs. Lincoln's Ball," *Mt. Pleasant (Iowa) Daily News*, Oct. 17, 1895.
13 Ibid.
14 "An Elegant Entertainment, Mrs. Lincoln At Home," *Mount Pleasant (Iowa) Journal*, Oct. 17, 1895.
15 "Mrs. Lincoln's Ball," *Mount Pleasant Daily News*, Oct. 17, 1895.
16 Smith, "L is for Lincoln," 78-79.
17 "An Elegant Entertainment, Mrs. Lincoln At Home," *Mount Pleasant Journal*, Oct. 17, 1895.
18 Smith, "L is for Lincoln," 78-79.
19 Ibid.
20 "An Evening of Gayety," *Mount Pleasant Daily News*, Nov. 7, 1895; "A Brilliant Reception," *Mount Pleasant Journal*, Nov. 7, 1895.
21 Ibid.
22 Ibid.
23 "A Brilliant Reception," *Mount Pleasant Journal*, Nov. 7, 1895.
24 Robert Barewald, "Recall When the Lincolns Lived in Iowa," *Des Moines Register*, Feb. 11, 1957.
25 "Miss Lincoln Elopes," *Mount Pleasant Daily News*, Nov. 11, 1897.
26 Haselmayer, "Jessie Harlan Lincoln," 420; Christie Vilsack, "A Look Back at a Lincoln Family 'Scandal,'" *Mount Pleasant Daily News*, April 24, 1941, IWC.

27 Seymour Korman, "Lincoln Family Story Turns Up a New Chapter," *Chicago Tribune* story reprinted under the title "Another Phase of Lincoln Story Has Interest Here," *Mount Pleasant Daily News*, March 22, 1952.
28 Haselmayer, "Jessie Harlan Lincoln," 421; *RTL's Hildene: Volunteer Manual*, 57.
29 "Romance in Life of Lincoln's Granddaughter Drew Frowns," *Milwaukee Journal* quote in *Republican Times* (Ottawa, Illinois), June 19, 1958, LML.
30 Haselmayer, "Jessie Harlan Lincoln," 421; *RTL's Hildene: Volunteer Manual*, 57; "Beckwith's Good Base Ball Record," *Mount Pleasant Daily News*, Nov. 18, 1897; "The Beckwith-Lincoln Marriage," *Mount Pleasant Journal*, Nov. 18, 1897.
31 "Beckwith's Good Base Ball Record," *Mount Pleasant Daily News*, Nov. 18, 1897.
32 "Romance in Life of Lincoln's Granddaughter Drew Frowns," *Milwaukee Journal* quote in *Republican Times* (Ottawa, Illinois), June 19, 1958, LML; Christie Vilsack, "A Look Back at a Lincoln Family 'Scandal,'" *Mount Pleasant Daily News*, April 24, 1941, IWC; "Bypaths of History: Grid Player, Sweetheart Elope," unlabeled news clipping, LML; "Miss Lincoln Elopes," unlabeled news clipping with the dateline "Chicago, Nov. 11," IWC; "Miss Lincoln Elopes: In Spite of Parental Objections She Marries Warren Beckwith," *Mount Pleasant Daily News*, Nov. 11, 1897; "Without His Bride," *Mount Pleasant Daily News*, Nov. 12, 1897; "Beckwith is Still Here," *Mount Pleasant Daily News*, Nov. 13, 1897; "United at Last," *Mount Pleasant Daily News*, Nov. 15, 1897; "Lincoln-Beckwith

Story," *Mount Pleasant Daily News,*
Nov. 18, 1897; "The Beckwith-
Lincoln Marriage," *Mount Pleasant
Journal,* Nov. 18, 1897.

33 Christie Vilsack, "A Look Back at a
Lincoln Family 'Scandal,'" *Mount
Pleasant Daily News,* April 24, 1941,
IWC; "Miss Lincoln Elopes: In Spite
of Parental Objections She Marries
Warren Beckwith," *Mount Pleasant
Daily News,* Nov. 11, 1897.

34 Ibid.

35 "Without His Bride," *Mount
Pleasant Daily News,* Nov. 12, 1897.

36 Ibid.

37 Ibid.; "Romance in Life of Lincoln's
Granddaughter Drew Frowns,"
Milwaukee Journal quote in
Republican Times (Ottawa, Illinois)
June 19, 1958, LML.

38 Ibid.

39 "The Beckwith-Lincoln Marriage,"
Mount Pleasant Journal, Nov. 18, 1897.

40 Randall, *Lincoln's Sons,* 333-34.

41 Goff, *Robert Todd Lincoln,* 233.

42 "Without His Bride," *Mount
Pleasant Daily News,* Nov. 12, 1897.

43 Christie Vilsack, "A Look Back at a
Lincoln Family 'Scandal,'" *Mount
Pleasant Daily News,* April 24, 1941,
IWC.

44 "Without His Bride," *Mount
Pleasant Daily News,* Nov. 12, 1897.

45 "Beckwith is Still Here," *Mount
Pleasant Daily News,* Nov. 13, 1897.

46 Christie Vilsack, "A Look Back at a
Lincoln Family 'Scandal,'" *Mount
Pleasant Daily News,* April 24, 1941,
IWC.

47 "The Beckwith-Lincoln Marriage,"
Mount Pleasant Journal, Nov. 18, 1897.

48 "United at Last," *Mount Pleasant
Daily News,* Nov. 15, 1897.

49 "Lincoln-Beckwith Story," *Mount
Pleasant Daily News,* Nov. 18, 1897.

50 Ibid.

51 "Romance in Life of Lincoln's
Granddaughter Drew Frowns,"
Milwaukee Journal quote in
Republican Times (Ottawa, Illinois)
June 19, 1958, LML; Goff, *Robert
Todd Lincoln,* 233-34.

52 "The Beckwith-Lincoln Marriage,"
Mount Pleasant Journal, Nov. 18, 1897.

CHAPTER TWELVE:
"Who Has a Better Right?"

1 Haselmayer, *Harlan-Lincoln
Tradition, 1977 ed.,* 23.

2 Isabel Parris interview, Hildene.

3 Haselmayer, *Harlan-Lincoln
Tradition, 1977 ed.,* 22-23.

4 Seymour Korman, "Lincoln Family
Story Turns Up a New Chapter,"
Chicago Tribune story reprinted
with the title "Another Phase of
Lincoln Story Has Interest Here,"
Mount Pleasant Daily News, March
22, 1952.

5 Ibid.

6 "Divorces Kin of Lincoln," unlabeled
news clipping with the dateline
"Mount Pleasant, Ia., Feb. 12," LML.

7 Seymour Korman, "Lincoln Family
Story Turns Up a New Chapter,"
originally published by the *Chicago
Tribune,* reprinted with the title
"Another Phase of Lincoln Story
Has Interest Here," in *Mount
Pleasant News,* March 22, 1952;
"Warren Wallace Beckwith," *RTL's
Hildene: Volunteer Manual,* 57-58.

8 Earhart, *The Fun of It,* 11.

9 Photo in Hildene archives.

10 Randall, *Lincoln's Sons,* 312.

11 Goff, *Robert Todd Lincoln,* 239.

12 Randall, *Lincoln's Sons,* 336-37; *RTL's
Hildene: Volunteer Manual,* 27;
Keelan, *Hildene and How It Was
Saved,* 5.

13 "1871: The Great Fire," Chicago
Public Library,
www.chipublib.org/004chicago/time-

line/greatfire.html (accessed Dec. 28, 2004).

14 *RTL's Hildene: Volunteer Manual*, 26.

15 Goff, *Robert Todd Lincoln*, 91-93, 96-99.

16 Now an elegant inn, a short history of the Inn at Ormsby Hill building is available at *www.ormsbyhill.com/history.html*.

17 *RTL's Hildene: Volunteer Manual*, 26.

18 Mary Porter interview, Hildene.

19 Lynn Walker interview, Hildene.

20 *RTL's Hildene*, souvenir booklet, 3; *RTL's Hildene: Volunteer Manual*, 68-69.

21 Lynn Walker interview, Hildene.

22 Helen Pearson interview and speech, Hildene.

23 Ibid.

24 *RTL's Hildene: Volunteer Manual*, 69; Helen Pearson interview, Hildene.

25 Theresa Zullo interview, Hildene.

26 Ibid.

27 *RTL's Hildene: Volunteer Manual*, 105.

28 Ibid., 102.

29 Clarence Roberts interview, Hildene.

30 Bessie Bushee interview, Hildene.

31 *RTL's Hildene: Volunteer Manual*, 105; Oscar Johnson interviews and tour of Hildene with the author, Aug. 12, 1991 and June 17, 1993.

32 Robert Todd Lincoln Letterpress Book #40, ISHL. Thanks to the late John Goff for sharing these references with me.

33 Mary Porter interview, Hildene.

34 Mrs. George (Virginia Pierce) Smith letter to the author, April 21, 1994.

35 Bernice "Beanie" Graham interview, Hildene.

36 Flora G. Orr and Edith Porter, "President Lincoln's Living Descendants," ©1931, *Every Week Magazine*, ISHL.

37 Mary Porter interview, Hildene.

38 Ibid.

39 Helen Pearson interview, Hildene.

40 Bruce Smart and Mary Porter interviews, Hildene.

41 Sherman, *Fast Lane on a Dirt Road*, 7.

42 Bigelow and Otis, *Manchester, Vermont*, 290.

43 Sherman, *Fast Lane on a Dirt Road*, 7.

44 Associated Press, "Lincoln's Anniversary Work Day for Descendant," *Stamford (Ct.) Advocate*, Feb. 12, 1962, LML; Alice Colonna e-mail to the author, Feb 27, 2005.

45 Alice Colonna e-mails to the author, Oct. 19, 1998 and Feb. 27, 2005.

46 Anthony and Harper, *History of Woman Suffrage*, 4: 134-35.

47 Nancy Otis, "Two of Lincoln's Descendants Live in Bennington County," *Bennington (Vt.) Banner*, April 14, 1965.

48 Bernice "Beanie" Graham interview, Hildene.

CHAPTER THIRTEEN:
Tractors and Fast Cars

1 Sherman, *Fast Lane on a Dirt Road*, 13.

2 Ibid.

3 Ibid., 24-26.

4 Ken Hill interview, Hildene.

5 Ibid.

6 Ibid.; Paul and Myrtle Bullock interview, Hildene.

7 These handwritten lists from Peggy Beckwith's sugaring operation are in the Lincoln family files at the ISHL.

8 Ken Hill interview, Hildene.

9 Letters from W.H. Shaw to Miss Mary L. Beckwith: April 15, 1932; April 18, 1932; April 25, 1932, Hildene; "Symposium to Tour Lincoln Family Homes," *News From Historic Hildene*, Spring 1998, 1-2; Mary Hard Bort, "Bullhead Pond," *Manchester Journal*, Aug. 11, 2000.

10 Information from author's tours of Hildene and from Ken Hill, Lynn

Walker, and Mrs. Herbert (Wynona)
Walker interviews, Hildene.

11 Pat Broderson, "Remembering the
Lincoln Family," *Manchester
Journal,* June 8, 1988.

12 "Great Granddaughter of Lincoln
Takes to Air," unlabeled news clip-
ping, Washington, Feb. 12, 1930,
LML.

13 Ken Hill interview, Hildene.

14 Handwritten letter to "Peg" from
"Ellamae," undated, ISHL.

15 Ken Hill interview, Hildene.

16 Ibid.

17 Ibid.

18 Ibid.; Oscar Johnson interviews
with the author, Aug. 12, 1991, and
June 17, 1993.

19 Ken Hill interview, Hildene.

20 Ibid.

21 Bruce Smart interview, Hildene.

22 Lynn Walker interview, Hildene.

23 Ken Hill interview, Hildene.

24 Pete and Charlotte Brooks interview, Hildene.

25 Ibid.; Oscar Johnson interviews
with author.

26 Ibid.

27 Ibid.; David Wilson interview with
the author, Sept. 3, 1993.

28 Oscar Johnson interviews with the
author; "Peggy Lincoln Beckwith: A
Particular Taste in Cars,"
Manchester Journal Hildene Car
Show Special Section, June 10, 1992.

29 Ken Hill interview, Hildene.

CHAPTER FOURTEEN:

Manchester's Amelia Earhart

1 Earhart, *The Fun of It,* 152-154.

2 Haselmayer, *Harlan-Lincoln
Tradition, 1977 ed.,* 23.

3 "A Great-Granddaughter of Lincoln
Trains for a Pilot's License," photo
and caption, *The New York Times,*
Feb. 9, 1930.

4 Associated Press, "Descendant of
Lincoln Prefers Plane to Teas,"
unlabeled news clipping with the
dateline "Washington, D.C.," IWC.

5 "Great Granddaughter of Lincoln
Takes to Air," unlabeled news clip-
ping with dateline "Washington,
Feb. 12, 1930," LML.

6 Heath, "Women's Activities," 58.

7 Flora G. Orr and Edith Porter,
"President Lincoln's Living
Descendants," ©1931, *EveryWeek
Magazine,* ISHL; FAA form sent to
the author, signed by Verla
Coleman and dated July 23, 1993.

8 Earhart, *The Fun of It,* 30-39.

9 *Newark (N.J.) Star-Eagle,* Feb.
12, 1930.

10 Earhart, *The Fun of It,* 163-65.

11 Earhart, *The Fun of It,* 175-76.

12 Earhart, *The Fun of It,* 181-84.

13 Ibid.

14 Gordon, *American Heritage History
of Flight,* 204-05, 230.

15 Ibid., 118, 201, 204, 208, 242, 247.

16 Gordon, *American Heritage History
of Flight,* 243.

17 Earhart, *The Fun of It,* 146.

18 Earhart, *The Fun of It,* 28.

19 Rich, *Amelia Earhart: A Biography,*
23-24.

20 Earhart, *The Fun of It,* 8, 26.

21 Earhart, *The Fun of It,* 11.

22 Earhart, *The Fun of It,* 143-146.

23 Earhart, *The Fun of It,* 25-26.

24 Bigelow and Otis, *Manchester,
Vermont,* 97-98.

25 Ibid.

26 FAA facsimiles of aircraft record
NC-970H, purchased by the author,
July 29, 1993.

27 Ibid.

28 FAA facsimiles of aircraft record
NC-772V, purchased by the author,
Aug. 10, 1993.

29 Lee D. Bowman letter to Miss
Beckwith, June 19, 1931, Hildene.

30 Jones, "Lincoln's Great
Granddaughter," B17; letter from
Larry Wilson, (Archives, National
Air and Space Museum,
Smithsonian Institute), to John R.
Howe, Jan. 29, 1992, Hildene; letter
from G. Maxine Bennett, (Aircraft
Registration Branch, FAA), to
author, Jan. 31, 1994.
31 Pete and Charlotte Brooks inter-
view, Hildene.
32 Flora G. Orr and Edith Porter,
"President Lincoln's Living
Descendants," ©1931, *Every Week
Magazine*, ISHL.
33 Pat Broderson, "Remembering the
Lincoln Family," *Manchester
Journal*, June 8, 1988.
34 Earhart, *The Fun of It*, 28.
35 Earhart, *The Fun of It*, 42.
36 Bigelow and Otis, *Manchester,
Vermont*, 97.
37 Isabel Parris interview, Hildene.
38 Ken Hill interview, Hildene.
39 Pat Broderson, "Remembering the
Lincoln Family," *Manchester
Journal*, June 8, 1988.
40 Earhart, *The Fun of It*, 27.
41 Jones, "Lincoln's Great
Granddaughter," B17.
42 Pat Broderson, "Remembering the
Lincoln Family," *Manchester
Journal*, June 8, 1988.
43 Bernice "Beanie" Graham interview,
Hildene.
44 Isabel Parris, Ken Hill, Bernice
"Beanie" Graham, Clarence "Clark"
Kelley IV, Pete Brooks interviews,
Hildene; Pat Broderson,
"Remembering the Lincoln Family,"
Manchester Journal, June 8, 1988.
45 Pat Broderson, "Remembering the
Lincoln Family," *Manchester
Journal*, June 8, 1988.

CHAPTER FIFTEEN:
*Peggy's One-Woman
Humane Society*

1 Rhoda Orvis Wriston interview,
Hildene.
2 James Campbell interview, Hildene.
3 Helen Coburn interview, Hildene.
4 Bessie Bushee interview, Hildene;
Donna Nemhauser, "Memories of
Hildene in Its Heydey," *Manchester
(Vt.) Journal*, Oct. 30, 1991.
5 Bessie Bushee interview, Hildene.
6 Pat Broderson, "Remembering the
Lincoln Family," *Manchester (Vt.)
Journal*, June 8, 1988.
7 Letter addressed to "dear Thacher"
and signed "R.T.L.," Box 2, Robert
Todd Lincoln Collection, CHS;
"Manchester's Distinguished
Resident," *Troy Times*, Aug. 23,
1904, 1861-1905 folder, Robert Todd
Lincoln Collection, CHS.
8 Bigelow and Otis, *Manchester,
Vermont*, 200-201, 216, 280; Goff,
Robert Todd Lincoln, 245.
9 Letters between Jessie Lincoln
Randolph and Save the Children
adoptees, ISHL.
10 Ken Hill interview, Hildene.
11 Christopher Madkour conversation
with the author.
12 Mabel Knapp interview with the
author.
13 Pat Broderson, "Remembering the
Lincoln Family," *Manchester (Vt.)
Journal*, June 8, 1988.
14 Mabel Knapp interview with the
author.
15 Isabel Parris interview, Hildene.
16 Ken Hill interview, Hildene.
17 Ibid.
18 Nancy Otis, "Stylish, Aristocratic,
Kindly: Manchester Remembers
Robert Todd Lincoln," *Bennington
(Vt.) Banner*, April 14, 1965.

19 Ken Hill and Ken Hill with Marie Pearson interviews, Hildene.

20 Bernice "Beanie" Graham interview, Hildene.

21 Oscar Johnson interview with the author, Aug. 12, 1991.

22 Isabel Parris interview, Hildene.

23 *Oxford Dictionary of Quotations,* 3rd ed., 201.

24 Bessie Bushee interview, Hildene.

25 Pat Broderson, "Remembering the Lincoln Family," *Manchester (Vt.) Journal,* June 8, 1988.

26 Associated Press, "Bobby Kennedy Goes Too Fast, Says Lincoln Kin," unlabeled story with "Manchester" dateline, February 1963, LML; Tim Powers, "Mary Lincoln Beckwith: One of the Last Lincoln Descendants," *Bennington (Vt.) Banner,* July 15, 1975.

27 "Says Abe Would Reflect: Lincoln's Descendant Opposed to Aggressive Desegregation," *Post & Times-Star (Cincinnati, Ohio),* Feb. 12, 1963, LML.

28 Pat Broderson, "Remembering the Lincoln Family," *Manchester (Vt.) Journal,* June 8, 1988.

29 Isabel Parris interview, Hildene.

30 Bernice "Beanie" Graham interview, Hildene.

31 Isabel Parris interview, Hildene.

32 Bessie Bushee interview, Hildene.

33 Bigelow and Otis, *Manchester, Vermont,* 153.

34 Isabel Parris interview, Hildene.

35 Ken Hill interview, Hildene.

36 Isabel Parris interview, Hildene.

37 Pete and Charlotte Brooks interview, Hildene.

38 Pete and Charlotte Brooks and Isabel Parris interviews, Hildene.

39 Bernice "Beanie" Graham interview, Hildene.

40 Pat Broderson, "Remembering the Lincoln Family," *Manchester (Vt.) Journal,* June 8, 1988.

41 Beverly Polant interview and tour of Hildene with the author, Aug. 6, 1993.

42 Pete and Charlotte Brooks interview, Hildene.

43 Marie Pearson interview, Hildene; Beverly Polant interview and tour of Hildene with the author, Aug. 6, 1993.

44 Beverly Polant interview and tour of Hildene with the author, Aug. 6, 1993.

45 Ibid.

46 Ibid.

47 Ibid.

48 Pete and Charlotte Brooks interview, Hildene.

49 Beverly Polant interview and tour of Hildene with the author, Aug. 6, 1993.

50 Ibid.

CHAPTER SIXTEEN:

For the Sake of the Family

1 Associated Press, "Bobby Kennedy Goes Too Fast, Says Lincoln Kin," unlabeled story with Manchester dateline, February, 1963, LML. (A United Press International wire story from the *Cincinnati Post and Times-Star,* Feb. 12, 1963, contains similar comments.)

2 "Lincoln's Anniversary Work Day for Descendant," *Stamford (Ct.) Advocate,* Feb. 12, 1962.

3 Beschloss, "Family Tree: Last of the Lincolns," 54-59.

4 Brenda You, "Historians Track Elusive Lincoln Clan," *Chicago Tribune* story reprinted in *Sunday Rutland (Vt.) Herald,* May 15, 1994.

5 Beschloss, "Family Tree: Last of the Lincolns," 54.

6 Oates, *With Malice Toward None,* xv.

7 Louise Hutchinson, "102 Years After Lincoln Died: A Call on His

Great-Grandson," *Chicago Tribune,*
April 16, 1967, LML.

8 Beschloss, "Family Tree: Last of the
Lincolns," 57; "R. Beckwith, 81:
President Lincoln's Great-
Grandson," *Times Wire Service* obit-
uary with the dateline "Hartfield,
Va.," Dec. 27, 1985, LML.

9 Louise Hutchinson, "102 Years
After Lincoln Died: A Call on His
Great-Grandson," *Chicago Tribune,*
April 16, 1967, LML.

10 Don Guy, "Lincoln's Kin Forgot It
Was His Birthday," unlabeled
Associated Press story with the date-
line "Manchester, Vt.," Feb. 12, 1959.

11 Ibid.

12 Phebe Ann Lewis interview, Hildene.

13 Goff, *Robert Todd Lincoln,* 253-57;
Randall, *Lincoln's Sons,* 316-320;
Carson, "The Other Tragic Lincoln:
Robert Todd," 255-57. See also
David C. Mearns, *The Lincoln
Papers.*

14 Ibid.

15 Randall, *Lincoln's Sons,* 320-22.

16 Ibid.

17 "Robert Todd Lincoln," *Boston
Herald,* July 27, 1926, LML.

18 Goff, *Robert Todd Lincoln,* 223.

19 Keelan, *Hildene and How It was
Saved,* 4-6; *Chicago Tribune* Press
Service, "Robt. T. Lincoln Estate
Victor in Tax Appeal," Oct. 16 (no
year given), ISHL; Goff, *Robert Todd
Lincoln,* 257, 261.

20 Keelan, *Hildene and How It was
Saved,* 9.

21 "Mary Lincoln Isham" and "Charles
Isham," *Hildene Volunteer Manual,*
42, 45; author's tours of Hildene.

22 Keelan, *Hildene and How It was
Saved,* 7-8.

23 Unidentified news clipping beginning with the words "No prettier
idyl...," ISHL.

24 Frank Johnson letter to "Mr.
Lincoln," from Havana, Cuba,
April 18, 1921, ISHL.

25 Ibid.

26 Mary Harlan Lincoln letter to
"Dearest Petticoat" (her pet name
for Jessie), June 10, 1921, ISHL.

27 See Keelan, *Hildene and How It Was
Saved,* 1-9, for more details about
Robert and Mary Lincoln's decision
to will Hildene to Peggy Beckwith.

28 Goff, *Robert Todd Lincoln,* 288.

29 Bernice "Beanie" Graham interview,
Hildene.

30 U.S. Navy, *Launching Program;*
"Mary Lincoln Beckwith Christens
Sub Abraham Lincoln," unlabeled
United Press International news
story with the dateline
"Portsmouth, N.H.," May 14, 1960,
IWC; "Mary L. Beckwith Born Here,
Will Sponsor New Sub," unlabeled
UPI news clipping with dateline
"Portsmouth, N.H." and the hand-
written date of March 26, 1960,
IWC. (Mary Lincoln Beckwith was
born in Mount Pleasant, Iowa.)

31 Ibid.

32 Ibid.

33 Ibid.

34 Ibid.

35 Ralph G. Newman and James T.
Hickey, "Robert Todd Lincoln
Beckwith," 1-3; Beschloss, "Family
Tree: Last of the Lincolns," 57.

36 Louise Hutchinson, "102 Years
After Lincoln Died: A Call on His
Great-Grandson," *Chicago Tribune,*
April 16, 1967, LML.

37 Haselmayer, *Harlan Lincoln
Tradition, 1977 ed.,* 25-26.

38 "Robert Todd Lincoln Beckwith,"
Hildene Volunteer Manual, 65.

39 "Lincoln Isham," *Hildene Volunteer
Manual,* 46, 48.

40 Ibid.

41 Ibid.

42 Ralph G. Newman and James T. Hickey, "Robert Todd Lincoln Beckwith," 1-3.

43 "Robert Todd Lincoln Beckwith," *Hildene Volunteer Manual,* 65.

44 "Great-grandson's Death Ends Lincoln Family Line," *Chicago Tribune,* Dec. 26, 1985, LML; "Robert Todd Lincoln Beckwith Dies," unlabeled and undated news story, LML; Keelan, *Hildene and How It Was Saved,* 80-81.

45 Ralph G. Newman and James T. Hickey, "Robert Todd Lincoln Beckwith," 1-3; Keelan, *Hildene and How It Was Saved,* 18, 25.

46 James T. Hickey, "Reminiscences of Robert Todd Lincoln Beckwith," Hildene Symposium, July 30, 1993.

47 Keelan, *Hildene and How It Was Saved,* 25-27; Neely and McMurtry, *Insanity File,* ix.

48 Louise Hutchinson, "102 Years After Lincoln Died: A Call on His Great-Grandson," *Chicago Tribune,* April 16, 1967, LML; Ralph G. Newman and James T. Hickey, "Robert Todd Lincoln Beckwith," 1-3; Times Wire Services, "R. Beckwith, 81; President Lincoln's Great-Grandson," Dec. 27, 1985, LML.

49 Beschloss, "Family Tree: Last of the Lincolns," 57; Ralph G. Newman and James T. Hickey, "Robert Todd Lincoln Beckwith," 1-3.

50 Yvonne C. von Fettweis (History Manager, First Church of Christ, Scientist), letter to author, July 13, 1993.

51 Howard B. Blanchard letter to Ralph G. Lindstrom, August 17, 1939, LML.

52 Keelan, *Hildene and How It Was Saved,* 4.

53 Howard B. Blanchard letter to Ralph G. Lindstrom, August 17, 1939, LML.

54 Yvonne C. von Fettweis, "Christian Science and its Historical Appeal," Hildene Symposium, June 15, 2001.

55 Howard B. Blanchard letter to Ralph G. Lindstrom, August 17, 1939, LML.

56 Judith Huenneke (Christian Science senior researcher) email to the author, April 8, 2003; Yvonne C. von Fettweis, "Christian Science and its Historical Appeal," Hildene Symposium, June 15, 2001.

57 *Painting a Poem,* 131.

58 Keelan, *Hildene and How It Was Saved,* 11-12.

59 Oscar Johnson interview with author, Aug. 12, 1991.

60 Ibid.

61 Ken Hill interview, Hildene.

62 Keelan, *Hildene and How It Was Saved,* 45.

63 Keelan, *Hildene and How It Was Saved,* 34-35.

64 Oscar Johnson interview with the author, June 17, 1993.

65 Ibid.

66 Keelan, *Hildene and How It Was Saved,* 36-37.

67 Keelan, *Hildene and How It Was Saved,* 40-41; Goff, *Robert Todd Lincoln,* v-vii.

68 Ibid.

69 Ibid.; Oscar Johnson interview with author, Aug. 12, 1991. For more details about the protracted negotiations and "miracles" that saved Hildene, see Keelan, *Hildene and How It Was Saved.*

70 Keelan, *Hildene and How It Was Saved,* 105.

71 Oscar Johnson interview with the author, Aug. 12, 1991.

72 Keelan, *Hildene and How It Was Saved,* 1.

Sources

Books, Pamphlets, Journal and Magazine Articles

Note: newspaper citations are given in full in endnotes.

Aldrich, Charles, ed. "Mrs. Ann E. Harlan, Late Wife of Ex-Senator James Harlan." *Annals of Iowa* (Des Moines, Iowa: Historical Department of Iowa) 2, NO. 7 (October 1896): 489-508.

Annual Register of the Iowa Wesleyan University, 1890-91. Journal Print, Mount Pleasant, Iowa: Iowa Wesleyan Univ., 1891.

Annual Register of the Iowa Wesleyan University, 1892-93. Journal Print, Mount Pleasant, Iowa: Iowa Wesleyan Univ., 1893.

Annual Register of the Iowa Wesleyan University, 1894-95. Journal Print, Mount Pleasant, Iowa: Iowa Wesleyan Univ., 1895.

Anthony, Susan B. and Ida Husted Harper, eds. *History of Woman Suffrage.* Vol. 4, 1883-1900. New York: Arno and The New York Times, 1969.

Arthur, T.S. *Advice to Young Ladies on Their Duties and Conduct in Life.* Boston: Phillips, Sampson, 1858. (Amherst College library microfilm).

Baker, Jean H. *Mary Todd Lincoln: A Biography.* New York, Norton, 1987.

Beckwith, Robert Todd Lincoln. "Foreword," in *The Insanity File: The Case of Mary Todd Lincoln*, Mark E. Neely, Jr. and R. Gerald McMurtry. Carbondale, Ill.: S. Ill. Univ. Press, 1986: IX.

Bennett, Rev. John. *Strictures on Female Education.* New York: Source Book, 1971 (reprint; orig. pub. 1795).

Beschloss, Michael R. "Family Tree: Last of the Lincolns." *The New Yorker*, Feb. 28, 1994: 54-59.

Bigelow, Edwin and Nancy Otis. *Manchester, Vermont—A Pleasant Land Among the Mountains.* Town of Manchester, Vt., 1961.

Brigham, Johnson. *James Harlan: Iowa Biographical Series.* Benjamin Shambaugh, ed. Iowa City, Iowa: State Historical Society of Iowa, 1913.

———. "The Wedding of James Harlan." *The Palimpsest* (Iowa City: State

Historical Society of Iowa) 3, NO.4 (April 1922): 101-05.

Carson, S. L. "The Other Tragic Lincoln: Robert Todd." *Manuscripts* (Tempe, Ariz.: Manuscript Society) 30, NO. 4 (Fall 1978): 242-59.

Cott, Nancy F., ed. *Root of Bitterness: Documents of the Social History of American Women.* Boston: Northeastern Univ. Press, 1986.

Donald, David Herbert. *Lincoln.* London: Jonathan Cape, 1995.

Drake, Ross. "Duel!" *Smithsonian*, March 2004: 96-97.

Earhart, Amelia. *The Fun of It.* Chicago: Academy, 1932.

Evans, Sara M. *Born for Liberty: A History of Women in America.* New York: Free Press/Macmillan, 1989.

Friends of Hildene. *Robert Todd Lincoln's Hildene* (souvenir booklet). Manchester, Vt.: 1980.

———. *Robert Todd Lincoln's Hildene: Volunteer Resource Manual.* Manchester, Vt.: 2002.

———. "Symposium to Tour Lincoln Family Homes." *News From Historic Hildene*, Spring 1998: 1-2.

Fullbrook, Earl S. "Relief Work in Iowa during the Civil War." *Iowa Journal of History and Politics* (Iowa City: State Historical Society of Iowa) 16 (1918): 155-274.

Goff, John S. *Robert Todd Lincoln: A Man in His Own Right*, 2ND ed. Manchester, Vt.: Friends of Hildene, 1990.

Goldsmith, Barbara. *Other Powers: The Age of Suffrage, Spiritualism, and the Scandalous Victoria Woodhull.* New York: Harper, 1999.

Gordon, Arthur. *American Heritage History of Flight.* Alvin Josephy, Jr., et al, eds. New York: American Heritage, 1962.

Gregory, John M.D. *A Father's Legacy to His Daughters.* Boston: Hosea Sprague, 1805. (Univ. of Mass./Amherst library, Special Collections and Archives).

Harlan, Alpheus H. *History and Genealogy of the Harlan Family*, 5TH ed. Gateway Press, Baltimore, Md.: Harlan Family in America, 1998 (1ST ed., 1914).

Harlan, Louis R. *Harlan Family in America: A Brief History.* Booklet published by the Harlan Family in America for its 1997 national reunion (see *www.harlanfamily.org/book.htm*).

Harper, Marjorie, ed. *The History of Henry County, Iowa.* Mount Pleasant, Iowa: Henry County Bicentennial Commission, 1982.

Haselmayer, Dr. Louis A. *The Harlan-Lincoln Tradition at Iowa Wesleyan College.* Mt. Pleasant, Iowa: Iowa Wesleyan College, 1977.

———. "Jessie Harlan Lincoln in Iowa." *Annals of Iowa* (Des Moines, Iowa: Historical Department of Iowa) 39, NO. 6 (Fall 1968): 415-25.

———. "Memorandum on Mary Harlan Lincoln (1846-1937)." Private memorandum, does not circulate, March 1968.

Heath, Lady Mary. "Women's Activities." *Popular Aviation,* September 1930: 58.

Heilbrun, Carolyn G. *Writing a Woman's Life.* New York: Ballantine, 1988.

Helm, Katherine. *The True Story of Mary, Wife of Lincoln.* New York: Harper and Brothers, 1928.

Johnson, Charles W. *The Nature of Vermont—Introduction and Guide to a New England Environment.* Hanover, N.H.: Univ. Press of New England, 1980.

Jones, Ruth Owen. "Lincoln's Great Granddaughter Was Vermont Aviation Pioneer." *Atlantic Flyer,* September 1992: B17.

Keelan, Donald B. *Robert Todd Lincoln's Hildene and How It Was Saved, 1975-1978.* Arlington, Vt.: Keelan Family Foundation, 2001.

Kerber, Linda K. *Women of the Republic: Intellect and Ideology in Revolutionary America.* Chapel Hill, N.C.: Univ. of N.C. Press, 1980.

Laver, James. *A Concise History of Costume.* London: Thames and Hudson, 1969.

Lewis, Lloyd. *The Assassination of Lincoln: History and Myth.* Lincoln, Neb.: Univ. of Neb. Press/Bison Book Ed., 1994. (orig. *Myths after Lincoln.* New York: Harcourt, Brace, 1929).

Lewis, Phebe Ann. *The Equinox— Historic Home of Hospitality.* Manchester, Vt.: Johnny Appleseed Bookshop, 1996.

Lunardini, Christine. *What Every American Should Know About Women's History.* Holbrook, Mass.: Bob Adams, 1994.

Mayo, Edith P. and Lisa Kathleen Graddy. *First Ladies: Political Role and Public Image.* London: Scala Publishers/Smithsonian, 2004.

Mearns, David C. *The Lincoln Papers: The Story of the Collection.* Garden City, N.Y.: Doubleday, 1948.

McGoldrick, Monica and Randy Gerson. *Genograms in Family Assessment.* New York: Norton, 1985.

McMurtry, R. Gerald. *The Harlan-Lincoln Tradition at Iowa Wesleyan College.* Harrogate, Tenn.: Lincoln Memorial Univ., 1946.

———. *The Harlan-Lincoln Tradition at Iowa Wesleyan College.* Mount Pleasant, Iowa: Iowa Wesleyan College, 1959.

———. "Some Intimate Glimpses into the Private Lives of the Members of the Robert Lincoln Family." *Lincoln Lore* (Lincoln National Life Insurance, Fort Wayne, Ind.) NO. 1525 (March 1965): 1-4.

Neely, Mark E., Jr. and R. Gerald McMurtry. *The Insanity File: The Case of Mary Todd Lincoln.* Carbondale, Ill.: S. Ill. Univ. Press, 1986.

Newman, Ralph G. and James T. Hickey. "Robert Todd Lincoln Beckwith." *Lincoln Newsletter,* Lincoln College, Lincoln, Ill., Spring 1986. In Friends of Hildene, *Robert Todd Lincoln's Hildene: Volunteer Resource Manual.* Manchester, Vt.: 2002: 65A-65C.

Oates, Stephen B. *With Malice Toward None: The Life of Abraham Lincoln.* New York: Harper & Row, 1977.

Old Kennett Meeting. "History of Old Kennett Meeting." Flyer provided for the Harlan Family in America 2002 national reunion (contact *www.harlanfamily.org*).

Orr, Flora G. and Edith Porter. "President Lincoln's Living Descendants." *EveryWeek Magazine,* February 1931, ISHL

Osmond, Mary, ed. "A P.E.O.'s Wedding in London, Reprints from the Past, 1889-1988." *P.E.O. Record* 100 (June 1988): 10-11.

Painting a Poem: Mary Baker Eddy and James F. Gilman Illustrate "Christ and Christmas." Boston: Christian Science Publishing Society, 1998.

Randall, Ruth Painter. *Mary Lincoln: Biography of a Marriage.* Boston: Little, Brown, 1953.

———. *Lincoln's Sons.* Boston: Little, Brown, 1955.

Rich, Doris L. *Amelia Earhart: A Biography.* Washington, D.C.: Smithsonian, 1989.

Rose, Phyllis, ed. *The Norton Book of Women's Lives.* New York: W.W. Norton, 1993.

Sandburg, Carl and Paul M. Angle. *Mary Lincoln: Wife and Widow.* New York: Harcourt, Brace & World, 1932.

Schreiner, Samuel A., Jr. *The Trials of Mrs. Lincoln.* New York: Donald I. Fine, 1987.

Sherman, Joe. *Fast Lane on a Dirt Road: Vermont Transformed 1945-1990.* Woodstock, Vt.: Countryman Press, 1991.

Smith, Joy. "L is for Lincoln." *History of Henry County, Iowa.* Marjorie Harper, ed. Mount Pleasant, Iowa: Henry County Bicentennial Commission, 1982.

Turner, Justin G. and Linda Levitt Turner. *Mary Todd Lincoln: Her Life and Letters.* New York: Knopf, 1972.

U.S. Navy, Portsmouth Naval Shipyard. *Launching Program, Fleet Ballistic Missile Submarine Abraham Lincoln.* Portsmouth, N.H.: U.S. Navy, May 14, 1960.

Warren, Louis A., ed. "Hon. Robert Todd Lincoln: The First Born Son of Abraham and Mary Todd Lincoln." *Lincoln Kinsman* (Lincolniana, Lincoln National Life Foundation, Fort Wayne, Ind.), NO. 10 (April 1939): 1-8.

Welter, Barbara. "The Cult of True Womanhood: 1820-1860," in *Women's Experience in America: An Historical Anthology,* Esther Katz and Anita Rapone, eds. New Brunswick, N.J.: Transaction Books, 1980.

Wise, Rev. Daniel. *Young Lady's Counselor, or, The Sphere, the Duties and the Dangers of Young Women.* Cincinnati: Hitchcock & Walden, 1851. (Univ. of Mass./Amherst library microfilm).

Woloch, Nancy. *Women and the American Experience: A Concise History.* New York: McGraw-Hill, 1996.

Wood, Ann Douglas. "The War Within a War: Women Nurses in the Union Army," in *Women's Experience in America: An Historical Anthology,* Esther Katz and Anita Rapone, eds. New Brunswick, N.J.: Transaction Books, 1980.

Interviews and Speeches

Audio or video tapes available for Hildene symposiums and Otis interviews.

Baker, Jean H. "Mary Todd Lincoln." Hildene Symposium: "The Lincoln Women: Five Generations of Triumphs and Tragedies," Equinox Hotel, Manchester, Vt., August 21, 1998.

———. "Varieties of Spiritual Experience: Mary Todd Lincoln and Religion." Hildene Symposium: "The Lincoln Family and Religion," Equinox Hotel, Manchester, Vt., June 15, 2001.

Brooks, Pete and Charlotte. Interview by Alison Otis, S. Dorset, Vt., Sept. 17, 1979. Hildene archives.

Buck, Anna. Interview by Alison Otis, Manchester, Vt., Sept. 4, 1979. Hildene archives.

Bullock, Paul and Myrtle. Interview by Alison Otis, Manchester, Vt., Sept. 5, 1979. Hildene archives.

Bushee, Bessie. Interview by Alison Otis, Manchester, Vt., Sept. 11, 1979. Hildene archives.

Campbell, Irene (Mrs. G.M.). Interview by Alison Otis, Manchester, Vt., Sept. 13, 1979. Hildene archives.

Campbell, James. Interview by Alison Otis, Manchester, Vt., Sept. 21, 1979. Hildene archives.

Coburn, Helen and Buz. Interview by Alison Otis, Wells, Vt., Sept. 14, 1979. Hildene archives.

Ellsworth, Lynn. "Mary Harlan Lincoln, Mary Lincoln Isham, and Jessie Lincoln Randolph." Hildene Symposium: "The Lincoln Women: Five Generations of Triumphs and Tragedies," Equinox Hotel, Manchester, Vt., August 21, 1998.

Fenton, Will. Interview probably conducted by Larry Belles, Mount Pleasant, Iowa, Feb. 9, 1959, HLH.

Gaudette, Howard. Interview by Alison Otis, Manchester, Vt., Sept. 5, 1979. Hildene archives.

Graham, Bernice "Beanie." Interview by Alison Otis, Manchester, Vt., Sept. 15, 1979. Hildene archives.

Hickey, James T. "Reminiscences of Robert Todd Lincoln Beckwith." Hildene Symposium: "From Log Cabin to Hildene: Comparing the Lives of Father and Son," Equinox Hotel, Manchester, Vt., July 30, 1993.

Hill, Ken. Interview by Alison Otis, Manchester, Vt., Sept. 17, 1979. Hildene archives.

———. Interview with author, Manchester, Vt., notes undated.

Hill, Ken with Marie Pearson. Interviewed Manchester, Vt., May 1, 1979. Hildene archives.

Holzer, Harold. "The Image of the Lincoln Family." Hildene Symposium: "From Log Cabin to Hildene: Comparing the Lives of Father and Son," Equinox Hotel, Manchester, Vt., July 30, 1993.

———. "Pictorial Overview of the Lincoln Women." Hildene Symposium: "The Lincoln Women:

Five Generations of Triumphs and Tragedies," Equinox Hotel, Manchester, Vt., August 20, 1998.

———. "Icons for the Domestic Altar: The Lincoln Family in Portrait and Print." Hildene Symposium: "The Lincoln Family and Religion," Equinox Hotel, Manchester, Vt., June 14, 2001.

Johnson, Oscar. Interview/tour of Hildene with author, Manchester, Vt., August 12, 1991.

———. Interview/tour of Hildene with author, June 17, 1993.

Kelley, Clarence IV ("Clark"). Interview by Alison Otis, Manchester, Vt., August 30, 1979. Hildene archives.

Knapp, Mabel. Interview with author, Arlington, Vt., notes undated.

Lewis, Phebe Ann. Interview by Alison Otis, Manchester, Vt., Sept. 7, 1979. Hildene archives.

Loatman, Dr. Paul Jr. "Elmer E. Ellsworth: Citizen Soldier." Speech delivered at the conclusion of the Ellsworth Parade, Mechanicville, N.Y., May 21, 2000. *www.mechanicville.com/history/ellsworth/citizensoldier.htm* (accessed Jan. 26, 2005).

Otis, Nancy and Don. Interview by author, Manchester, Vt., June 8, 1993.

Ott, Hallie. Interview probably conducted by Larry Belles, Mount Pleasant, Iowa, Feb. 9, 1959, HLH.

Parris, Isabel. Interview by Alison Otis, Manchester, Vt., Sept. 11, 1979. Hildene archives.

Pearson, Helen. Interview by Alison Otis, Manchester, Vt., August 28, 1979. Hildene archives.

————. Public address about history of Manchester Village (tape incomplete, group and date not noted). Hildene archives.

Polant, Beverly. Interview/tour of Hildene with author, Manchester, Vt., August 6, 1993.

Porter, Mary. Interview by Alison Otis, Manchester, Vt., Sept. 20, 1979. Hildene archives.

Roberts, Clarence. Interview by Alison Otis, Manchester, Vt., Sept. 10, 1979. Hildene archives.

Simon, John Y. "Mary Todd Lincoln." Hildene Symposium: "The Lincoln Women: Five Generations of Triumphs and Tragedies," Equinox Hotel, Manchester, Vt., August 21, 1998.

Smart, Bruce. Interview by Alison Otis, Peru, Vt., Sept. 7, 1979. Hildene archives.

Thompson, Mabel and Norman. Interview by Alison Otis, Manchester, Vt., August 29, 1979. Hildene archives.

Von Fettweis, Yvonne C. "Christian Science and its Historical Appeal: The New Woman and the New Church." Hildene Symposium: "The Lincoln Family and Religion," Equinox Hotel, Manchester, Vt., June 15, 2001.

Walker, Mr. Lynn. Interview by Alison Otis, E. Dorset, Vt., Sept. 14, 1979. Hildene archives.

Walker, Wynona (Mrs. Herbert). Interview by Alison Otis, Manchester, Vt., Sept. 13, 1979. Hildene archives.

Wessner, Herbie. Interview with author, Manchester, Vt., notes undated.

Wilcox, Grace (Mrs. Burton). Interview by Alison Otis, Manchester, Vt., August 29, 1979. Hildene archives.

Wilcox, Howard "Dutch" and Dorothy. Interview by Alison Otis, Manchester, Vt., Sept. 21, 1979. Hildene archives.

Wilkins, Anne Pettibone. Interview by Alison Otis, Manchester, Vt., Sept. 21, 1979. Hildene archives.

Williams, Frank. "Mary Todd Lincoln's Influence on Abraham Lincoln and Robert Todd Lincoln." Hildene Symposium: "The Lincoln Women: Five Generations of Triumphs and Tragedies," Equinox Hotel, Manchester, Vt., August 22, 1998.

Wilson, David. Interview with author, Manchester, Vt., Sept. 3, 1993.

Wriston, Rhoda Orvis. Interview by Alison Otis, Manchester, Vt., Sept. 6, 1979. Hildene archives.

Zullo, Theresa. Interview by Alison Otis, Manchester, Vt., August 30, 1979. Hildene archives.

Photographs

Plates 1, 2: The Ostendorf Collection, courtesy of the Library of Congress, Washington, D.C.

Plate 3: Courtesy of the National Archives, College Park, Maryland.

Plates 4-6, 10, 11, 13, 15-17, 19, 21-35: Courtesy of Hildene Archives, Manchester, Vermont.

Plates 7-9, 12, 14, 18, 20: Courtesy of the Harlan-Lincoln House Collection, Iowa Wesleyan College, Mount Pleasant, Iowa.

Index

ABOUT THE AUTHOR

 C.J. King first became interested in the Lincoln women when she learned she is related to them through the Harlan family. After visiting Hildene, the Lincoln family home in Manchester, she moved to Vermont and began this research. A resident of Jamaica, Vermont, and a native Hoosier, she holds a B.A. in journalism from Ball State University and an M.F.A. in writing from the University of Massachusetts-Amherst. As a professional writer for 25 years, she has published many articles in newspapers and magazines. This is her first book.